Electoral competition in Ireland since 1987

MANCHESTER
1824

Manchester University Press

Electoral competition in Ireland since 1987

The politics of triumph and despair

Gary Murphy

Manchester University Press

Copyright © Gary Murphy 2016

The right of Gary Murphy to be identified as the author of this work has been asserted
by him in accordance with the Copyright, Designs and Patents Act 1988.

Published by Manchester University Press
Altrincham Street, Manchester M1 7JA
www.manchesteruniversitypress.co.uk

British Library Cataloguing-in-Publication Data
A catalogue record for this book is available from the British Library

Library of Congress Cataloging-in-Publication Data applied for

ISBN   978 0 7190 9765 2   hardback

ISBN   978 0 7190 9766 9   paperback

First published 2016

The publisher has no responsibility for the persistence or accuracy of URLs for any
external or third-party internet websites referred to in this book, and does not guarantee
that any content on such websites is, or will remain, accurate or appropriate.

Typeset
by Toppan Best-set Premedia Limited
Printed in Great Britain
by CPI Group (UK) Ltd, Croydon CR0 4YY

Contents

Acknowledgements

I have been thinking and researching about the politics of modern Ireland for many years and have accumulated significant intellectual and personal debts. I have spent my working academic life at Dublin City University where my interest in Irish politics has been supported and encouraged by many colleagues and friends over the years. I thank Eileen Connolly, John Costello, Brenda Daly, Yvonne Daly, Michael Doherty, John Doyle, Robert Elgie, Barbara Flood, Billy Kelly, Eugene Kennedy, Christine Loscher, Adam McAuley, Iain McMenamin, Brian MacCraith, Declan Raftery and Ferdinand von Prondzynski for making DCU such a stimulating place in which to work. I have had the privilege of being the Head of the School of Law and Government at DCU since 2012 and have gained enormously from the support, counsel, and encouragement of my colleagues in the School and of our students. For that I thank them all.

For conversations, insights and advice about the nature of modern Irish politics which have informed this book I thank Nicholas Allen, Alex Baturo, Fiona Buckley, Elaine Byrne, Sarah Carey, Raj Chari, Mick Clifford, John Coakley, Shane Coleman, Matt Cooper, Larry Donnelly, Seán Donnelly, David Farrell, Odran Flynn, Michael Gallagher, Yvonne Galligan, John Garry, Eoghan Harris, John Hogan, Peadar Kirby, Joe Lee, the late Peter Mair, Michael Marsh, Shane Martin, Andrew McCarthy, Conor McGrath, Seán McGraw, Tim Meagher, Ciara Meehan, Elizabeth Meehan, Brian Murphy, Mary Murphy, Donnacha Ó Beacháin, John O'Brennan, Mark O'Brien, Deiric Ó Broin, Philip O'Connor, Michelle O'Donnell Keating, Niamh Puirséil, Theresa Reidy, Rob Savage, Jane Suiter, Damian Thomas, Ben Tonra, Liam Weeks, and Noel Whelan.

I particularly want to thank my DCU colleagues, Eoin O'Malley and Kevin Rafter for stimulating conversations on modern Irish politics, research advice, assistance and friendship. Kevin in particularly made me sharpen my argument in response to his many queries and ultimately told me to finish this book, for which I am most grateful. My good friends and long-standing mentors Brian Girvin, John Horgan and Eunan O'Halpin have also helped me in more ways than they can imagine over the years and I take this opportunity to thank them once again for support, guidance and encouragement.

I started to think seriously about this book and the arguments presented in it during a sabbatical as a Fulbright scholar at the Center for European Studies at the University of North Carolina at Chapel Hill in 2011–12. I thank Frank Baumgartner, Phil Daquila, Erica Edwards and John Stephens of UNC for hosting me so generously. In Chapel Hill I benefited greatly from the friendship of Mary Beth Oliver, John Christman, Sri Kalyanaraman and Jock Lauterer and thank them for it. I also thank Cathy Frost, Breda Griffith, Dave Hannigan, Niamh Hardiman, Bill Kissane, Donal McGettigan, Mary Ann O'Neil and Tim O'Neil for their friendship, guidance and support during that sabbatical. Many thanks also to Colleen Dube and Sonya McGuinness at Fulbright Ireland for their support and help and to the Fulbright Commission for awarding me a fellowship to UNC.

I thank Tony Mason and his team at Manchester University Press, particularly Dee Devine, for their professionalism, support, and, in Tony's case, considerable patience. I am also grateful to the anonymous referees who first assessed the proposal for this book and made many helpful suggestions and to the anonymous reader of the full text. I thank DCU's Faculty of Humanities and Social Sciences Research Support Scheme for supporting this work.

Away from my desk my friends Michael O'Brien, Colm O'Callaghan, Michael Moynihan, Aengus Nolan, Joe O'Hara and Colm O'Reilly continue to remain pillars of support. This book has its beginning in 1987, the year I first entered university life as an undergraduate history student in University College Cork. Although I lived and was brought up exactly five minutes' walk from UCC it was in many ways a different world. I began my academic journey then and am still on it. From that time I thank Ashley Kenny, Niamh Counihan, Fiona Crowley, Seamus Cullinan, Brian Cunningham, Neil Hackett, Judith Kelleher, Tom Lawton and Esther Moriarty for helping me begin the journey.

Finally I cannot repay my debts to them but would like to pay particular thanks to my wife Mandy and children Amy, Aoife and Jack for living with this project as much as I have, wondering would it ever be finished, putting up with the delays and absences, and for persevering with me. I dedicate this book to my late father, Jack Murphy (1939–2012), who often shook his head at the nature of the politics of modern Ireland. I hope this book goes some way to explaining it.

Gary Murphy
Dublin
September 2015

Introduction:
The conservative revolutionaries

If we want things to stay as they are things will have to change.
Giuseppe de Lampedusa, *The Leopard*, 1958

In February 2011 Fine Gael and Labour, although running as separate parties, were swept to power on a wave of anti-Fianna Fáil resentment by an electorate deeply unhappy with austerity. Twenty-four years earlier in 1987 the same two parties had been unceremoniously dumped out of office by the electorate after presiding over a deep and lasting recession in which division and dissension were at the heart of the coalition government. After a quarter of a century in which the Irish state fluctuated from the brink of bankruptcy in 1987 through to the vulgar heights of the Celtic Tiger in the early to mid-2000s, to the spectacular collapse of the banks in 2008–9 one constant remained: politically the Irish electorate would look to traditional solutions when it came to the ballot box. The Irish voter, while occasionally happy to flirt with minor parties and independents, ultimately rejected new-comers, forcing them either to disband or to join with one of the larger parties.

The ultimate test of this was the 2011 general election when a Fianna Fáil party which had dominated modern Ireland would face a vengeful and angry electorate, who felt somehow conned that the party which had given them the prosperity of the Celtic Tiger went on to present them with the cata-strophic results of its dramatic end. And what an end it was. Exemplified both economically and politically by the accepting of access to an €85 billion rescue package for the Irish state from the so-called Troika of the International Monetary Fund, the European Union and the European Central Bank in November 2010, the decision to seek and take access to an emergency fund was the culmination of a catastrophic collapse in the economy which saw the very survival of the Irish state at risk. The political aftershock of the fall of the Celtic Tiger and the threat to the sovereignty of the state would be the collapse of the Fianna Fáil–Green government in almost farcical circum-stances in January 2011. The resultant general election would be the most dramatic in Ireland since Fianna Fáil first came to power in 1932. At its heart the election was about two potential results: how bad would the damage be for Fianna Fáil, and could Fine Gael form a majority government of its own or would it have to form a coalition with the Labour Party? There were no other possible alternative governments. That in itself tells us something extraordinarily significant about Irish politics and the state of the Irish party system; at a time where practically no family in the land was unaffected by the dramatic collapse of the Irish economy the only political solution to the crisis was to go back to the two parties who had failed in the 1980s.

Three months after the arrival of the Troika, Fianna Fáil suffered its worst ever electoral performance, polling only 17 per cent of the first preference vote in the February 2011 general election and winning 20 of the 166 seats. Less than four years earlier it had won 78 seats in the May 2007 general election. Its government partner the Greens were wiped out, losing all their six seats. But the Irish public did not take its revenge by looking to new political parties. Instead it turned to Fine Gael and Labour, the traditional alternatives to Fianna Fáil since the foundation of the state.

And yet it was all so different. From the time Fianna Fáil won the 1997 general election to when it was re-elected for a third time under Bertie Ahern in 2007, Ireland was the economic success story of modern Europe. A soaring economy, nicknamed the Celtic Tiger, based primarily on a construction boom and massive borrowings, saw full employment, a rise in standards of living, and an end to emigration, long the scourge of Irish people. There were significant decreases in both personal and corporation tax rates and substantial increases in the numbers of people at work, with the creation of 600,000 jobs in that ten-year period leading to over two million people at work. Moreover the government was 'in the black' for the first time in thirty years in the late 1990s, with the exchequer able to meet day-to-day spending without recourse to borrowing. The political consequence of this boom was Fianna Fáil hegemony. However, once the Irish banks collapsed in September 2008, all changed utterly.

In that context the aim of this book is to assess the quarter-century of political competition in the Republic of Ireland from the time of the ending of the 1987 recession up to the 2011 general election where Ireland was ruled by the Troika and austerity was a byword both for policy-making and for how many people lived their lives. It is not intended as a comprehensive history of modern Ireland. Rather it is an attempt to ascertain in a thematic way the forces which shaped the decisions the political elites in Ireland took over the course of this crucial quarter-century in modern Irish life. The year 1987 is an important starting date as, after the election of a minority Fianna Fáil government that year, Ireland hauled itself out of the mire of the recession of the 1980s through the twin prongs of foreign direct investment and social partnership. These two precepts of macroeconomic policy-making combined with EU membership were central to the boom in economic development in modern Ireland. The Irish government was able to advertise itself to investors as an ideal location owing to its low corporation tax rates, membership of the EU, stable social partnership process and its young, educated workforce. None of these elements was enough, however, to stave off the vicious recession that hit Ireland once its banks literally went bust in 2008. Still, there have been other severe recessions in Ireland: think of the 1950s when over 600,000 people emigrated from Ireland during the course of that grim and dismal decade, or the 1980s when emigration and unemployment were a staple of family life. Yet neither of those recessions spawned either the dramatic collapse in party support we saw for Fianna Fáil in 2011 or a complete realignment of the party system. This book attempts to explain why the politics of recession have been so much different in the Ireland of the bank guarantee, bailout and Troika from what they were in previous depressed economic eras.

Disenchantment with public life has been a feature of Irish politics in the recent past where tribunals of inquiry and the collapse of the banks have opened up all sorts of questions about the nature of undue influence in Irish public life. In that context these years are also a story of political corruption, epitomised by tribunals of inquiry into payments to politicians, tribunals that for all their faults showed up a covert and complex system of payments from developers to politicians in charge of the re-zoning of public lands. Such re-zoning decisions taken by local councillors to allow planning permission for residential housing had the potential to vastly increase the value of lands owned or controlled by developers. In that context the decisions had significant consequences for Irish public life and for the private lives of those made rich by these deals and those whose lives were blighted by negative equity, ghost estates and shoddy building. There has long been a view held by practically all sections of Irish society that the main political parties, but Fianna Fáil in particular, had an especially close relationship with property developers and the construction industry. This was vitally important at local government level where local councillors were charged with making planning decisions on land re-zoning, and were continuously and vigorously lobbied by property developers. A crucial result of this was the blight of unfinished housing estates across the Irish state, estimated by the Department of the Environment at over 2,700, comprising between 40,000 and 50,000 equally unfinished houses by the time of the 2011 general election.

But this is not simply a story of economics and its consequences. The Irish people rejected a proposal to allow for divorce in the Constitution in 1986 before narrowly agreeing to it in 1995. More fundamentally a referendum to constitutionally outlaw abortion was comfortably passed in 1983 by a margin of two to one, but thirty years later, in the summer of 2013, a government constituting the same two parties as in 1983 passed legislation which allowed for abortion in very narrow circumstances based on a Supreme Court judgement in 1992. That Supreme Court judgement in theory turned the 1983 referendum decision on its head in that an amendment designed to ensure that abortion would be constitutionally prohibited was interpreted by the state's highest court as allowing for just such a development in the famous X case. The Supreme Court basically made abortion legal in Ireland if the life of the mother was at risk by the continuance of the pregnancy, including through the potential threat of suicide. However no abortions were carried out in Ireland despite the Supreme Court's ruling, and the will of the people as expressed in the 1983 referendum remained in place. Yet that abortion referendum and subsequent referendums on abortion and divorce have spawned deep social divisions in modern Ireland. The 1982–87 coalition government led by Garret FitzGerald, which was committed to secularising Irish society by dint of a so-called constitutional crusade, instead within a year of its formation put a deeply divisive referendum to the people emphasising a distinctly conservative position on abortion – notwithstanding the liberal credentials and disquiet about the wording of the abortion referendum of its own Taoiseach (the leader of the government).

The battle lines between conservatism and liberalism were drawn in the 1980s and hardened over the intervening quarter-century. Further referendums followed in 1992, to deal in the first place with the so-called substantive issue of abortion, along with guaranteeing the rights of Irish citizens to travel and to information. In 2002 yet another referendum to clarify the abortion situation was put to the people, who narrowly defeated the government's new proposal and instead decided basically to uphold the Supreme Court decision and reject government-sponsored efforts to copperfasten the original 1983 result, notwithstanding that it remained effectively in place. With the narrow rejection of the 2002 referendum, abortion as an issue seemed to be taken off the public policy agenda. However in 2013 it resurfaced as one of the most controversial of all issues in Irish life when, following the death of a young Indian woman in childbirth, both pro-life and pro-choice groups mobilised, demanding a variety of legislative changes and indeed another referendum. The government eventually legislated for the X case twenty years after the decision was handed down by the Supreme Court amidst significant disquiet from many Fine Gael members, a number of whom lost the Party whip when they voted against the legislation and eventually left the Party and set up their own. In the period since 1987 there have been over twenty referendums held to amend the 1937 Constitution, Bunreacht na hÉireann, including the historic 2015 decision to allow for same-sex marriages. The seemingly never ending cycle of referendums in Ireland particularly on social and European issues has helped the political class to remove a variety of controversial issues from the policy-making arena where the political parties have to all intents and purposes outsourced leadership on these issues to the courts and the people through the mechanism of the constitutional referendum.

The politics of Ireland between 1987 and 2011 was one of triumph and despair. A boom to bust story of economic policy-making characterised by recklessness in banking and regulation was both implicitly and explicitly endorsed by the Irish people, in a variety of elections and through a lax approach to the dangers of corrupt influence, epitomised in particular by a strengthening of the clientelist system whereby the people expected their politicians to get things done for them on an individual level. This worked in creating the conditions for a booming but essentially false economy. It worked in land re-zoning. It worked in reassuring citizens on moral questions like abortion and divorce. It worked on the European level where politicians oftentimes blamed Europe when they were not able to deliver on specific issues. However, once it failed when the banks collapsed and the lax regulatory framework inevitably flopped, the electorate would take brutal revenge on the peddlers of this clientelist system: Fianna Fáil. The Irish people, however, went seeking answers from an alternative proffering similar wares. This book charts how this happened and seeks to explain why.

It is organised into six chapters and a conclusion which analyse the course of political competition in modern Ireland since 1987. Chapter 1 assesses the crises of the 1980s. Throughout the mid-1980s Ireland went through a ruinous recession which saw unemployment and emigration reach levels not seen since the 1950s. The Fine Gael–Labour government of 1982–87, unable to get a handle on either problem, eventually came to an end when Labour withdrew from office, forcing an election in February 1987. Both government parties lost heavily but the outcome was particularly disastrous for Fine Gael as it lost 20 seats, falling to 50. Although it had come within five seats of Fianna Fáil in the previous election of November 1982, the voters had enough of the party they had put into office to fix the economy. Instead the electorate went back to the old reliable voice of Fianna Fáil. Falling just two seats short of an overall majority, Fianna Fáil embarked on a political journey which aimed to restore the state's financial position by promoting a twin-pronged approach of social partnership and foreign direct investment. This chapter assesses the Ireland of 1987, examines the general election of that year and analyses the birth of the process of social partnership, widely seen as being the launchpad for two decades of macroeconomic stability which provided the conditions for economic success in Ireland. It also assesses the complex relationship between the state and its citizens regarding the moral questions of abortion and divorce that convulsed Irish society in the 1980s, leading to a number of deeply divisive referendums.

Chapter 2 examines the politics of coalition. The minority Fianna Fáil government fell in April 1989 when it lost a vote in the Dáil (the lower house of the Irish parliament) on the issue of providing additional funding to haemophiliacs suffering from the Aids virus. Although that government had lost six other Dáil votes, the Taoiseach, Charles J. Haughey, decided that his government could not be held to ransom on issues of money and finance and so requested from the President a dissolution of the Dáil, which was granted. The election of June 1989 had far-reaching consequences for the Irish party system and Irish politics in general when Fianna Fáil, having failed to convince the people to give it an overall majority, ultimately went into coalition with the Progressive Democrats (PDs) and so ended one of Fianna Fáil's core values: that of single-party government. The lure of power was too great for Charles Haughey, and he negotiated a coalition government with his arch-nemesis and former Fianna Fáil colleague Des O'Malley, who was thrown out of Fianna Fáil in 1985 for conduct unbecoming a member, and set up his own party, the PDs. The 1989–92 government continued the policies of fiscal rectitude that Fianna Fáil had begun in 1987. Stringent cutbacks in public services aligned to tax benefits for foreign direct investment, all underpinned by a process of social partnership, appeared to be having some success in restoring Ireland's economic fortunes. However Fianna Fáil would begin to implode from late 1990 when it lost a presidential election for the first time in its history, its candidate, Brian Lenihan, losing out to Mary Robinson in rather bizarre and dramatic circumstances. Its leader, Charles Haughey, faced a number of internal revolts and was eventually forced from office in January 1992 but not before he had changed the face of Irish politics by bringing coalition to Fianna Fáil.

Chapter 3 examines Fianna Fáil's difficulties with coalition. Charles Haughey's replacement as Fianna Fáil leader, Albert Reynolds, is one of the great mysteries of Irish politics. A self-made man who had previously enjoyed a successful business career, he entered politics determined to get things done and certainly lived up to his promise. He was, however, singularly unsuitable for coalition government and holds grave responsibility for the failure of Fianna Fáil's first two attempts of governing with another party. Once the Fianna Fáil–PD government collapsed amidst a wave of recriminations, Fianna Fáil continued its coalition dance after the 1992 general election by going into government with the Labour Party. The great irony here was that Labour had spent pretty much all of its time in opposition lambasting Fianna Fáil. Nevertheless once the numbers stacked up after the election, both parties decided to coalesce and the new government had, in Irish terms, a massive majority of 18 seats. Fianna Fáil had, however, gained its lowest ever share of the first preference vote, falling below 40 per cent for the first time in its history. This government proved short-lived, lasting just under two years. It fell as a result of a political miasma of events which had at their heart distrust between the Fianna Fáil leader, Albert Reynolds, and the Labour leader, Dick Spring. Chief among these events were their differing reactions to the outcome of the so-called Beef Tribunal report which examined allegations of malpractice in the beef-processing industry and whether political favours were granted to a number of companies in the industry. But while this government failed, no general election was held to find a replacement. Rather a new government was found using the arithmetic from within the then Dáil, as Labour rescued Fine Gael from potential political oblivion by agreeing to coalesce with it and the small left-wing party Democratic Left. This government also grappled with issues of morality and corruption and, while stable, it ultimately proved unpopular with the public by failing the re-election test.

Chapter 4 examines the tribunals of inquiry that co-existed uneasily with the electorally successful governments of Fianna Fáil and the PDs from 1997. Fianna Fáil and the PDs managed to unseat the then rainbow coalition governing in the 1997 general election, and were decisively re-elected in 2002 where Fianna Fáil nearly won an overall majority. Yet the tribunal of inquiries into payments to politicians and into the planning process in Dublin, both of which finished only in 2010, would haunt the political class throughout this period. But it was a strange kind of haunting which had little impact when it came to political competition and electoral success. While the evidence of the Taoiseach, Bertie Ahern, to the Mahon Tribunal on planning brought his, in many ways successful, career to a shuddering end, the wider consequences for political life in Ireland were relatively inconsequential. In that context this chapter examines the various tribunals of inquiry that stalked the Irish political landscape for practically two decades, and assesses the impact they had for Irish politics and society in that period.

Chapter 5 focuses on the reasons for the political success of Fianna Fáil and the PDs. Pursuing generally neoliberal economic policies which had low corporate and personal levels of taxation at their core, this coalition government oversaw an Irish economy which reported spectacular levels of economic success on a whole range of indices. Public spending by government remained high and was imitated by levels of personal spending by an electorate slightly dumbstruck with new-found wealth. The ultimate result was that Fianna Fáil was re-elected for a third time in 2007 amidst warnings from some quarters of an impending economic crash, which were dismissed by all parties. Economic boom seemed to presage perpetual Fianna Fáil government, and this chapter examines the conditions that would ultimately lead to the political hubris which in no small way contributed to the collapse of the Irish economy and the fracturing of the Irish state. The crash, however, did come. It was foreshadowed by the bank guarantee scheme when on the fateful night of 29 September 2008 the government decided to guarantee all the deposits and obligations of the commercial banks without knowing the cost of their liabilities. This was trumpeted at the time as the solution to the impending crisis that was surrounding the Irish economy. It would later prove to be a millstone of gigantic proportions around the necks of the Irish people.

Chapter 6 focuses on the Fianna Fáil-led government's attempts to fix the economy and stave off political collapse. The collapse of the banking system was but one sign of an economy in free fall. Emigration, long the scourge of the Irish people, returned with a savagery that few could have predicted. Unemployment skyrocketed, with the government coming up with plan after plan, all of which went nowhere. Membership of the European Union and the Euro, long trumpeted as central to the Irish economic success story, proved little help when the crash came. Most of the government's plans were based around implementing austerity measures to ease Ireland's colossal debt crisis which magnified significantly once the private debt of the banks became the public debt of the state. They all failed. Ultimately the failure of the regulatory regime in Ireland, which allowed a massive orgy of property speculation by developers funded by the banks, overwhelmed the political organs of the Irish state. The economic mayhem in Ireland caused by such recklessness by bankers and property developers alike ended up decimating Fianna Fáil. But while the dominant party of independent Ireland was crushed, it was not killed off. The shambolic way in which the Fianna Fáil–Green coalition collapsed is discussed in this chapter, as is the election result itself which saw the Irish people revert to the traditional and comfortable alternative of Fine Gael and Labour.

At its heart the story of political competition in Ireland between 1987 and 2011 is one of decisions made and not made by politicians and voters alike. These decisions which came close to wrecking the Irish state cannot simply be explained by structural forces operating in Europe, Washington DC, the EU, the ECB or the IMF, or by the dismal science of economics or by the invisible hand of the market. They have their home in decisions made in Ireland. In that context this is a book which seeks to explain how political agency and clientelist relationships in modern Ireland have shaped political competition within the Irish state. To borrow a phrase from Christopher Clark's magisterial account of the origins of World War One, *The Sleepwalkers*, this is a book 'saturated with agency' (Clark, 2012: xxvii). Bailout Ireland was a country dominated by explicit choices made by specific politicians and voters which resulted in a euphoric state of triumph for a while but one which quickly turned to disaster and despair.

1

Of constitutional and economic crusades: Ireland in the 1980s

A major achievement for the nation.

Charles J. Haughey on social partnership, 9 October 1987

I would deprecate any attempt to make this a political issue in the House because there are certain things that the parties in the House are united on and this is one.

Garret FitzGerald on abortion, 26 January 1982

Social partnership and the corrosion of intellectual thought

Since the collapse of social partnership in 2009, the model heralded by many politicians in the two decades since its inception in 1987 as crucial to the success of modern Ireland has become the whipping boy for much of the political and economic ills that stalk the landscape of the Irish state. In his introduction in 2006 to the then agreement *Towards 2016* the Taoiseach, Bertie Ahern, pointed out that

> Social Partnership has helped to maintain a strategic focus on key national priorities, and has created and sustained the conditions for remarkable employment growth, fiscal stability, restructuring of the economy to respond to new challenges and opportunities, a dramatic improvement in living standards, through both lower taxation and lower inflation, and a culture of dialogue, which has served the social partners, but more importantly, the people of this country, very well. (Government of Ireland, 2006: 2)

In December 2008, just over two months after the infamous bank guarantee scheme, the Fianna Fáil–Green–PD coalition government presented to the public its plan to deal with the increasingly grim economic crisis of 2008. Informally titled the *Plan for Economic Renewal* – its more formal title was the cumbersome *Building Ireland's Smart Economy: A Framework for Sustainable Economic Renewal* – it was the government's response to six months of catastrophic economic news after over a decade of boom of which the twin processes of social partnership and EU membership were seen as pillars of the country's economic success. Amongst a number of initiatives, the plan called for heavy investment in research and development which would incentivise multinational companies to locate more such capacity in Ireland, ensuring the commercialisation and retention of ideas that flowed from that investment. Two months earlier, Minister for Finance, Brian Lenihan, had issued the 2009 budget which he described as nothing less than a call to patriotic action to face the deterioration in the government's fiscal position. The 2009 budget was introduced in, as Lenihan put it, one of the most 'difficult and uncertain times in living memory' where the global credit crunch had created turmoil in the world's financial markets, and steep increases in commodity prices placed enormous pressures on economies across the globe, including Ireland (Lenihan, 2008).

In the *Plan for Economic Renewal* the Taoiseach, Brian Cowen, renewed his government's commitment to social partnership, noting that it was the government's intention to work with the social partners on the development and implementation of the plan, which was consistent with the principles and vision underpinning *Towards 2016*, using the well-established mechanisms of the social partnership process. The *Plan for Economic Renewal* sank without trace, and social partnership in essence went with it when the trade union movement, amongst the greatest supporters of social partnership since its inception in 1987, refused in January 2009 to sign up to a new deal. A pay deal, agreed in September 2008 and linked to the social partnership process, was reached only after mammoth negotiations which were described as the toughest in the twenty years of pay talks since social partnership began (*Irish Independent*, 18 September 2008). When after the bank guarantee the government wanted to restructure the process, the unions said no.

It was all so different over twenty years earlier. Social partnership was born in crisis at a time when the Irish state had stagnated economically and when the panacea of membership of the EEC seemed nothing but a chimera. The heady optimism that accompanied entry to the EEC after the overwhelming yes vote in the 1972 referendum on membership had dissipated by the time of the 1987 general election. Recession had taken hold of the Fine Gael–Labour government of 1982–87 and a political depression took hold of its constituent parties. Into this breach stepped Charles Haughey and Fianna Fáil.

It was during this period of deep depression in the mid-1980s that the social partners, acting in the tripartite National Economic and Social Council, agreed a strategy to overcome Ireland's economic difficulties. Titled *Strategy for Development* (1986), this document formed the basis upon which, in 1987, the new Fianna Fáil government and the social partners negotiated the Programme for National Recovery. This would be followed by six other agreements. While in many ways these agreements did bring a certain economic stability to the Irish state they also left a deeply troubling legacy.

Although the Taoiseach, Brian Cowen, was insisting up to early 2009 that social partnership was alive and well, despite the trade union movement refusing to sign up to an economic recovery plan, the final death knell for the process came with the government's refusal in November of that year to agree to the trade unions' proposal for public sector reform in return for no pay cuts for public sector workers. With this act, the government had actually overcome one of the criticisms of social partnership and by extension sectional interest group activity, namely that it is an exercise in non-legitimate power, whereby the leaders of such groups are not publicly accountable and their influence bypasses the representative process. If the government had accepted this deal, it would, in effect, have indeed bypassed any democratic representative process. The main opposition to this deal came from back-bench Fianna Fáil TDs (members of Parliament) who, at least some of them claimed, were merely reiterating the views of their private sector constituents. Moreover, this deal, if it had gone through, would also have confirmed the idea of interest groups and governments being engaged in a closed and secretive policy process, where the groups exerted influence through negotiation, and a deal that was not subject to any public scrutiny. But of course that is exactly what happened in the social partnership process between 1987 and 2009 under mainly Fianna Fáil-led governments.

One critical result of this was that the public was effectively excluded from the main nature of economic governance within the state. While trade unionists got to vote on whether their unions should participate in these agreements, and while one could perhaps plausibly argue that the electorate got to have a say on such issues at subsequent general elections, it nevertheless was the case that these agreements were negotiated in secret. Even within trade union circles social partnership remained a contested process. While the trade union leaders were enthusiastic supporters, the agreements were usually passed by a small majority (Adshead, 2011). At a more public level social partnership agreements were not open to any real scrutiny, with opposition parties, for instance, having no idea of what was going on with regard to these deals, notwithstanding the fact that on conclusion they would be legally binding beyond the outcome of general elections. The problem for the Irish state was that once social partnership had run its course the government had little idea of what exactly to do in terms of economic policy. Over twenty years of social partnership had led to a corrosion of intellectual thinking in Irish policy-making whereby no one in power seemed to have the slightest idea of how to get the Irish state out of the morass it found itself in from the middle of 2008. This vacuum of political thinking in many ways led to the famous bank guarantee scheme of September 2008.

What made social partnership agreements from 1987 onwards different from those of the 1960s and 1970s was that they were not simply centralised wage mechanisms but agreements on a wide range of economic and social policies such as tax reform and the evolution of welfare payments (O'Donnell and Thomas, 1998: 118). The social partnership agreements had evolved considerably from 1987, when the first agreement was developed strictly as a means of responding to a grave fiscal crisis. They developed into a strategy for facilitating steady growth and the inward investment that fuelled such growth, over a much longer period than was originally expected, and this strategy was clearly central to the successes of the Irish economy from the mid-1990s.

There remains a substantive debate about the exact nature of social partnership in Ireland. O'Connor (2002: 164) maintains that it was born in 1987 out of the then Taoiseach Charles Haughey's need to neutralise trade union opposition to a series of swingeing cuts in public spending implemented by his Fianna Fáil minority government. Allen (2000) claims that the whole concept of social partnership is a myth which has functioned mainly as a means of sustaining inequalities in the outcome of growth by incorporating union leaders into the process and reinforcing their control over the ordinary membership. For O'Donnell and O'Reardon (2000: 252), it is best described as the 'formulation of a new concept of post-corporatist concertation' as the range of interests represented in social partnership goes beyond that arising from functional interdependence between business and labour. This challenges the representational monopoly of the confederations on each side that one would find in a classically corporatist arrangement. They argue that new relationships have emerged between government policy-making institutions and interest groups at different levels, with the result that traditional conceptions of neo-corporatism, premised on the effectiveness and power of central government, are outdated.

For Roche and Cradden (2003: 80–7), both these approaches have faults, and they argue that social partnership can best be understood in terms of the theory of competitive corporatism. The resurgence in the 1990s of neo-corporatist social pacts in a number of European countries, including Ireland, differed substantially from superficially similar agreements in the 1960s and 1970s. The later agreements concentrated on pay deals that were consistent with the enhancement of national competitiveness, on sustainable levels of public expenditure, the reform of taxation and welfare systems, and the upskilling of the labour force. Previous aspirational policies such as managing income distribution gave way to the promotion of business objectives – particularly in terms of competitive advantage. To that end the social partnership pacts of the 1990s can be seen as examples of competitive corporatism, which has also been termed 'supply side' or 'lean' corporatism.

Significantly, nine of the then fifteen members of the European Union – Belgium, Finland, Germany, Greece, Ireland, Italy, the Netherlands, Portugal and Spain – put in place social partnership pacts of this competitive neo-corporatist kind in the 1980s and 1990s (Roche and Cradden, 2003: 73). In that context Ireland's social partnership experiment since 1987 can be seen as one of a number of similar agreements across the EU. O'Donnell (2008: 97) has criticised this view, noting that Irish social partnership is but one case of a new approach to negotiated public governance that is emerging in many EU countries and at EU level where such approaches are 'fragile and incomplete and sit alongside traditional public systems: hierarchical administration, centralised policy-making, adversarial industrial relations and, in varying degrees, clientelistic or ideological politics'. Moreover it is important to note that the type of tripartite agreement which is not rooted in strictly corporatist structures has the tendency to be 'only as good as its last deal' (Gallagher, Laver and Mair, 2006: 448). In that context it is significant to note that each successive agreement had become increasingly difficult to negotiate before social partnership, a bit like the Irish state itself, went bust.

The Haughey effect

The simple reality about social partnership is that it was a political construct driven by a singular politician, Charles Haughey, which aimed at bringing some stability to the Irish economy and political success to Fianna Fáil. Haughey's own view of social partnership was that it had essentially contributed to

> initiating and sustaining the transformation of our economy from a near-disaster type situation in 1986 to a prosperous and progressive economy … There were, of course, other factors which assisted that transformation but Social Partnership from its inception and for twenty years has provided the essential bedrock on which sound public finances and progressive fiscal, social and economic policies could be firmly based. Should any proof of its basic soundness be required, it must surely be the number of individuals and bodies who have laid claim to its parenthood. (Haughey, 2011)

And indeed Haughey was insistent that he was the founding father, architect and midwife of social partnership all rolled into one. The official memorial website devoted to his life and times notes that as 'the driving force behind Social Partnership, he expressed mild amusement at attempts by others to claim ownership of this concept' (Haughey, 2011).

According to Haughey, the stimulus and need for social partnership came directly from the near-disastrous state of the Irish public finances caused both by adverse economic trends, most notably the oil crisis of the 1970s, and by the application of unsuccessful policies during the 1970s and 1980s brought in by other politicians of course. The result was a spiral of high inflation and equally high interest rates, contracting output and unprecedented levels of unemployment. Haughey's critique goes something like as follows. High inflation, caused by external pressures, exceeded 20 per cent in 1975 and 1981 and, concomitantly, caused massive increases in public sector pay, thus greatly increasing the servicing of the growing National Debt. Aligned to this, social welfare payments had to be similarly increased because of inflation and also because of growing unemployment, which rose from 90,000 in 1980 to 227,000 in 1986. Then, sticking the boot into his own party and particularly his political nemesis from the mid-1960s until he took power in 1979, Jack Lynch, Haughey noted that the 'transfer of the bill for domestic rates to the Exchequer was a further burden on the public finances in that period: in 1980 the cost to the Exchequer was €135 million' (Haughey, 2011). Abolishing rates was of course at the heart of the Fianna Fáil manifesto of 1977 on the back of which Fianna Fáil romped home to the largest ever majority in the history of the Irish state. It did Jack Lynch no favours and he was gone as Taoiseach within two and a half years, to be replaced, much to his own chagrin, by Haughey, who in December 1979 had outwitted Lynch's chosen successor, George Colley, to become both leader of Fianna Fáil and Taoiseach.

In the same year the then twenty-nine-year-old Fianna Fáil backbencher Charlie McCreevy, at the beginning of his long and often controversial career, noted that: 'the way in which the 1973 General Election was conducted, with both parties putting up their ideas on what they would do, led me to feel that in future elections there would be more of putting up the best goodies and seeing who would vote for them'. He went on to say that in the 1977 election, when both parties published their policies, he reached a different conclusion. Declaring that the document Fianna Fáil placed before the electorate was well-researched and caught their attention, he nevertheless noted that 'our victory at that time gave us to understand that, whereas we may have won on 16 June, the attitude of the electorate was: If you do not deliver, when the next election comes around, the electorate will give you their answer' (Dáil Debates, vol. 312, col. 672, 1 March 1979). Going on to praise the integrity of the Fianna Fáil government, McCreevy argued that they were setting about achieving their targets from the 1977 election, despite many commentators being of the view that these objectives were impossible to reach. Between the 1977 and 1981 general elections, borrowing, direct taxation, inflation and the National Debt all soared, leaving Haughey somewhat bewildered in office. This grim economic news then became the context for the resurgence of Fine Gael, which won an increase of 22 seats, bringing it to a total of 65 in the election of June 1981. Fianna Fáil's loss of 7 seats, leaving it with a total of 77, denied the Party an overall majority, and seemed to confirm McCreevy's hypothesis on delivering the goods.

Fianna Fáil gained the largest share in its history of 84 seats, and its second largest percentage of the vote share with 50 per cent, in the 1977 general election. This result followed a campaign which has gone down in history as the quintessential example of auction politics, with Fianna Fáil making an array of spending promises, most spectacularly pledging to abolish car tax and local government rates to mention just two, promises unlike any other in the history of the state. Such promises were based on the government's proposals to pump-prime the economy through a form of deficit-financing fiscal policy which was to achieve significant growth rates and bring about full employment by 1983. The 1977 manifesto opened with the words 'the real threat to the future of our country lies in the economy', and with that Fianna Fáil, committed itself to a full employment strategy (Fianna Fáil, 1977: 1). Nevertheless there were some in Fianna Fáil who were sceptical about these claims, including, from the minuscule Health and Social Welfare brief, the brooding but essentially silent Haughey. McCreevy, for one, while mentioning a growth rate of 6 per cent per annum in Gross Domestic Product in 1979, did point out that this did not mean that jobs would grow by an equivalent amount. In any event all this was to be driven by the newly formed Department of Economic Planning and Development: a classic Fianna Fáil statist response to the economic conditions of the time. This sort of étatisme, as Foster (2007: 17) points out, came easily to an Ireland with a tradition of governments, mostly Fianna Fáil, used to restricting property rights, compulsorily acquiring land and monopolising energy and transport on behalf of the state. In other words this was Fianna Fáil equating the state with itself. The minister chosen to head up the new department, Martin O'Donoghue, has, however, continued to insist ever since that the manifesto was properly costed and could have been delivered but for external circumstances, particularly the second oil crisis. Over the years he has offered a trenchant defence of the economic strategy, pointing out that the employment targets were actually exceeded and that the critics of the policy had never defined an alternative way of meeting the massive employment problem the country faced (O'Donoghue, 1990). Many others involved in Fianna Fáil at the time and who have subsequently put pen to paper, such as Pádraig Faulkner (2005), John O'Leary (2015) and Des O'Malley (2014), have also continued to defend the 1977 manifesto. In any event, despite their personal antipathy to each other, using the state to pump-prime economic growth was something O'Donoghue and Haughey could both agree on.

The 1977 victory actually set in train a series of events which led to the dramatic electoral upheaval of the early 1980s with three elections within the space of eighteen months between June 1981 and November 1982. The ominously large 20-seat majority led to a situation in Fianna Fáil where, once the economy began to decline, unsavoury jealousies emerged between individuals with the result that many deputies became susceptible to the argument that the party needed a new and dynamic leader if their seats were to be made safe (Arnold, 2001: 213). That new leader was to be Charles Haughey, who after his surprise victory over George Colley in December 1979, mainly on the back of support from the backbenches, promised a new era of Fianna Fáil dominance. He was to be denied, as Fianna Fáil could not give the voters the economic goods they were looking for.

On becoming leader, Haughey, in his own narrative, had to do something about the dire situation he found the state of the public finances to be in. According to Haughey he formed the view in 1982 that the corrective action needed in the public finances was possible only in the context of a comprehensive and balanced economic and fiscal plan with the support of the main social partners: namely the trade unions, the business organisations and the farmers. Such a plan would need to contain positive proposals for economic growth as well as more essentially negative measures to contain public expenditure. This is how Haughey describes his Eureka moment when it came to his brainchild of social partnership:

> I vividly recall the occasion that, in all probability, was the first time I began to think along the lines of this concept of Social Partnership. A European Summit in Brussels on 28th / 29th June 1982 had just concluded and Chancellor Schmidt of Germany and I were chatting together when I asked him what he would spend the forthcoming week-end on. He said: 'This week-end is the most important one in my annual calendar – I meet with the employers and the Trade Unions to hammer out an agreement on the rates of pay and salaries appropriate for the coming year in the light of the economic situation anticipated.' I was immediately struck with this commonsense approach and began, in my mind, as I listened to Chancellor Schmidt, to develop and expand the concept. (Haughey, 2011)

Earlier that year, while Taoiseach of a minority government, Haughey had arranged for a Cabinet Committee of economic ministers, chaired by himself, as not only Taoiseach but de facto Minister for Finance, to prepare yet another national economic plan. The Committee was assisted by a steering committee composed of civil servants from the economic departments and agencies with some outside expert assistance. It was specified by Haughey from the outset that the social partners should be consulted in the preparation of this plan. Following his meeting with Schmidt, Haughey was insistent that this new plan, of which he and his close civil service confidante, Padraig O'hUiginn, secretary of the Department of the Taoiseach, were principal authors, would be written in such a way as to obtain the agreement of the social partners who would sign up to it and to the new concept of social partnership. Unfortunately for him, Haughey then lost office. Governing with a minority is never easy, particularly in times of economic crisis, and Haughey miscalculated the support he could count on from the independent left-wing deputy Tony Gregory, with whom the Taoiseach shared a fraught relationship, not helped by the fact that they represented neighbouring Dublin city constituencies, and from three Workers' Party TDs. They eventually pulled down the government by withdrawing their political support over what they saw as unnecessarily harsh spending cuts based on the publication in the autumn of Fianna Fáil's economic plan *The Way Forward*, which placed some emphasis on redistributing wealth but was most associated in the public mind with swingeing public service cuts. Written by O'hUiginn at his home in Templeogue, and drawing on his admiration for Seán Lemass, who had originally devised a type of proto-corporate state in the 1960s by being the first politician to bring the social partners into the charmed circle of power, *The Way Forward* also drew on the experience of other small European states both as a development model for the future and as a reference point on the need for social consensus. *The Way Forward* was derided by official Ireland. The Department of Finance, sore enough over the whole idea of the Department of Economic Development and Planning, contemptuously dismissed it as *The Way Backwards* and briefed incessantly against it, insisting that it, the Department, alone was the repository from which economic policy should derive and that anything else was to be treated with suspicion (Dunlop, 2004: 294). It was not impressed with so-called national economic plans. Two weeks after *The Way Forward* was published, the government fell and the document became a historical artefact. Though it was written off by the then press secretary Frank Dunlop in his memoirs as 'a one-day wonder ... the document that had caused so much sound and fury signified little and was largely forgotten' (Dunlop, 2004: 296–7), the reality was that it was certainly not forgotten by either Haughey or O'hUiginn, who would return to its basic premise in 1987.

For now Haughey's social partnership dream was in ruins. Barely in power nine months, he was turfed out by the electorate, who instead turned to a coalition of Fine Gael, led by Garret FitzGerald, and Labour led by Dick Spring. Haughey found himself out in the political cold again and his civil service Svengali O'hUiginn was diplomatically pushed aside by FitzGerald and sent to the wasteland of chairing the National Economic and Social Council, well away from the new Taoiseach. According to Jacobsen (1994: 149), the fact that Fine Gael gained power from the November election 'might well be a tribute to the potency of free market ideology'. However, it is much more likely that, in an era of white-collar protest about taxation and declining union membership, all the parties realised there simply was no other choice but to reduce public spending in an attempt to retain control over macroeconomic policy, and stave off the spectre of IMF domination that would haunt Irish politicians of the same mainstream parties three decades later.

The Fianna Fáil–Fine Gael dichotomy

Social partnership, or any variation thereof, was not something Fine Gael considered when it took office in November 1982, and the 1982–87 Fine Gael–Labour government would be a cold house for the trade union movement. Garret FitzGerald came to power in November 1982 clearly believing that the influence of the trade unions on Fianna Fáil government policy was insidious, and he resolved not to let the same happen to his government. Noting that in the period 1979–81 'the trade unions ... had such an easy time of it with Fianna Fáil', he maintained that by the end of his government in 1987 the industrial relations situation in the country was transformed; this allowed Fianna Fáil to negotiate better national agreements in 1987 and 1991 (FitzGerald, 1991: 453–4). It is more than a little puzzling why FitzGerald's government could not negotiate its own agreement with the unions, as for one it might have kept the Labour Party from walking out of government in February 1987 and given that government a chance of re-election. While FitzGerald strongly argued that he was neither a neoliberal nor even more pejoratively a Thatcherite, it is clear that this is how the trade union movement viewed him. And certainly the trade union movement was close to Fianna Fáil. In the words of Jack Lynch himself, the basic objectives of Fianna Fáil and the Irish Congress of Trade Unions were 'close and perhaps identical' (Hardiman, 1988: 211). But Fianna Fáil's main priority was itself and not the trade unions. When the 1979 national understanding had initially been rejected by that Congress, Brian Lenihan famously remarked that it was the fault of 'reds' with 'alien ideologies' (Foster, 2007: 17), which was more than a touch ironic given the closeness of Fianna Fáil to the unions. As the Fine Gael–Labour government imploded towards the end of 1986 and the beginning of 1987 Fianna Fáil stood on the sidelines desperate for power and to implement its new toy: social partnership.

Fianna Fáil has long been characterised as a catch-all party with a chameleon-like ability to appeal to all sections of society, and historically it has dominated the Irish party system. A classically populist party since its foundation in 1926, it has always defied easy analysis. It garnered support from all sections of the population since it first entered government in 1932. Originally founded out of the split in the Sinn Féin Party, the success of which in the 1918 Westminster election led to Irish independence in 1922, Fianna Fáil quickly set out its stall as a radical anti-establishment party. It soon lost much of its early radicalism, however, and by the end of its first sixteen-year period in power in 1948 the Irish party system had developed into 'Fianna Fáil versus the rest' in terms of party competition. Over the course of the following fifty years Fianna Fáil continued to espouse policies imbued with nationalist rhetoric while also maintaining close links to the trade union movement and an appeal to farmers both large and small. Moreover it also attracted support from both big business and the working class. Fianna Fáil was well summed up by Peter Mair in 1987 where he noted that through 'a combination of economic expansion, a commitment to welfare, and a persistent opposition to the politicisation of social conflict, the party developed what might be termed a corporatist ideology congruent with but also at quite a remove from its traditional appeal to territorial nationalism' (Mair, 1987a: 141). It also significantly dominated the Irish bureaucracy through its dominance of the higher echelons of the civil service, with Garvin noting in 1981 that 'the penetration of Fianna Fáil into the bureaucracy appears to be very great, and is due mainly to the fact that the party has had a near monopoly on public office for almost fifty years and has, by its own success, generated social categories created in its own image'. Although perhaps overstating things, Garvin goes on to note that one member of the 1973–77 coalition government occasionally felt during his tenure as minister that he was 'an interloper at a Fianna Fáil *comhairle ceanntair* [area council] in perpetual session' (Garvin, 2005: 224).

But despite these deep roots in the Irish administrative system and its remarkable ability to attract over 40 per cent of the vote at every election it entered up until 1992, Fianna Fáil under Haughey in the 1980s was showing a distinctly conservative hue. In its devotion to the 1937 Constitution, Bunreacht na hÉireann, Fianna Fáil articulated a defence of sovereignty, nationalism, family values and a belief in the transformative power of the state to bring economic progress. This enabled it to oppose the government's proposal to allow for divorce in 1986 and to advocate trenchant opposition to the Anglo Irish Agreement the year previously. Fianna Fáil's moral traditionalism had clearly some support given the defeat of the divorce referendum but its opposition to the Anglo Irish Agreement is more puzzling if one takes the view that Fianna Fáil was basically a bunch of huckster opportunists who would oppose everything in opposition and then shamefacedly perform voltefaces once they were in power. On its signing in 1985 the Agreement had wide popular support, and Fianna Fáil opposition towards it is probably most simply to do with the fact that it did not sit with its constitutional nationalism and in particular its devotion to Articles Two and Three of the Constitution which laid claim to the thirty-two counties and which eventually were deleted after the referendum ratifying the 1998 Good Friday Agreement. This as much as any political opportunism lies behind that specific decision. Defending the Constitution was at heart a core raison d'être of Fianna Fáil. As

Haughey pointed out in October 1986: 'Fianna Fáil today is more than ever left alone as the guardian of the republican tradition and the Constitution of this state, in which that transition is enshrined. We are a Constitutional party in the fullest sense in that we support totally and unequivocally the Constitution of our country. Fianna Fáil see that Constitution as giving substance and meaning to Irish national life and to our freedom and independence' (Girvin, 1987a: 13).

But it would not be family values in relation to abortion, contraception and divorce that would see Fianna Fáil back in government, or any trumpeting of the nationalist clarion, but plain simple economics. A people fed up with the mid-1980s recession would look to a familiar voice and one that always been of the view that the state would be at the heart of ensuring economic prosperity. Moreover it was an alternative with a leader in Haughey who was able to claim that, notwithstanding the dire state of the national finances between 1979 and 1981 when he was first in power, people were better off with a Fianna Fáil government rather the inept if well-meaning amateurs from Fine Gael and Labour who according to him had certainly made the country much worse economically during their period in power. For Haughey, Fine Gaelers were more interested in theory than practice – Garret FitzGerald's supposed phrase 'it sounds great in practice but how will it work in theory' summed them up in the minds of most Fianna Fáilers – and had little feel for how voters actually lived their lives and paid their bills. Fianna Fáil of course did, and it would be by using the power of the state that people's lives would be improved. The trouble was that there was actually very little money in the public purse for the state to play with. That was Haughey's dilemma as the Fine Gael–Labour government played out its lonely existence in the last days of 1986, memorably described by the Minister for Social Welfare, Gemma Hussey, as 'a sort of gloom has settled over us all … Long Dáil session, Cabinet meetings that get nowhere' (Hussey, 1990: 246).

The Dáil never reconvened after Christmas, and Labour finally pulled out in January 1987 when it could not agree with various proposed cuts for that year's budget. The election was called for 17 February, with Fianna Fáil in an ideal position to benefit from not only from the grim economic situation most notably summed up by the 18 per cent unemployment rate but also from the departing coalition government's ideological incoherence. Who could possibly re-elect a government paralysed by indecision and unable to come up with any strategy to take the state and its people out of the economic morass it was mired in throughout the 1980s? The monetarism of Fine Gael, summed up by its overt concentration on reducing debt, borrowing and state spending, was contrasted with Labour's view of the state as a vehicle for economic growth and social justice. Going in to the general election Labour stood at barely 5 per cent in the polls while Fine Gael's vote seemed ready to collapse, standing at just 18 per cent when the election was called (Girvin, 1987a: 28). On these numbers not only had the Fine Gael–Labour government no hope of being re-elected even if it wanted to be, but the very survival of Labour was at stake and Fine Gael's status as the state's second largest party was at grave risk as the Irish people took a long look at the newcomer on the right, the PDs. The new party born in a wave of optimism was a threat not only to Fine Gael but also to Fianna Fáil as it threatened the elusive dream of a Fianna Fáil overall majority so dear to the heart of Charles Haughey.

Who were these apostates from the right and where did they come from? Economically right-wing or neoliberal, and socially liberal, the PDs had been formed in December 1985 in a breakaway from Fianna Fáil, mainly over one thing: the leadership of a certain Charles Haughey. Nevertheless, once they started to organise and fund themselves and offered a policy programme to the Irish people it quickly became clear that the PDs would pose a significant and probably more ominous threat to Fine Gael than Fianna Fáil. Support for the new party was drawn mostly from the middle class, and much of it seemed to be from disaffected Fine Gael supporters rather than from Fianna Fáilers who had followed Des O'Malley and others out from the Soldiers of Destiny. Initially treated by Fianna Fáil as a traitorous O'Malley rump who had jumped ship, the PDs proved doughty political operators and throughout 1986 polled consistently in the mid- to high teens. The new destiny as the 1987 general election campaign got under way seemed to be that the PDs would transform Irish politics, given that they were polling at 15 per cent, within striking distance of Fine Gael and a full 10 points higher than Labour. While performing well in the polls and taking seats are two very different things, for a people weighed down by recession, joblessness and emigration the PDs seemed to offer some concrete hope. However, for many of these poor and indigent people who looked to the state for help, the PDs offered little succour with their mantra of low taxation and low public spending, and a retreat of the state which looked suspiciously and decidedly like what Margaret Thatcher was engaging in across the water in Britain. In their 1987 election manifesto grandiosely entitled *Message to the Irish People* the PDs left no one in any doubt about their ideological assault on, and commitment to, reducing the role of the state: 'we believe that the state must play a less dominant role in the economic and social life of the country'. What the country needed, they argued, was a 'truly Republican view of the state where the individual is master, and not slave to the system; where the state protects the needy but encourages the brave' (Mair, 1987b: 38).

The retreat from the state utopia so beloved of the PDs did not stop them, however, from voting against the proposed closure of Barrington's Hospital by the minority Fianna Fáil government in Limerick city in 1988. That the hospital happened to be at the centre of Des O'Malley's constituency was good enough reason to oppose any cutbacks or closure. Political ideology worked for the PDs when it suited them. When it did not, as with Barrington's, they simply abandoned it on the altar of political expediency and resorted to the clientelism they had so railed against since their inception in 1985. Excuses offered at the time by O'Malley, that the wrong hospital was being closed in Limerick and that Barrington's should be kept open with the neighbouring St John's closed, sounded suspiciously like special pleading on behalf of the PDs and offer a stark reminder that, for all their probity and promise to bring high-minded ethics to public life, the PDs were as susceptible to clientelism and localism as anybody else and especially the great satans of Fianna Fáil. Subsequently a number of high-profile PDs voiced opposition and disquiet about the incident, with the future leader Mary Harney noting 'I was totally against what we did on Barrington's hospital ... Here was an issue in Des O'Malley's backyard and the party adopted a position that did not fit with its overall policy.' This view was echoed by the Party stalwart and backroom apparatchik Stephen O'Byrnes, who bemoaned the fact that Barrington's Hospital did enormous damage to the Party: 'Here we were, the party of fiscal rectitude, not being prepared to follow the prescription in the leader's own constituency. In my view it was fundamental as it represented a failure of the party to live up to one of its fundamental principles' (Collins, 2005: 82–3). But the PDs had succumbed to the iron rule that all politics is local. Despite the later protestations of practically every PD bar O'Malley that Barrington's should have been let close, the reality was that no one was prepared to tell their leader that he was in the wrong. For all the PDs' protestations that Fianna Fáil was an Il Duce organisation ruled with an iron fist by Charles Haughey, senior PDs were unable to tell their own leader that on this issue he was in the wrong. But the pressure on O'Malley in his native Limerick was too strong to ignore and he became an enthusiastic opponent of the closure. It classically illustrated one of the core tenets of Irish politics. Notwithstanding any ideological held beliefs, local issues and the clientelistic holds of people on their public representatives were constantly on the surface of Irish politics. O'Malley's beliefs that Haughey had chosen Barrington's rather than St John's on the grounds of lobbying by the then Bishop of Limerick to close what he called 'the Protestant Barrington's' and keep the Catholic St John's open (O'Malley, 2014: 177), and that furthermore it had been part of ongoing dastardly attempts by Fianna Fáil and Haughey in particular to undermine O'Malley, have a bit of the he-doth-protest-too-much about them.

In any event, for the needy and those without any political influence, Fianna Fáil, the traditional party of the poor and working class, seemed a safer bet at the 1987 election. The trick for Fianna Fáil would be in ensuring that other parts of its electoral Hydra held up. Protecting the poor, memorably described in an infamous political advertisement as 'Health cuts hurt the old, the sick and the handicapped: there is a better way', would only get them so far. The real trick for Fianna Fáil was in persuading the electorate that the recovery of the economy was linked to its success in the general election. Economic growth, whatever that was, would be at the heart of its economic policy and would provide extra benefit to the state's coffers, thus enabling people to get back to work and to provide enough moneys to protect services. This linked back to the Fianna Fáil of Seán Lemass in the late 1950s and 1960s where an economic engagement with the social partners of business, farming and unions would join together with the government in an economic scenario in which a Keynesian rising tide lifts all boats. The clever advertisement would come back to haunt Fianna Fáil, which took to cutting services with a gusto that would surely have made Fine Gael blush.

For their part Fine Gael and Labour had not quite given up during the 1987 election campaign but had little to offer the electorate. This was particularly the case for Labour, which stressed its commitment to state-led intervention to achieve a 4 per cent growth rate per annum and a promise to protect the needy, but faced a sceptical electorate who wondered why Labour was unable to achieve this in government over the previous four years. In reality Labour was in the election to try to hold on to as many of its 16 seats as it could. Fine Gael had had an intriguing four years in power. Coming into office having closed to within a historic 5 seats of Fianna Fáil in the November 1982 general election, the Fine Gael of Garret FitzGerald promised three things to the electorate: it was not Fianna Fáil; it would deliver prudent effective economic governance; and it would unleash a constitutional crusade that would liberalise Irish society. Within a year that crusade would be significantly frayed as Fine Gael foisted a bizarre constitutional referendum on the public to constitutionally prohibit abortion.

The constitutional crusade

Nobody who knows anything at all about modern Irish politics could possibly doubt Garret FitzGerald's commitment to liberal social values and support for the personal liberties of individuals. Yet as Meehan (2013: 3) astutely points out, the constitutional crusade was immediately derailed by FitzGerald's decision to hold a referendum to insert prohibition on abortion into the Constitution following intense lobbying from pro-life groups. In essence it was a government led by probably Ireland's foremost intellectual politician who kowtowed to a bunch of unelected lobbyists by putting the abortion referendum to the people in 1983 that sowed serious social division throughout the state. It was those groups, who wished to impose a distinctly Catholic view of morality on the Irish state, who would become the acknowledged leaders in the field of pressure-group politics. Indeed, the Society for the Protection of the Unborn Child sprung up completely unannounced in 1981 and within two years had, along with other likeminded groups, under the umbrella of the Pro-Life Amendment Campaign (PLAC), successfully persuaded the government of the day to call a referendum with the purpose of introducing an amendment that would, in effect, guarantee the rights of the unborn child and constitutionally outlaw abortion (Girvin, 1986: 61–81). In Ireland, restrictive abortion legislation had remained intact and virtually unchallenged since 1861 under Section 58 of the Offences against the Person Act. Section 59 of the same act also provided that anyone helping a woman have an abortion would be liable to considerable penalties (Hesketh, 1990: 1–2). Why, if such a situation existed, did the government of the day put a deeply divisive referendum to the people in 1983, when up to just a few years previously there had been virtually no calls for any repeal of the existing legislation?

In essence, the so-called pro-life campaign was pre-emptory in that its aim was to prevent the future legalisation of abortion in Ireland. It anticipated that abortion might become legal through either parliamentary action or court activity or both. It seemed to fear that a simple amendment of the existing act could legalise abortion, notwithstanding that the idea of replacing the existing act with a more permissive or liberal act was simply not an option that any government would be willing to sign up to or even want to do. Secondly, the pro-life campaign feared that, if abortion was not constitutionally prohibited, there would be a danger that an action could be taken in the Irish courts to challenge the then existing legislative prohibition of abortion in an attempt to have it declared unconstitutional: something akin to the famous Roe versus Wade decision in the United States in 1973. Again the likelihood of this in a state noted for its social conservatism since its foundation in 1922 was extremely unlikely as there was no liberal cadre of jurists or constitutional lawyers of any type advocating for such a judgement or state of affairs to come about.

Nevertheless in the hectic political atmosphere of 1981–82, which saw three general elections in the space of eighteen months, the question of an anti-abortion amendment to the Constitution forced its way on to the political agenda. In April 1981 FitzGerald, then in opposition, was approached by a group of people who said that they were concerned about the possibility that the Irish Supreme Court might copy its American counterpart's decision in the case of Roe versus Wade, which eight years earlier had declared state legislation against abortion to be unconstitutional in the US. The Fianna Fáil government of Charles Haughey had also been approached by the same group. FitzGerald has since written that it seemed highly improbable to him that the Irish Supreme Court would ever challenge the existing abortion legislation. Nevertheless, such was his personal antipathy to abortion, and conscious as he was of the opposition of the vast majority of the people of Ireland, he was willing to support a constitutional amendment that would limit the court's functions in this matter (FitzGerald, 1991: 416). Rather confusingly, over a decade later FitzGerald would write:

as it seemed to me sensible that this complex matter be left to the legislative power of the Oireachtas, I agreed that an amendment among such lines should be introduced and later confirmed that it would be included with other constitutional changes which I proposed to introduce with a view to removing sectarian elements from our 1937 Constitution. (*Irish Times*, 2 March 2002)

If FitzGerald believed that such a matter should be left to the Oireachtas (Parliament), then why would he be supporting any new insertion to the Constitution, which by its very nature removes power from the Oireachtas and places it explicitly in the hands of the people at the ballot box?

FitzGerald, as Taoiseach, had met PLAC in late 1981 to tell the group that a constitutional change in relation to abortion would be incorporated into a general constitutional review that he had proposed. PLAC was dissatisfied with his response and continued to demand that there should be a singular referendum to outlaw abortion (FitzGerald, 1991: 416). PLAC also met with Fianna Fáil, which was more receptive to the idea of a single referendum. Haughey wrote to PLAC stating:

I am glad to be able to confirm to your executive committee that when elected to office the new Fianna Fáil Government will arrange to have the necessary legislation for a proposed constitutional amendment to guarantee the right of the life of the foetus initiated in Dáil Éireann during the course of this year, 1982, without reference to any other aspect of constitutional change. (O'Reilly, 1992: 75)

The singularity of this proposal was in direct contrast to the FitzGerald view on the amendment as part of a constitutional package. PLAC continued to keep up the pressure on Fine Gael and the result was that, by the time of the November 1982 general election, both Fianna Fáil and Fine Gael had declared they would, if elected, introduce a pro-life abortion amendment into the Irish Constitution. Nowhere in FitzGerald's memoirs (1991) does he state what sorts of pressure tactics were brought to bear on him from such groups. Yet the reality is that his government, and indeed that of Haughey in the same period, were hopelessly ill equipped to deal with such a highly organised pressure group as PLAC. The reason they were so ill equipped was that they had not thought through the implications of any such referendum nor had they taken a position as to whether it was a good idea to start tinkering with the Constitution when there was no urgent demand for it to be amended. This was not a crucial economic and foreign policy question such as joining the

EEC or an attempt to change the voting system. Constitutions as guiding posts for societies should be treated carefully and not be changed without significant public engagement. Yet this referendum was basically an attempt by a well-resourced and vocal pressure group to use the Constitution as its own special plaything. For both Fianna Fáil and Fine Gael this did not seem too problematic, as after all who in the Ireland of the early 1980s was actually advocating to make abortion legal? The answer put simply was pretty much no one, and certainly no one with any political or judicial influence.

In essence, the original referendum on abortion came about quite simply because of the incessant lobbying of a number of highly vocal interest groups who argued that the legal ban on abortion could be overturned in the courts and that a constitutional ban on abortion was imperative. Eventually, the wording that Fianna Fáil put forward, which was acceptable to PLAC, was forced through by the Fine Gael–Labour government against the advice of its own attorney-general, Peter Sutherland. FitzGerald has subsequently written that he should never have accepted 'the original referendum proposal put to me, however harmless it may have appeared at the time, for that commitment to introduce a constitutional amendment on the issue led me into a position that, while intellectually defensible, was much too complicated to secure public understanding or acceptance' (FitzGerald, 1991: 446). While the reference to the proposal being much too complicated suggests a certain intellectual superiority on behalf of FitzGerald, the question must be asked: why did this most intelligent of Taoisigh actually support a referendum that he was sure the electorate would not understand? His reaction to his first meeting with PLAC has been described as 'grovelling' by one PLAC member present (O'Reilly, 1992: 68).

The perceived electoral power of influence that such groups might well pose is the most plausible explanation behind such political acquiescence to PLAC's demands. While such groups have had a negligible effect when they have presented themselves to the electorate in national elections, the fear in the early 1980s of being perceived as 'soft on abortion', as FitzGerald himself alluded to a rumour then doing the rounds about him (FitzGerald, 1991: 416), was thought to have been enough to have been electorally suicidal in the fluid political situation then in existence and in which Fine Gael would come historically close to overtaking Fianna Fáil as the leading party in the state. PLAC was an umbrella group that formed with the intention of getting a single piece of legislation enacted and did everything in its power to ensure such an outcome. But the question must be asked as to how much political influence these groups actually had when it came to citizens voting at the ballot box in general elections. The trouble for FitzGerald and Fine Gael was that once Fianna Fáil, out of purely political considerations, had agreed to hold a referendum to outlaw abortion, then Fine Gael was surely damned if it did not agree to hold one as well. Once the FitzGerald gambit of attempting to hold an abortion referendum as part of a wider constitutional referenda framework was rebuffed by PLAC, he had really no political choice but to agree to hold one as well. While all the evidence was that Irish voters in this period voted on economic grounds (Laver, Mair and Sinnott, 1987), no major political party could leave its social flank unguarded by being accused of not protecting the unborn and being soft on abortion. Thus FitzGerald felt himself as having really no choice but to put an abortion referendum to the people. His major failing in many ways was deciding to have it so early in his government's tenure when he clearly was uneasy with it himself. Moreover there was no real political capital to be gained, as Fianna Fáil also supported the referendum, and more to the point it was the latter's wording that was eventually put to the people. In that context no political credit would come to either government party from the abortion referendum. The referendum was passed two to one on a 53.67 per cent turnout which for comparison was some 17 percentage points lower than the turnout for the 1972 referendum on Irish entry to the EEC. One wonders, given the fact that practically half the population did not turn out to vote, whether the decision to hold a referendum was worth it all. This would prove to be even more the case when within a decade the people were back voting on more abortion referendums.

Matters on the social front would become much worse for FitzGerald and his government when he failed in his bid to remove the prohibition of divorce from the Constitution in 1986. Women's interest groups had been at the centre of political life since the early 1970s. Organisations such as AIM (Action, Information, Motivation) and Cherish (a single mothers' organisation) became important lobbying agencies for changes in family law and the status of women. Moreover the National Women's Council of Ireland, which represented established women's organisations, also sought to influence government policy in a wide range of areas affecting women (Galligan, 1998: 54). While AIM was very influential in placing specific and narrowly defined reforms in the field of family policy on to the political agenda, it had much greater difficulty in finding parliamentary and governmental approval of the need for the introduction of divorce legislation. AIM joined with the Divorce Action Group and the Irish Council for Civil Liberties in lobbying for divorce from 1981 onwards. The Divorce Action Group formed in 1980 proved very effective in attracting support from the Labour Party and the liberal wing of Fine Gael (Girvin, 1987b: 94). With the election of the Fine Gael–Labour coalition government in 1982, such lobbying held out the hope of success as the introduction of divorce was one of the tenets of Garret FitzGerald's constitutional crusade. Moreover the issue had been a live one within Fine Gael since the late 1970s when strong support was given at the Fine Gael Ard Fheis (Annual Meeting) of 1978 to the removal of the Constitutional ban on divorce (FitzGerald, 1991: 623). Any success would, however, entail the use of a Constitutional referendum, which by its very nature would be much more public and controversial than the reform agenda pushed by AIM up to that point.

In July 1983 the government established an all-party joint committee on marital breakdown with a view to obtaining cross-party consensus on a family law agenda including divorce. This committee received over seven hundred written and twenty-four oral submissions including the views of AIM, the Divorce Action Group, the Free Legal Aid Centres, the Catholic Marriage Advisory Council and the Irish Council for Civil Liberties (Galligan, 1998: 102). When the committee finally reported in 1995, it stopped short of recommending the removal of the ban on divorce as the then opposition Fianna Fáil members opposed such a move. Notwithstanding such a position, the government, buoyed by a series of opinion polls, decided that the time was right to tackle the issue of divorce. Yet after the decision to hold a referendum was taken, FitzGerald procrastinated for months while he attempted to convince the churches, particularly the Catholic Church, that the time was right to introduce a modest measure of reform. The delaying of the referendum, however, also delayed the preparation of the necessary background papers to enable the government to deal with any issues that might arise in the course of a referendum campaign. The result was that when the referendum was called, with little advance public or political discussion, the government was woefully unprepared (Finlay, 1998: 33). FitzGerald had basically outmanoeuvred himself. So desperate was he to bring everyone onside after the division of the abortion referendum that he appeared weak. His cherished aim of a civilised debate and an overwhelming Yes vote dissipated, and after the referendum was over his beloved Constitutional crusade was in ruins.

The campaign itself was deeply divisive and bitter, and resulted in defeat for the government's proposed removal of the ban on divorce by 63 per cent to 37 per cent on a turnout of 60.84 per cent. A poll carried out at the beginning of the campaign showed 57 per cent in favour of the amendment and 36 per cent against (Girvin, 1987b: 93–8). The opposition of the Catholic Church had proved crucial. Rather naively, FitzGerald at the outset of the campaign had assumed that, given the Catholic Church's stated position that it did not seek to impose its theological views on the civil law of the state, then the only relevant consideration would be whether the balance of social good would or would not be served by a restricted form of divorce: 'I recognised that there could of course be divided views on this issue – it was essentially a matter of judgement – but the fact that the two sides of this crucial question were never addressed by the church during the course of the campaign disturbed me' (FitzGerald, 1991: 631). Furthermore in a country where ownership of property means so much, doubts raised in the public mind by those on the No side as to the equitable distribution of property proved hugely influential in returning a No vote. As Fergus Finlay, who was intimately involved in the Yes campaign, has written:

> The opponents of divorce were able to rely on a mixture of fear about property and land, and a message that this was a government which couldn't be trusted. I came to believe in the course of that campaign that a great many women, who had been prepared to vote for divorce before it started, began to see divorce as a reward for philandering husbands. (Finlay, 1998: 33)

While at a fundamental level the defeated amendment had for the first time placed the issue of marital breakdown firmly on the political agenda, the loss of the referendum and, even as importantly, the size of it was a crushing blow for FitzGerald. With an economy all but collapsing around him and now a defeated referendum behind him, the government's reputation, and by extension FitzGerald's, for economic competence and for constitutional innovation had dissipated. Not being Fianna Fáil would not save him or his government as they limped to the inevitable early general election.

No national government for Ireland

The 1987 election campaign itself was a tame enough affair. Garret FitzGerald's cunning plan was based around the idea of a national Economic Forum along the lines of the New Ireland Forum established by his government in 1983, which allowed for Irish political parties of a nationalist persuasion to discuss potential political solutions to the Northern Ireland problem so that a nationalist consensus could be achieved. The trouble for FitzGerald was that, while such an idea was plausible in discussing the rather abstract if certainly lethal problems of Northern Ireland, it was completely unrealisable when it came to facing economic questions in the Republic. It also had the faint notion of being a desperate bid by FitzGerald to hold on to some form of power in post-election Ireland. Fianna Fáil had never been keen on the idea of national governments to deal with the economic woes of the state. National governments in democracies usually derive from circumstances of extraordinary crisis such as world wars and political revolutions. In Ireland there had been significant calls for a national government at various times – during World War Two or *The Emergency* as it was quaintly known in Ireland, and again in the 1950s – which were always rebuffed by Eamon de Valera (Murphy, 2009: 150). Similar calls in late 2008 and 2009 as that economic crisis deepened were also dismissed by Fianna Fáil. In 1987, having been out of power for over four long years, Fianna Fáil was certainly in no mood to share office or even ideas on how to overcome the continuing economic difficulties facing the state especially when, according to itself, it had the solution at hand; a solution that was very different to the one espoused by Finc Gael. Haughey particularly rejected the idea of a national government as an affront to the democracy of the ballot box. The minor parties all followed suit.

Once FitzGerald's national government idea predictably went nowhere, he resolved to try to keep Haughey out of power by, in the last week of the campaign, encouraging all Fine Gael voters to give their second preferences to the PDs. This was certainly an audacious move to stay in power, and of course in reality a repudiation of the government he had led for four years. He couched it in terms of the fact that, with Fianna Fáil slipping in the polls with the voters – in his own correct analysis they not willing to give Haughey an overall majority – there was now an alternative coalition willing to save the state: 'The only alternative Government is a Fine Gael Government with support from the Progressive Democrats, who have shared broadly our analysis of the problem and who have faced the fact that for some years to come we have to control public spending.' The trouble for FitzGerald was that the PDs did not buy into his analysis when O'Malley refused to advise his supporters on who to give their second preferences to beyond an anodyne statement that they should 'vote for candidates, whose principles and policies are in the voter's judgement closest to our own' (Girvin, 1987a: 27). The reasons the PDs took this position are relatively straightforward. While the PD and Fine Gael manifestos were closely aligned, the reality was that very few voters actually read manifestos carefully. By making a call for PD voters, who after all would be casting their votes for the party for the very first time, to transfer specifically to Fine Gael, the PDs' independence as a new political entity ready to break the mould of Irish politics, as they themselves evangelically saw it, would have been placed immediately in jeopardy. More fundamentally, despite relatively good poll numbers no political pundits or politicians could actually say how well the PDs would fare when the voters entered the ballot box. Finally the last MRBI poll of the campaign found that 34 per cent of Fine Gael and PD voters would transfer to one another but that 21 per cent of the PDs would transfer to Fianna Fáil, showing that, despite being accused of traitorous behaviour by Fianna Fáil, there were plenty of would-be PD voters who were more comfortable with Fianna Fáil than they were with Fine Gael.

The electorate of 1987 was the most volatile Ireland has seen since World War Two. The entry into the mix of the PDs, who made the most impressive debut of any political party since Clann na Poblachta in the 1940s, lent significant uncertainty to the political contest. (Clann na Poblachta was a small Republican party established by Seán MacBride in 1946 which for a brief while prior to the 1948 general election threatened the political hegemony of Fianna Fáil. It entered government as part of a grand coalition led by Fine

Gael in 1948. It was ultimately dissolved in 1965.) This led to a scenario where, once the votes were counted, it transpired that the three major political parties Fianna Fáil, Fine Gael and Labour all recorded their lowest first preference vote share in the modern era. Fianna Fáil's vote was its lowest since 1961. It fell just 2 seats of the holy grail of an overall majority it had assumed was its right having spent over four years in the purgatory of opposition. Fine Gael saw its vote slip to its lowest since 1957 when it had last presided over an economy in severe and seemingly never-ending recession. The outcome in seats was, if anything, even worse for the Party as it lost 20 seats, falling to 50. With Fine Gael having come within 5 seats of Fianna Fáil in the previous election of November 1982, the voters had enough of the party they had put into office to fix the economy, and it now languished an astonishing 30 seats behind Fianna Fáil. The Labour Party did as poorly as most commentators had predicted and recorded its lowest vote since 1933. It managed to survive, however, coming back to the new Dáil with twelve TDs, a loss of four, on just over 7 per cent of the vote. It looked as if the traditional two-and-a-half party system was finally at an end and had been broken by a specifically ideological right-wing party. The shape of Irish politics was to change even further, however, as, unbeknown to the political system or to anyone within it, Ireland was to see its last single-party government when Charles Haughey was elected Taoiseach of a minority Fianna Fáil government with tacit support to fix the economy from Fine Gael.

2

Charles J. Haughey and the politics of coalition

I don't believe in coalitions.

Charles J. Haughey, 29 June 1989

The Haughey election

In the late morning of 12 July 1989 the Fianna Fáil leader, Charles J. Haughey, took a decision that changed the nature of Irish politics when he agreed to lead a coalition of Fianna Fáil and the PDs following the inconclusive result of the election held on 15 June. Generally perceived as having done a pretty decent job in bringing the Irish state out of the mire of recession, the minority Fianna Fáil government elected after the 1987 election with the tacit support of Fine Gael fell on its own sword in April 1989. On losing a vote in the Dáil on the issue of providing additional funding to haemophiliacs suffering from the Aids virus, Haughey, recently returned from Japan, decided that his government could not be held to ransom on issues of money and finance and so requested a dissolution of the Dáil from the President a month later on 25 May. Although the government had lost six other Dáil votes during its two years in office and the opposition was of the view that a defeat on this issue would not necessarily mean an election, Haughey had had enough of minority government. This was no fit of pique but a serious calculation that he could win an overall majority. Thus he went to the country on a campaign based not around policy but on the more nebulous question of governance and the necessity and goodness of strong, stable single-party government versus the evils of weak coalitions and minority-led governments.

A continuing series of minor parliamentary defeats, while uncomfortable for Haughey and Fianna Fáil, was not exactly debilitating in terms of actually governing. It was, however, sapping to morale and was breeding uncertainly and instability. Moreover, given that the government had now lost a vote on a financial matter, the chances of passing deeply contested health estimates on the government's terms were unlikely. Having campaigned in 1987 promising to spend lavishly on health, the minority Fianna Fáil government quickly went into austerity mode once in power and began cutting public spending in all ministries, including health. Having been defeated on providing additional funding on the haemophiliac issue, it seemed unlikely that it could persuade the opposition to accept its health estimates. Beyond that, passing another difficult budget would also inevitably prove problematic given the emboldened nature of the opposition. In that context those ministers in Haughey's cabinet who advocated continuing in government on the reasonable grounds that the electorate did not want an election quickly found themselves drowned out (Farrell, 1990: 181).

The thinking amongst those who favoured a dissolution of the Dáil and a snap election was based around the twin prongs of public opinion favouring the party, the leader and its policies, and the fact that Fianna Fáil simply detested not being able to govern independently and baulked at the idea of sharing power with any other party or individuals. On the first prong Fianna Fáil stood at just over 50 per cent in some polls in early 1989 and the thinking within the Party was that if it could receive 45 per cent in an election then it would certainly gain a majority. On the second it had governed effectively in a minority capacity before under its two legendary leaders Eamon de Valera and Seán Lemass, but under Haughey the goal of majority government had become an article of faith in itself. Tiring of what it regarded as an 'artificial arrangement', Fianna Fáil and Haughey lost their patience and gambled on a quick early summer election in the expectation of getting that elusive overall majority (Girvin, 1990: 13).

For those who were against any notion of an early election, such as Albert Reynolds and Bertie Ahern, the calling of the election was an act of supreme folly. With an improving economy, the restoration of the public finances to some order and the fear that calling an unnecessary election would prove unpopular with the voters, the majority of the cabinet attempted in vain to talk Haughey out of this course of action but he was having none of it. According to Ahern, Haughey 'just found it a personal affront to his dignity that he had to rely on the goodwill of the opposition to keep him Taoiseach' (Ahern, 2010: 105). Both Collins (2005: 89) and Whelan (2011: 231) have offered the intriguing snippet on the basis of evidence from the Flood and Mahon Tribunals that those most in favour of an election, Haughey and senior ministers Pádraig Flynn and Ray Burke, all collected substantial amounts of donations during that election campaign, some of which ended up being used for their own ends. This is unlikely to have been a reason in itself for Haughey's decision to go to the country but it certainly adds an extra dimension to the calling of perhaps Ireland's most pointless general election.

For the opposition the calling of this unwanted election presented some difficulties. Fine Gael, still traumatised over the scale of its defeat at the 1987 election and the replacement of Garret FitzGerald with Alan Dukes, had very little interest in fighting another election. FitzGerald maintained that Fine Gael had not changed its mind on supporting the government on the main fiscal issues to be addressed and, given that none of the government's defeats had been on confidence issues, there was no need to call an election. He went on to cast doubt on Haughey's motive for calling the election, noting that 'the only Fianna Fáil government which people have found in any way acceptable is one with Fine Gael support' (Girvin, 1990: 14). This was seen by most commentators as a dig at Haughey's behaviour in power in the one period he had an overall majority, between December 1979 and June 1981. Questions of Haughey's fitness for power and his use of the state for personal enrichment had been aired since he first took office on succeeding Jack Lynch, and denying Haughey an overall majority would be a central vehicle for Fine Gael and indeed all other opposition parties during the election campaign.

The catastrophic election of 1987 did not only result in a change of leadership in Fine Gael but it also led to one of the most selfless political acts in modern Irish history when the new leader of the Party, Alan Dukes, vowed that Fine Gael would support the government in the broad thrust of its economic policy provided that Fianna Fáil was serious about tackling the mounting public debt. This also had the effect of immediately increasing public and investor confidence in the Irish economy (O'Malley, 2011a: 41). Dukes's so-called Tallaght Strategy speech of September 1987 promising budgetary support for the government was in essence formalising a statement made by Garret FitzGerald on Haughey's election as Taoiseach on 10 March 1987 when he stated that, as long as Fianna Fáil took corrective action to rectify the public finances, Fine Gael would 'not oppose such measures or legislative action required to implement the necessary budgetary provisions' (Dáil Debates, vol. 371, col. 50, 10 March 1987). Such noises had of course been made before in Irish politics. What made this one different and why we can see it as a type of heroic political act is that, unlike pretty much any opposition in the history of the state, Fine Gael under Dukes actually did support the general thrust of the government's fiscal rectitude programme. This was something unique in Irish politics. Bertie Ahern took the view that a minority government had to accept that it would lose some parliamentary votes during the duration of its tenure but that as long as these were not confidence votes it could govern effectively. Indeed, so as not to be accused of being the government's lapdog, Fine Gael for its own political well-being had no real choice but to oppose the government in certain votes. The Minister for Finance, Ray MacSharry, the man who benefited mostly from the Tallaght Strategy, offered the following summation of why Fine Gael took this course: 'the Tallaght Strategy was designed to serve the party and the country. It combined altruism with a degree of political self-interest, and in fairness to

Alan Dukes, perhaps more of the former than the latter' (MacSharry and White, 2000: 75). The strategy allowed Fine Gael to rebuild its tarnished reputation from the ashes of the horrors of the 1982–87 government, allowed it to have an input into the budgetary strategy being pursued by the government and, perhaps most important, allowed it to claim, perfectly legitimately, that it was putting the country first. Moreover it also ensured that if Fianna Fáil called an early general election no blame could be laid at Fine Gael's door.

With a certain grim sense of inevitability Fianna Fáil campaigned poorly. On the back foot from the off, with its promises on the health service from the 1987 election being repeatedly brought up by the opposition, it also constantly faced criticism on why a country ever so slowly coming out of the grip of a grim recession had to tolerate an election at all. The health cuts issue reached a nadir for Fianna Fáil when Haughey admitted that he personally had not been aware of 'the problems and difficulties and hardships' they had caused (Girvin, 1990: 20; Corless, 2007: 233). He then went on to claim that there would be no more expenditure cuts once Fianna Fáil was returned to office as all the necessary cuts had already been made. To an electorate that remembered Fianna Fáil's memorable slogan from just two years earlier, that health cuts hurt the old, sick and handicapped, this was hardly reassuring. If health was a crucial issue for Fianna Fáil's core working-class vote, then the calling of the election itself seemed to have alienated its middle-class constituency. The 50 per cent it had polled in early spring of 1989 dramatically disappeared to a situation whereby once the election had been called the Fianna Fáil vote sunk to its lowest since February of 1988. It quickly became apparent that the party could not win an overall majority. Given that this was the only reason for calling the election, this came as a crushing blow to Haughey. He made a desperate attempt to stave off such a scenario in the last days of the campaign by noting that Fianna Fáil was not looking for a landslide of 1977-style proportions but simply wanted 'a working majority that will give us the capacity to implement our policies on a long term basis without insecurity or instability' (Girvin, 1990: 21). Given that these policies of fiscal rectitude were very much the same in macro terms as Fine Gael's and that the idea of Haughey making a grab for overall power by calling an early election gained traction throughout the campaign, the country was not willing to give him his prized overall majority.

If not an unmitigated disaster, the results were deeply disappointing for Fianna Fáil, which lost 4 seats to fall to 77, on 44 per cent of the first preference vote, some 7 seats short of an overall majority. Both Fine Gael and Labour made modest gains. With Alan Dukes on his first outing as party leader, Fine Gael won an extra 5 seats to bring it to 55, still a long way shy of 1982 when FitzGerald had the Party within touching distance of Fianna

Fáil. Labour gained 3 seats, leaving it with 15, nowhere near forming a coalition with Fine Gael even if it had wanted to. It decided to settle down in opposition to attempt to rebuild the Party, a seemingly perennial task in its history. Besides Fianna Fáil the big losers were the PDs. After their sensational breakthrough two years earlier, hopes were high in the Party that once they entered the Dáil they would reshape Irish politics. Then reality hit home. Fianna Fáil governed in a way that the PDs with their emphasis on fiscal rectitude could hardly complain about. Fine Gael in its adoption of a similar austerity agenda firmly positioned itself as the only responsible party of opposition. The PDs were thus squeezed by the two traditional warhorses of Irish politics. Moreover their original 1987 vote was fluid in the extreme: a concoction of an urban middle-class protest vote, combined with the remnants of the old personal Jack Lynch Fianna Fáil vote now epitomised by Des O'Malley. The PDs' poll numbers for the first year of their life in the Dáil were a steady 14 per cent; up slightly on what they received at the general election of 1987. These numbers were to drop precipitously over the next year and reached a barely believable 5 per cent by the time the election was called. Certainly O'Malley did not believe them (Collins, 2005: 94). Life in the drudgery of the opposition benches proved unexpectedly dull for most of their firstly elected TDs, to the extent that a number of them decided not to run in 1989. Most prominent here was the Party's deputy leader, Michael Keating, who not only was Dublin-based but also had the advantage of having defected from Fine Gael rather than Fianna Fáil. His decision not to run came as a shock and left the Party in some disarray. While he had made no real impact in the Dáil and was a somewhat isolated figure within the Party, his departure left the public somewhat nonplussed about both the inner workings and the electoral prospects of the PDs.

More pertinent perhaps was the decision taken by the Party to enter into a pact with Fine Gael entitled rather cumbersomely the 'Agreed Agenda for Action'. This was in response to Haughey's view that only Fianna Fáil could form a strong government after the election. Inflicted with a type of hubris that a good – miraculous would be more accurate – election by both parties could see them form a coalition, Fine Gael and the PDs agreed that the formation of a stable government was essential and thus presented themselves to the Irish people as one in waiting. In reality neither party was very comfortable with what it had agreed to. Dukes as leader was wary both of O'Malley on a personal level and of the PDs as a party, seeing them not unreasonably as a threat to his own long-established party. He was persuaded of the merits of the deal by his deputy leader John Bruton but in reality his heart was never in it. Moreover none of Fine Gael's chief strategists was enthused by the deal. Dukes even went as far as refusing to give a guarantee that Fine Gael voters should transfer lower preferences to PD candidates, which made many wonder what the point of the pact was at all. For their part the PDs were actually happy enough with the arrangement. It gave them publicity in terms of being spoken about as part of a potential alternative government to Fianna Fáil. It also unsettled Fianna Fáil and achieved the neat trick of having Fianna Fáil being attacked from the right by Fine Gael and the PDs and from the left by Labour and the Workers' Party. Later O'Malley reckoned that the PDs had 'made a strategic mistake in agreeing a pre-election pact with Fine Gael when the correct decision was to have maintained our full independence' (O'Malley, 2014: 176–7). In any event the pact never really attracted the enthusiasm of the public in an election that came increasingly to be dominated by the crisis in the health service. When the votes were counted, the PDs took a terrible hammering, returning with only 6 seats on 5.5 per cent of the vote, below their polar ideological opposites, the Workers' Party. There was very little sympathy for them from any quarter, with Ray Burke caustically remarking on RTÉ radio that it 'couldn't happen to a nicer bunch of people' (Collins, 2005: 95).

The Haughey coalition

With the results ruling out any obvious anti-Fianna Fáil coalition, Haughey immediately claimed that it was his intention to form another minority government and that he would be consulting with other party leaders including Alan Dukes. This predictably enough went nowhere, with Dukes taking the reasonable view that as Haughey had called an unnecessary election he would have to take the consequences. The first of these was that, if he was hoping to rely on Fine Gael's help, he would have to do it within a formal coalition government where Fine Gael would have 7 seats at the cabinet table and where there would be a revolving Taoiseach (Whelan, 2011: 232). The grand coalition of Fianna Fáil and Fine Gael might have been the manna from heaven that those who wanted to see a left–right cleavage emerge in Irish politics had always wished for. It was never going to happen for two reasons. Firstly, coalition government of any type remained anathema to Fianna Fáil. Secondly, coalition government with Fine Gael was the last of all possible options that would be explored. The history of both parties practically forbade it. While technically the idea of the grand coalition had much to recommend it, particularly in terms of its huge majority and the fact that once an agreement was reached it should theoretically be able to withstand defections and backbench revolts, the reality was that there was no way such an agreement could be reached. Enmity simply ran too deep in Irish politics.

Given that Haughey's opening gambit of another minority government had met with this brutal rebuff by Dukes, Fianna Fáil found itself in an extremely difficult position. Its gamble on securing an overall majority was

lost. Its preferred alternative of another minority government had fallen at
the first hurdle when Fine Gael made clear it was not willing to play ball.
The left-wing parties, Labour and the Workers' Party, were implacably
opposed to Fianna Fáil. That just left the apostates of the PDs as potential
supporters of a minority government or coalition partners. Before the election any thought of a Fianna Fáil–PD coalition government seemed ludicrous. After the votes were counted it seemed equally far-fetched. Both
parties had lost votes. The PDs existed at all only because of the schism
within Fianna Fáil. All six PD TDs were former Fianna Fáilers. And, probably most importantly, no greater enmity existed on a personal level within
Irish politics than that between Charles Haughey and Des O'Malley. The
numbers were too small for a minority government. What would be the point
of the PDs supporting Fianna Fáil when they would receive none of the
spoils of office and most likely no credit for their support? The numbers for
a coalition would work only if there was an independent Ceann Comhairle
(Speaker of the House). This was hardly an impediment. And there was certainly something to be said for a coalition with no slack where party and
governmental discipline would be central to its continuance and ultimate
success. As Albert Reynolds pithily pointed out, the price of PD backing was
coalition (Reynolds, 2009: 131).

Thus negotiations began and would last for close to two weeks. A week
into the deliberations Pádraig Flynn, one of the main proponents of an early
general election, jumped back into the fray buffoon-like by declaring 'the
Government is very strong. All the members of the Cabinet are unanimous
for no coalition. The national executive, the parliamentary party and the grass
roots have indicated that this is a core value which we must preserve' (Farrell,
1990: 185). This seemed to miss the pretty important point that the people
had decided not to give Fianna Fáil its longed-for holy grail of an overall
majority. Once Haughey, or anyone else in Fianna Fáil for that matter, could
not persuade one of the minor parties to support them in a minority government, then coalition rapidly became the only alternative, no matter how much
the whole idea and ultimate prospect was anathema to Fianna Fáil. The fact
was that Flynn was too stupid to see this. Haughey most certainly was not.
The reality was that no such unanimity existed and it certainly did not exist
in the mind of the one man who was all-important in Fianna Fáil: Charles J.
Haughey. Flynn accused Haughey of acting out of personal gain, out of a lust
for power, and for putting himself above the needs of Fianna Fáil (Collins,
1992: 163). He might well have had a point. Haughey wanted to remain
Taoiseach above all else. Abstract theories about coalition were not much use
to him if he could not operate a minority government. The idea of hanging
tough and fighting another general election, as articulated by those within
Fianna Fáil who had been most enthusiastic for an election in the first place,

seemed spectacularly misplaced, and Haughey gave it little credence. Just two days after Flynn's statement on the sanctity of single-party government Haughey told the Dáil that, while such an option was his preferred view, 'if our entry into some form of political alliance is the only possible way forward at this stage, the only way in which a government can be formed in this Dáil without causing another immediate general election, then clearly in the higher national interest our duty is positively and constructively to explore the possibility of finding some agreed basis for government' (Farrell, 1990: 186). That in essence was the Rubicon crossed. It was only a matter of agreeing the details after that.

At the heart of this process was Haughey himself. Simply put, he liked being Taoiseach. He not only liked the trappings of power but he also enjoyed getting things done. He considered himself to have a done a good job in rescuing the country from the shambles as he saw it of the Fine Gael–Labour coalition. An ungrateful public had not recognised that he needed an overall majority to govern the country and do things even better. But he certainly was not going to let the loss of a number of seats threaten his desire to lead the next government. Whether Fianna Fáil could have governed in a minority with a different leader was a question he was not even going to be let be posed, never mind answered. Fianna Fáil's insistence on single-party government would have worked only if it had a leader who was willing to let such a situation ride out and develop into another general election if necessary. If this had happened, Haughey's own leadership would essentially have come under significant pressure and been seriously jeopardised as there was no real appetite in the country for another general election (Laver and Arkins, 1990: 206). Haughey kept his own party and his chief negotiators, Albert Reynolds and Bertie Ahern, in the dark and essentially did his own deal with O'Malley. This infuriated both would-be successors, with Reynolds noting that once he became aware of Haughey's own secret negotiations 'I lost all faith and made up my mind – enough of Charlie Haughey!' (Reynolds, 2009: 132). Haughey left it as late as the morning of 12 July to cede a second cabinet seat to the PDs. Coalition theories, policy compatibility, personal animosity, articles of faith: none of these mattered to Haughey. What mattered was leading the government. 'Nobody but myself could have done it', he beamed Caesar-like to the PD delegation on finally agreeing to a deal that fateful morning (Collins, 1992: 167).

The die was cast. Ireland faced into its first ever coalition with Fianna Fáil at the helm. Irish politics and the Irish party system would never be the same again. There has been no single-party government since. Fianna Fáil did not, however, accept coalition with good grace. Up to the demise of the coalition three years later in late 1992 the vast majority of both the Fianna Fáil parliamentary party and the grassroots members were at best ambivalent about both coalition in general and the arrangement with the PDs in particular, and at worst downright hostile. Over eighteen months into the coalition, Albert Reynolds famously remarked to a grassroots Fianna Fáil meeting in Kanturk, Cork, that it was a 'temporary little arrangement' (Reynolds: 2009, 161). At the March 1991 Fianna Fáil Ard Fheis he bluntly told the audience of loyalists that 'Fianna Fáil does not need any other party to keep it on the right track or to act as its conscience'. A year later Reynolds's cabinet colleague, close friend and ideological soulmate Brian Cowen told a rapturous Fianna Fáil Ard Fheis that the way to deal with the PDs was 'if in doubt leave them out' (O'Toole, 2008: 43).

All this anti-coalition rhetoric, however, failed to recognise that the Fianna Fáil-PD government actually seemed to know what it was doing in terms of governing the country. Des O'Malley in his autobiography argues that the reason the government was a success was that Fianna Fáil in general, and Charles Haughey in particular, was kept in check by the PDs. Left to their own devices Fianna Fáil, or more particularly Haughey, was likely to do anything. O'Malley is of the view that Haughey's minority 1987–89 government was 'the most corrupt government in the history of the State' precisely because there was no one willing to stand up to Haughey (O'Malley, 2014: 178). O'Malley, having sat in Haughey's 1979–81 and 1982 governments, knew well the dangers of, as he saw it, Haughey governing without the check of at least some dissenting voices (namely O'Malley himself) in his government. Armed now with two seats at the cabinet table, O'Malley was determined to make this coalition work. He recognised the immense talent of Haughey and was convinced that with himself acting as watchdog Haughey could actually lead a good government:

> My status vis-à-vis Haughey had changed. I was now dealing with him as the leader of a party in government rather than just a member of his cabinet. In fairness, he acknowledged this position in that our dealings were always business-like. But I never trusted him. In fact, when I saw him taking an interest in a particular topic or policy area I tended to keep an even closer eye on proposals. Despite these reservations Haughey was well suited to running a coalition government. He was business-like and worked to ensure the coalition functioned properly. (O'Malley, 2014: 186)

So notwithstanding the vituperative antipathy towards Haughey displayed by O'Malley – in fairness the vitriol went both ways – the two men were nevertheless able to get things done in government.

The strategy Fianna Fáil had pursued since 1987 of enhancing international competitiveness through reduced taxation, cuts in public expenditure and a drive for increased foreign direct investment through a consensual approach was one which had the support in ideological terms of both Fine Gael and the PDs. Now in government the PDs were to the fore in insisting on a continuance of cutting taxes and public expenditure while Fianna Fáil, which had a much wider constituency to address, remained steadfast to its corporatist approach to macroeconomic planning. The 1987 Programme for National Recovery with its commitment to low inflation and export-led growth was bearing fruit, with the National Economic and Social Council report noting in 1990 that despite significant unemployment the overall performance of the economy was impressive, given the grim nature of the recession of the 1980s. For Haughey the key to continued growth and continued Fianna Fáil success at the ballot box was social partnership, and he was particularly anxious to keep both the trade union and business communities happy. The result was a new social partnership programme agreed in January 1991, *The Programme for Economic and Social Progress*. This programme, a bit like all the social partnership agreements, had something for everyone. It was seen by the unions as underwriting growth and development while the business and employers' groups were keen on its commitments to low taxation, its low public spending and its strategy whereby the government would continue to pitch aggressively for foreign direct investment. The trouble was that this agreement was really only held together by the sheer political will of Charles Haughey. Social partnership was led from the Taoiseach's office and Haughey had to intervene several times to secure agreement on the final draft to which all parties were happy to sign up. He was the political agent around which macroeconomic policy in the state revolved.

Notwithstanding the difficulties of negotiating social partnership agreements – and in truth the PDs were never too keen on the idea given their essentially anti-trade-union and pro-enterprise outlook – macroeconomic strategy was given a certain stability by the agreements, a stability the PDs found themselves happy enough to abide by. Politics was a very different matter, however. And here tension was never too far away from the government surface.

The 1990 presidential election

Presidential elections had been rather dull affairs in Ireland up to the 1990 contest. Clearly presidential elections are different from other contests in Ireland, offering as they do the only opportunity for citizens to vote for a national candidate as distinct from constituency politicians. As the position of president is supposedly an apolitical one in terms of the winning president becoming the first citizen of the people, candidates are quite constrained in the way in which they can project their candidacies. The elections of 1959, 1966 and 1973 were clearly straightforward political contests between Fianna Fáil and Fine Gael, but there was no question of the presidency being anything but a ceremonial type of role of father of the nation. In contrast the Mary Robinson candidacy of 1990 was clearly political as she articulated for the first time a different vision for the presidency.

The 1990 campaign marked a significant number of turning points in presidential elections. The contest took centre stage in the front and political pages of all the main newspapers, while television and radio programmes gave extensive coverage to the campaign. While elections to this point had at times involved personal attacks on the candidates from other candidates or within parties, the focus had been exclusively on the public personae of the candidates. Their private lives and those of their family members did not feature in the public commentary. This began to change in 1990. Probably most crucial of all, the 1990 presidential campaign saw for the first time a woman stand for Ireland's highest office. While initially Mary Robinson's entry into the fray was not seen by Fianna Fáil as a major threat to its hold on the presidency, this view soon began to change as Robinson's campaign began to gain traction on the ground never before seen in a presidential election campaign (Murphy and Reidy, 2012: 625)

By 1990, radio and television appearances were expected and debates and interviews with the candidates have since become a central feature of the campaign. Generally, candidate debates are not seen as being particularly decisive in determining election outcomes, although much of the research supporting that assertion is drawn from the analysis of US presidential debates. It is more difficult to assess the wider impact of media coverage. Nevertheless the 1990 campaign included a number of decisive broadcast moments.

Brian Lenihan, Tánaiste (deputy leader) and Minister for Defence in the then Fianna Fáil–PD coalition and a senior member of Fianna Fáil, was selected to be the Party's candidate and continued the long-standing tradition of grandees of the Party bearing the Party's standard at presidential election time. He was, however, blindsided during the campaign when in the midst of a panel discussion programme *Questions and Answers* he was questioned about phone calls he was supposed to have made to the then President Hillery in his official residence at Áras an Uachtaráin, on the collapse of the Fine Gael and Labour coalition government in 1982. On the programme Lenihan denied making calls to the President asking him not to dissolve the Dáil. When a student, Jim Duffy, produced a recording in which Lenihan admitted making the calls, Lenihan, in a famous political moment, stated that on 'mature recollection' he could confirm that he had not attempted to contact President Hillery. Lenihan in fact had phoned Áras an Uachtaráin but got through not to the President but to the army officer on duty who did not transfer the calls to the President. While Lenihan downplayed the controversy, describing it as a 'storm in a teacup' (*Irish Times*, 27 October 1990), it later transpired he had been on heavy medication when he had given the original interview to Duffy. The controversy was to overshadow the remainder of his campaign, culminating in his sacking as Tánaiste, although he remained as Fianna Fáil's candidate for president. Thus Irish politics was presented with a man whom the then Taoiseach Charles Haughey sacrificed as Tánaiste but kept as Fianna Fáil's presidential candidate. The irony was not lost on a majority of the electorate.

In essence the PDs insisted on Lenihan's head as a price for their continued participation in government, but the episode is scarcely treated in Des O'Malley's autobiography, where it barely merits a paragraph: '[i]t was not a problem we made, but it was a very real problem. Letters of resignation were prepared; we put the party on an election footing. But Haughey was not keen to face the electorate, and when Lenihan refused to resign he was duly sacked' (O'Malley, 2014: 188). Nowhere does O'Malley state why he insisted on this course of action. He subtly shifts the blame on to Haughey, stating that the Fianna Fáil leader was not willing to have an election, but we are left none the wiser why O'Malley himself thought such a course of action was preferable to leaving Lenihan in government. In her own memoir the former cabinet minister, and sister of Brian Lenihan, Mary O'Rourke, also offers up Haughey as the great culprit in the affair. She also simply notes that O'Malley insisted on Lenihan's resignation as the price of the PDs staying in government and paints the episode in heroic terms: '[a]ll the world loves a hero, and in the eyes of his loyal supporters, Brian was the hero battling against the might of Charlie Haughey' (O'Rourke, 2012: 75). Unfortunately the heroic does not extend to O'Rourke's own behaviour when the vote confirming the sacking of Lenihan by Haughey was passed by the Dáil on 31 October 1990: 'I had no choice but to side with the Fianna Fáil party in a vote of confidence of Charlie as Taoiseach and in the Cabinet. It was a terrible time for us all' (O'Rourke, 2012: 77). But of course there are always choices in politics, including resignation. This does not seem to have dawned on O'Rourke, however, for whom blood was certainly not thicker than party loyalty on this occasion. In his own recollection of the affair, in a book written especially to defend his actions and to insist that he had not telephoned the Áras on the fateful night, Lenihan, in a rather rambling account, attacks both Haughey and O'Malley, going as far as calling O'Malley 'dishonest' (Lenihan, 1991: 156). No such epithets are landed at the door of Haughey, but the disappointment felt by Lenihan in being sacked by his party leader and Taoiseach at the behest of the PDs' 'blackmail' as he calls it is palpable throughout (Lenihan, 1991: 163).

In any event the Lenihan presidential candidacy continued notwithstanding his sacking and his campaign actually seemed to have gained some momentum in the form of significant public sympathy until an apparently throwaway remark by minister Pádraig Flynn, in which he appeared to cast aspersions on Mary Robinson's maternal instincts, derailed the Lenihan fightback, swaying many female voters in particular to support Robinson (O'Sullivan, 1991: 94). The historic nature of Robinson's campaign, and the fact that she was doing better than most pundits and politicians had anticipated, effectively spooked Fianna Fáil into some woefully misplaced scaremongering. Increasingly desperate attempts to portray her as some sort of radical feminist would ultimately see Flynn accuse her of having a 'new found interest in the family', an interest that long-standing politicians who knew her had never seen before. The 1990 campaign affirms an old political adage: the campaign matters. Lenihan had entered the race as the clear front runner but a series of events saw Robinson's public support rise and a *Sunday Press* poll placed her in the lead just days before the election (*Irish Times*, 10 November 1990).

In the midst of the cultural battle between the traditional Lenihan and the liberal Robinson was the sideshow that was the Fine Gael campaign. After painful attempts to persuade a senior party grandee to run, Garret FitzGerald and Peter Barry were the obvious choices but both refused. Fine Gael eventually nominated the former Social Democratic and Labour Party (SDLP) MP and Northern Ireland civil rights activist Austin Currie to be their candidate. It would prove to be a disastrous choice. Currie had been elected a Fine Gael TD only at the 1989 general election and his selection was widely seen as the party's desperate final throw of the dice. Winning just 17 per cent of the popular vote, it was the worst performance of any Fine Gael candidate in a presidential election until 2011 and led to the ousting as party leader of Fine Gael of Alan Dukes, who stepped down just days after the election (Gallagher and Marsh, 2002: 33). It also presaged a loss of 10 seats for Fine Gael at the 1992 general election and threatened its position as Ireland's second largest party.

Mary Robinson technically ran on a non-party ticket and has always maintained that she was an independent candidate who was supported not only by the Labour Party who nominated her but also by the Green Party and many in the PDs, although that party was in coalition with Fianna Fáil. Robinson's share of the vote in 1990 at 38.9 per cent was nearly 30 percentage points more than the Labour Party received in the 1989 general election and close to 20 per cent more than it would receive in 1992 so it would really be a stretch to claim her victory as one for the Labour Party. But of course that is exactly what the Labour Party did. Nevertheless she had not been a member of the Party since 1985 when she famously resigned over the Anglo Irish Agreement, claiming it was a bad deal for unionists. Her victory can be attributed to many factors, not least the implosion of the Fine Gael vote, the controversy over Brian Lenihan's campaign and whether he did or did not place pressure on President Hillery in 1982, the fact that she was the first woman to stand for the office and, most importantly of all, that she herself ran an excellent campaign. Up to Robinson's victory the presidency was the preserve of Fianna Fáil candidates and would return to that party with Mary McAleese's victory in 1997. But what the 1990 presidential contest fundamentally signalled was the end to the two-party dualism in presidential elections. In essence enough voters were persuaded that Robinson's personal appeal was a strong enough reason to vote for her notwithstanding that Lenihan with 44 per cent of the vote received most first preference votes. Transfers from Fine Gael's Austin Currie were the deciding factor and went to Robinson over Lenihan in a ratio of 6:1 (O'Sullivan, 1991). Here we get the first evidence of voters turning away from party politics and relying on what Mair and Weeks (2005: 156) describe in Dáil terms as a heavier reliance on 'competing personal appeals of the party leaders or even the local candidates, which could lead to even greater successes for independent, single-issue candidates'. While Sinnott (1995) found that support for the divorce referendum worked best to explain the Robinson vote in 1990, that election did continue in the tradition of the Fianna Fáil versus the rest dynamic of electoral politics. What was different was that a strong third candidate, with a wide appeal, entered the fray and took non-core Fianna Fáil voters away from potentially supporting the Fianna Fáil candidate.

The consequences of this result were politically seismic. Beyond Lenihan, the first real political casualty was Alan Dukes. Since his election as leader after the disaster of the 1987 general election Dukes had done little to inspire confidence in his party and remained unpopular in the country at large. He had downgraded party headquarters on his election as leader, was generally considered aloof by both his parliamentary party and the wider public and had proved no match for Charles Haughey in the cut and thrust of Dáil debate, where the Labour leader, Dick Spring, was the political leader who regularly got under Haughey's skin during leaders' questions. Dukes had a reputation as being a liberal in the FitzGerald mode but was unable to hold the support of that wing of the Fine Gael Party and had earned the outright hostility of the conservative wing whose criticism he was unable to contain. The bizarre nomination of Austin Currie as the Fine Gael candidate doomed Dukes's leadership. Currie gained no momentum during the campaign and was widely seen as sideshow to the Lenihan–Robinson battle for the office. Currie's reimagining of the presidency as a 'reconciling figure' was ignored by both media and public (Galligan, 2014: 129). With this coming on top of Fine Gael's poor showing in the 1989 general election, a majority of the parliamentary party, feeling the Party was going nowhere under Dukes's leadership, decided that it had had enough of him. He initially declared he would stay on to lead the Party but quickly recognised that his support within the parliamentary party had dissipated and he resigned as leader just six days after the election before a motion of no confidence that he was certain to lose (Gallagher and Marsh, 2002: 23). He was replaced by John Bruton, flag carrier for the Fine Gael conservative tradition and the man whose famous VAT on children's shoes budget of January 1982 had brought down that Fine Gael–Labour coalition government when he was Minister for Finance. The immediate impact of Bruton's election as leader was non-existent as neither Bruton's personal approval ratings as party leader nor the position of the Fine Gael Party itself rose in subsequent opinion polls (Girvin, 1993: 3).

While Mary Robinson went off to Áras an Uachtaráin, the real political winner from the presidential contest was the Labour leader, Dick Spring. After the turmoil of his time in the 1982–87 Fine Gael–Labour government, Spring didn't exactly rejuvenate Labour in the immediate aftermath of the 1987 election and his party picked up a modest 3 seats and 3 per cent of the first preference vote in the 1989 general election. Having barely hung on to his seat by just 4 votes in 1987, Spring took no chances with his own seat in the 1989 general election and was a much more visible presence in his Kerry North constituency in that campaign. Another spell in the opposition ranks but now with a much more secure seat would give him the opportunity to rebuild Labour. The fact, however, that Fianna Fáil had actually decided to go into coalition government made this a more complicated task as all sorts of possible government formulations were now on the table after future elections; if Fianna Fáil would go into government with the hated PDs, it would surely go into government with anyone else. In any event, while the Fianna Fáil–PD government settled into the task of governing in the late summer of 1989 with some aplomb, Spring and Labour seethed over their inability to offer a coherent critique of a government which, despite its unlikely provenance, was actually enjoying significant political support in its first year.

Then Dick Spring came upon the presidency as a way to improve Labour's fortunes by insisting that there should be a presidential election in 1990. Spring declared in January 1990 that Labour would contest a presidential election and he would be the candidate if he had to be (Collins, 1993: 174–5). In fact he soon found himself a much better candidate outside his parliamentary party fold in Mary Robinson. This was part of a deliberate strategy to raise the profile of the Party with an aim to increase electoral success in future general elections. Probably most crucial of all, the 1990 presidential campaign saw for the first time a woman stand for Ireland's highest office. The fact that she won changed the political dynamic of Irish politics and catapulted Spring into a position as the real leader of the opposition. Internally Spring had routed the Militant Tendency group within the Party and he and his supporters now had a tight grip around the Party's organisation and finances. Robinson's victory allowed Spring to pose Labour as a modern social democratic party which would appeal to a broad liberal coalition that had to some extent been tapped into by the Robinson victory. Harnessing this into support for Labour at subsequent general elections would now be the task for Spring.

While the 1990 presidential result was extraordinary, the reality was that it was a second-order election where Fianna Fáil still managed to gain 44 per cent of the first preference vote. It was not in any way a realignment of the Irish party system. While it had given Labour a significant boost and led to severe internal unrest for Fine Gael, it in no way threatened the stability of the Fianna Fáil–PD coalition once Brian Lenihan had been sacrificed. Reasonable macroeconomic indicators were, however, to prove inadequate for the government, as a variety of scandals were to emerge that would bring significant upheaval to Fianna Fáil and bring about a sudden end to the government. The first problem was that Haughey had alienated many within Fianna Fáil given his brutal treatment of Lenihan at the behest of the hated PDs. While Haughey, clinging to power, was quite comfortable with working alongside O'Malley, the reality for most Fianna Fáilers was that the PDs were a hindrance to be got rid of sooner rather than later.

The end of Haughey

A new and much more worrying view for Haughey, however, was beginning to form within Fianna Fáil, and that was that it was time for Haughey himself to be removed. Albert Reynolds, the most senior and most visceral opponent of coalition within Fianna Fáil, announced on the day of the presidential count that once there was a vacancy for the leadership of the Party he would be a candidate. This was certainly an odd time for the Party's Minister for Finance to be declaring leadership ambitions, considering Fianna Fáil had lost the presidency for the first time in its history. It presaged a period of practically open warfare within the Party, with 'tension bordering on animosity' as Reynolds described it between Haughey and himself. Haughey's put-down of Reynolds at a EU summit in Rome where, discussing British financial policy, he acerbically and maliciously noted that 'Chancellors of the Exchequer and Ministers for Finance are neurotic and exotic creatures whose political judgement is not always best' seemed to be the last straw for Reynolds (Reynolds, 2009: 140), who became much more truculent in his dealings with the PDs and openly began to build up support within Fianna Fáil for a putative leadership battle.

Coming on top of the Party's presidential election woes, the local elections of June 1991 brought more bad news for Fianna Fáil. Its first preference vote share fell by 7 points from its 1985 result to 37 per cent, well under the crucial 40 per cent it assumed was its bottom figure in any election. Moreover its vote in Dublin fell from 42 per cent to 31 per cent: an ominous result considering the importance of the capital in any general election contest. For now it seemed the Party was becoming more heavily dependent on its traditional rural support to do well in elections as the urban voter began to look elsewhere. The Party's poor result was laid at the door of its Dublin Taoiseach, while the rural Reynolds was increasingly seen as the man to bring Fianna Fáil back to the glory days of single-party government. This view, however, seemed to ignore the fact that it was the same voters who had initially rejected single-party Fianna Fáil government and who, particularly in urban areas, were unlikely to favour the so-called 'country and western' alternative in Reynolds.

Haughey's woes were not, however, confined to electoral politics. His status as Taoiseach itself was becoming severely undermined by an increasingly worrying number of scandals in the late summer of 1991 that the government he led was embroiled in. The easiest and most accurate way to describe these is a type of crony capitalism. Haughey was friendly with a number of senior businessmen such as the beef baron Larry Goodman, the chairman of the semi-state sugar company Greencore, Bernie Cahill, and the paper tycoon and chairman of Telecom Éireann Michael Smurfit, all of whom had ready access to the Taoiseach and to whom the government seemed readily helpful (Ryle Dwyer, 1999: 400). Cahill was also chairman of a mining company called Feiltrim which was owned by Haughey's son Conor. Irregularities in relation to the establishment of Greencore, the state purchase of Carysfort Training College in Blackrock, Dublin, and the purchase of a site in Ballsbridge by Telecom Éireann for what seemed a vastly overinflated sum brought the reality of a 'Golden Circle' into public life (O'Malley, 2014: 178; 188–9) and were all tangentially linked to Haughey. Although he denied any impropriety he was placed on the political defensive. A Fianna Fáil Taoiseach with two electoral defeats in just over six months behind him being linked to scandals where cronyism was their defining feature was a very weakened creature indeed.

After a difficult renegotiation of the programme for government in October 1991 when the PDs threatened to pull out of government and Albert Reynolds was of the view that they should be let go, an agreement was reached only after Bertie Ahern secured an uneasy compromise between both government parties. Fear of an early and publicly unwanted general election was the most plausible explanation for the compromise, but Reynolds was becoming increasingly exasperated by on the one hand Haughey's increasingly dictatorial style and on the other the seemingly sheer effrontery of the PDs in actually being in government with Fianna Fáil. By November of 1991 he clearly had had enough and launched a rather strange bid for leadership by proxy.

The main strength of putting the Fianna Fáil Party through another leadership challenge was that this time it was in essence organised by many of those who had actually supported Haughey in the 1979 leadership election when he had surprisingly beaten George Colley, and so could thus be painted as an initiative for saving the party. The main weakness of the challenge was that its supporters were very much of the conservative, rural, country and western wing of the party who could be accused by the Haugheyites of acting out of personal ambition and bitterness following the formation of the coalition government, and were hardly likely to regain political support in the large cities where Fianna Fáil's vote was most at risk. The decision to mount the challenge seems to have been taken in the firm belief that Fianna Fáil's most popular Dublin-based deputy the Minister for Labour and chief fixer, Bertie Ahern, would support the challenge. This did not materialise, as Ahern, always renowned for his caginess, refused to sign up, believing such a challenge could not possibly win. On Ahern's advice Haughey revealed to a parliamentary party meeting that he would step down after overseeing the budget of early 1992, but this was not enough for Reynolds. In his own memoir Ahern pithily notes that 'Albert wouldn't wait' (Ahern, 2010: 129). On 6 November 1991, after an extremely bitter and acrimonious parliamentary party meeting, a no confidence motion in Haughey was tabled, proposed by a little-known rural deputy from Kildare, Seán Power (part of a gang of four who had already made noises about Haughey's leadership), and Reynolds immediately came out saying he would support it. In his autobiography Reynolds claimed the motion to discontinue forthwith the leadership of Charles J. Haughey was taken 'without my prior knowledge or approval' but that once it was made he had 'no choice but to support it. I did not believe the motion would succeed, but I did not want to be labelled a hypocrite' (Reynolds, 2009: 141). Haughey promptly sacked him from government and also brusquely dismissed Pádraig Flynn, the Minister for the Environment, and a number of junior ministers all of whom stated they would support the motion. But Haughey still had strong support from many within the parliamentary party, including Ahern, whose job it was to secure the votes for a Haughey victory, Brian Lenihan, now back in the Haughey fold after the humiliation of the presidential election, Mary O'Rourke, Ray Burke and Gerry Collins. In the end Haughey, the wily old fox of Irish politics, defeated the no confidence motion comfortably by 55 votes to 22.

Fianna Fáil, and by extension the government, quickly lurched into another crisis when Haughey in his reshuffle of ministers decided to appoint Dr James McDaid, a relatively unknown Donegal backbencher, to the position of Minister for Defence. McDaid's appointment came as a proverbial bolt out of the blue, none more so than to the man himself: 'I would have been overjoyed had I been promoted to a junior post but when Mr. Haughey told me that he was appointing me to the cabinet as Minister for Defence I was left speechless' (McDaid, 1993: 41). A photo then emerged of a smiling McDaid

alongside an IRA suspect, and constituent of his, whom a court had decided
not to extradite to Northern Ireland. The PDs, although accepting that McDaid
had no sympathy with the IRA or with any subversive elements, threatened
once again to leave the government unless McDaid was in essence sacked.
Once again O'Malley is coy about this whole episode in his memoir,
commenting only that McDaid behaved 'honourably' in eventually deciding not to accept the appointment (O'Malley, 2014: 189). The whole non-
appointment of McDaid to the sensitive Defence portfolio generated much
sympathy for him within Fianna Fáil, more vitriol for the PDs from their
government partners, and most crucially a critical damaging of Haughey's
credibility within his party, where he was seen by most of his parliamentary
colleagues as having lost his touch in being completely unable to stand up to
the PDs, all in the name of keeping himself in office. Why Haughey appointed
McDaid is itself a bit of a mystery. He had been elected only for the first time
at the 1989 election and to most political observers had not made any lasting
impression that was deserving of promotion to ministerial office. That perennial issue in Irish politics, geography, may have had something to do with it
or he may just have simply caught Haughey's eye as an up and coming politician of talent. In any event McDaid's non-appointment was yet another blow
to Haughey's position, which was beginning to look more and more untenable. As the astute journalist John Waters noted in a perceptive column in the
Irish Times called 'Attempting to depose Fianna Fáil', Haughey's opponents
only had to be lucky once in order to oust him (*Irish Times*, 5 November
1991). Such luck was not long in coming.

The final dagger in Haughey's 'death of a thousand cuts' was inflicted by
his old Minister for Justice, Seán Doherty (Whelan, 2011: 252). The continuing series of scandals was becoming wearisome for all sides when Doherty
went on the popular late-night television programme *Nighthawks* to tell the
nation that Haughey as Taoiseach had had knowledge of the phone taps of
two journalists, Bruce Arnold and Geraldine Kennedy, during the ill-fated
government of 1982 when Doherty was Minister for Justice. He followed this
up with a carefully choreographed press conference at which he claimed that
Haughey had succumbed to PD pressure yet again, this time in relation to
introducing legislation on phone tapping which could only cause maximum
damage to Doherty as Cathaoirleach of the Seanad (leader of the upper
house), given that Doherty was the minister who ordered the original phone
taps (Whelan, 2011: 252). Haughey had not supported Doherty's nomination
for the position of Cathaoirleach but he was nevertheless elected anyway and
had apparently smarted ever since over what he regarded as Haughey's
betrayal of him.

Haughey immediately issued a denial which brought the familiar re-
frain from the PDs that he would have to go or they would bring down the

coalition. He reasonably pointed out that he had been consistent in his denials of not knowing anything about phone tapping whereas Doherty had changed his story from that of a decade ago. But the PDs were not about to let Haughey get away this time. It seems quite clear now that the Doherty intervention was orchestrated by opponents of Haughey. O'Malley in his memoir claims he had 'no doubt the intervention was orchestrated' but typically does not say by whom (O'Malley, 2014: 189). The historian T. Ryle Dwyer in his racy account of the affair argues that it was to do with the leadership struggle in Fianna Fáil and that Doherty knew he had the power to 'deliver a fatal blow by telling what he knew about the events of 1982' when he had lied for Haughey (Ryle Dwyer, 1992: 176). The veteran Fianna Fáil politician John O'Leary, no friend of Haughey, in his valuable political memoir places Pádraig Flynn at the centre of the intrigue, while also speculating that Albert Reynolds was fully aware of a plan to essential take Haughey down, noting that he 'was told that Flynn and Doherty were in cahoots and plotting the downfall of Haughey' on the night that a party was being held to celebrate O'Leary's twenty-five-year unbroken stint in the Dáil: '[t]he plan was to get Doherty to come out straight and name Haughey as one of those who knew about the phone tapping, something he hadn't done yet. I'd be very much surprised if Albert Reynolds didn't know what was happening behind the scenes' (O'Leary, 2015: 261).

Haughey for his part felt the allegation was part of a plot by those disaffected with his leadership but whom he had seen off in the leadership election of barely two months previously: the country and western alliance, of whom Doherty from Roscommon and Reynolds from Longford were clearly two (Whelan, 2011: 252). O'Malley went to see Haughey to tell him 'this can't go on' and that Haughey quickly recognised reality: '[t]he threat of a general election wasn't available to him. He knew he couldn't carry a majority in the Fianna Fáil parliamentary party. If he somehow had attempted to carry on he would have been removed as leader by his own colleagues' (O'Malley, 2014: 189). According to Bertie Ahern, he was approached by Bobby Molloy to give Haughey the resignation ultimatum, but on going to see Haughey he was somewhat surprised that the Taoiseach had decided to resign, declaring 'I've had my nine lives' (Ahern, 2010: 132). And thus the most controversial leader of modern Ireland, a man who inspired devotion and antipathy in equal measure, left the political stage, declaring on 30 January 1992 that he would resign as Taoiseach and leader of Fianna Fáil. The coalition maker had eventually fallen at the hands of his own party, but with a significant shove from the PDs.

The way was now open for Albert Reynolds to reach the pinnacle of Irish politics. Only one man could stand in his way: Bertie Ahern. Haughey was desperate that Ahern would succeed him but the innately cautious Ahern would contest the leadership only if he was guaranteed to win. Reynolds, having seen off Haughey, was not about to leave the prize to be taken from his grasp by yet another inner-city Dubliner. He arranged to meet Ahern, and essentially told him to wait his turn, which would not be long in coming; perhaps no longer that the rest of the Dáil term and one more election cycle considering that Reynolds was already sixty years of age. If Ahern pulled out of the race he would be the anointed number two; if he stayed in and lost he would suffer the consequences. Ahern took the advice, never officially entering the contest, and Reynolds romped home, winning 61 out of 76 votes to become the fifth leader of Fianna Fáil and eighth Taoiseach. On becoming Taoiseach on 11 February 1992 Reynolds made Ahern his Minister for Finance and putative successor and then in an act of unparalleled political savagery sacked over half of Haughey's cabinet, replacing eight ministers and ten ministers of state: 'I was a man with things to do and I wanted people in government who would do things with me', he rather grandiosely declared in his autobiography in defending his actions (Reynolds, 2009: 153). It left the political world in shock, including most of the Fianna Fáil parliamentary party and the entire PD establishment. Bertie Ahern considered it an unmitigated disaster: 'I wanted to put the division of the Haughey years behind us. Instead, Albert had made them worse' (Ahern, 2010: 139). O'Malley was equally unimpressed about the butchery of over half the cabinet but could do nothing about it. Things were about to get markedly worse for the junior partners in government, with O'Malley in his memoir plaintively noting that from the outset 'there was a change in mood and tone in the working relationship in the Government' (O'Malley, 2014: 191). There can be little doubt that Reynolds detested coalition government, detested the PDs a little bit more and was orchestrating a strategy whereby he could call an election and blame his junior partners in government, thereby showing once and for all that, notwithstanding Haughey's efforts, coalitions could not really work. The idea of single-party government could then be justified and vindicated in a subsequent general election. It was a fool's paradise of an idea but one which Reynolds engineered to bring about with predictably disastrous consequences.

3

The politics of changing coalitions

Grossly unwise, reckless and foolish.
Des O'Malley on Albert Reynolds, 3 July 1992

Reckless, irresponsible, and dishonest.
Albert Reynolds on Des O'Malley, 27 October 1992

Of beef and dishonesty

In the summer of 1992 Des O'Malley presented his evidence at the Beef Tribunal set up the previous year by the Dáil, under the chairmanship of Justice Liam Hamilton, to investigate allegations of illegal activities, fraud and malpractice in the beef processing industry. Until the establishment of the Hamilton Tribunal on the beef industry, judicial inquiries had for two generations been employed, not for investigating corruption, but for the purposes of investigating a range of calamities such as the Whiddy Island oil refinery explosion of 1978 and the Stardust disco fire of 1981, both of which were without significant political or administrative subtext. Some previous tribunals had more political overtones. In 1946 a tribunal was established to examine allegations of tax irregularities made against Dr Conor Ward, the parliamentary secretary to the Minister for Health, who was the driving force behind the 1947 Health Act, the principal legislation on the state's role in the provision of healthcare in Ireland, which had been vociferously opposed by varying medical interests over the extension of public health provision (Barrington, 1987: 174–5). Ward was ultimately found to have committed no wrongdoing but the tribunal did find that some income tax evasion had occurred. The episode essentially ended his political career as he became the first politician in the history of the Irish state to resign for alleged personal impropriety (Byrne, 2012: 49). The following year another tribunal was established by the Dáil to explore allegations of political influence in the affairs of Locke's Distillery, a whiskey firm in Westmeath, which was up for sale and for which a foreign consortium, later exposed as a bunch of charlatans, had received support from the Department of Industry and Commerce (Collins and O'Shea, 2000: 22). Apart from demonstrating that the main proponent of the charges, Deputy Oliver J. Flanagan, had lied in the course of his evidence, after originally making wild and lurid allegations in the Dáil, the tribunal found no substance in the claims (Horgan, 1997: 130). Seán Lemass, who had been smeared during the Dáil allegations, vowed never again to agree to the creation of a tribunal of inquiry on the basis of purely party political allegations (O'Halpin, 2000: 184).

Tribunals of inquiry are in essence amongst the last legacies of British to Irish law under the Tribunals of Inquiry (Evidence) Act of 24 March 1921 (O'Neill, 2000: 201). They have quite an array of powers and are equipped with the full armoury of High Court enforcement to compel the attendance of witnesses, the production of documents and the making of such orders as are deemed necessary for the purposes of carrying out their functions. Principal among these are to establish the facts about issues of 'urgent public importance'. The remit of the 1991 Beef Tribunal was explicitly political in that it was established to examine allegations of government favouritism towards certain companies, most particularly those of the beef baron Larry Goodman, in the beef processing industry. Its creation was a prerequisite for the continued survival, under Charles Haughey, of the governing coalition of Fianna Fáil and the PDs. The catalyst for the establishment of the tribunal was a number of allegations raised by the Granada Television programme *World in Action* relating to tax fraud, falsification of documents and weights, the use of bogus stamps and the switching of meat sent into intervention with a clearly inferior product. The programme was originally dismissed by the then government, or, as Des O'Malley says, the Fianna Fáil part of the government, as anti-Irish and designed to achieve sensationalist impact (O'Malley, 2014: 212), but Charles Haughey ultimately caved into PD demands that a judicial public inquiry be held, although he insisted it be about the whole beef industry and not simply the Goodman group of companies.

The tribunal ultimately sat for 231 days, from November 1991 to July 1993, heard from 475 witnesses, took three years to deliver its 904-page report on 29 July 1994, saw seven different applications for judicial review made to the High Court and Supreme Court, cost approximately £320 million and ultimately failed to deliver a clear result in the form of punishment, condemnation or significant policy change (O'Toole, 1995; Byrne, 2012). While the tribunal was exhaustive in detail and did uncover evidence of massive tax fraud, official connivance in systematic abuses of EU export rebates and reckless ministerial decision-making, it was also so opaque that almost any construction could be and was put on it (O'Halpin, 2000: 184–5).

With the tribunal having sat since November 1991 without any political damage to the government and with increasingly tedious evidence from a variety of witnesses, Des O'Malley finally gave his own testimony to the tribunal in July 1992. It proved to be explosive when he branded as 'grossly unwise, reckless and foolish' decisions made by the Taoiseach, Albert Reynolds, five years earlier in his capacity as Minister for Industry and Commerce, on export credit insurance for beef processing companies. A government spokesman insisted at the time that this 'does not impugn the Taoiseach's veracity or integrity' (*Irish Times*, 4 July 1992). Four months later Reynolds had his revenge when in his own evidence to the tribunal he maintained that O'Malley's evidence was 'reckless, irresponsible, and dishonest'. The ubiquitous government spokesman indicated to the media after the tribunal session ended that the Taoiseach was wholly unrepentant about describing O'Malley's evidence to the tribunal in such terms and had all along pledged that 'he would tell it as it was without any varnish or veneer' (*Irish Times*, 28 October 1992). The government press secretary, Seán Duignan, in his memoir of the period used a clever football analogy to sum up Reynolds's action: 'Like a footballer badly fouled in the first round of a cup-tie, Reynolds nursed his wrath until the second leg, and then put the boot in. Unfortunately as often happens in such circumstances, it instantly earned him the red card' (Duignan, 1995: 49).

The PDs, not used to having their moral probity questioned, reacted with hostility, describing Reynolds's remarks as 'outrageous' and saying that the Taoiseach's attacks on O'Malley would be dealt with 'in the first instance' at the tribunal itself by his lawyers. The opposition were quick to widen the fissure between the government parties, with the Labour leader, Dick Spring, telling the Dáil that the Taoiseach had 'deliberately accused one of his senior Ministers of, in effect, committing perjury'. The government spokesman pointed out that O'Malley in his evidence to the tribunal had 'accused the Taoiseach of untruths' and made a distinction between O'Malley's role as a member of the cabinet and as a member of another party when he said that the Taoiseach's point in his evidence to the tribunal the previous day was that 'Des O'Malley had made a dishonest presentation of the facts in his personal capacity' (*Irish Times*, 28 October 1992). Two days later, back in the witness box, Reynolds in an exchange with O'Malley's lawyer, Adrian Hardiman, repeated that O'Malley's evidence had been 'dishonest'.

Now in politics to call the leader of one's coalition partner 'grossly unwise', 'reckless', 'foolish', 'irresponsible', even 'incorrect' or 'wrong' would be troublesome but could be resolvable. To call one's partner 'dishonest', though, is clearly beyond the pale. Duignan pithily summed it up: 'I think we're bollixed' (Duignan, 1995: 52). O'Malley for his part two decades later stated it was simple perjury as all evidence was given on oath. He then proceeded to beautifully put the boot into Reynolds: 'It appeared that he made his gratuitous allegation of perjury against me on the strength of a spin-doctor's notion that he himself could not understand, or did not take the trouble to understand' (O'Malley, 2014: 192). There clearly is a lot of truth in this. Duignan maintains that he was told that 'a certain legal luminary advised him (Reynolds) not just that he could get away with the "D" word but that O'Malley would be forced to grin and bear it' (Duignan, 1995: 49). This was to spectacularly misread O'Malley, who, whatever else he would take to keep a coalition going, was not going to stand for being called dishonest under oath in a sworn tribunal of inquiry. Reynolds later plaintively told Duignan that when it came to his evidence and to calling O'Malley dishonest 'from a political point of view, and I stress the word political, I was badly advised' (Duignan, 1995: 49). In his own memoir Reynolds adopts a rather bemused and even detached air about the whole affair, as if it was somehow nothing to do with him, maintaining simply that 'In my book you are either honest or dishonest, and whether I was well advised to use it or not, I believed "dishonest" was the word that applied, and I used it' (Reynolds, 2009: 172). At the time he even went so far as to state 'if any party chooses to bring down this Government at this particular stage, the heavy responsibility lies with them and not me' (*Irish Times*, 2 November 1992). But he had gone too far. The PDs pulled out of the coalition on 4 November and the following day the government was beaten on a confidence motion by 88 votes to 77. The Dáil was dissolved, and with that the Fianna Fáil–PD coalition which had changed the nature of Irish politics was over. The loathing O'Malley and Reynolds had for each other turned out to be much worse than that between O'Malley and Haughey. Moreover Reynolds, unlike Haughey, simply could not get used to the idea of coalition, and finally O'Malley never rated Reynolds and considered him far inferior to the other Taoisigh he knew and worked with, namely Liam Cosgrave, Jack Lynch, Garret FitzGerald and even Charles Haughey, as this biting comment from his memoir shows: 'These four individuals had different strengths and weaknesses but they were head and shoulders above Reynolds, politically and intellectually. Personally, I don't think he was as up to being Taoiseach' (O'Malley, 2014: 192).

Coming somewhat late to political life, Albert Reynolds was in some ways an odd politician. First elected in the Fianna Fáil landslide of 1977 at the age of forty-four, he had great confidence in his ability to get things done but was also fatally undermined by crippling insecurities about his acceptance at the top table of Irish politics. Notwithstanding his later difficulties with Charles Haughey, he had been an early supporter of Haughey's leadership campaign in 1979 and was rewarded with his first ministerial office in Posts and Telegraphs, where he immediately began his, in an Irish context at least, inimitable entrepreneurial style of ministerial leadership. If he wanted something to happen he was determined that it would and in that aim and ambition he would not be bound by convention, precedent or dogma. Such an attitude invariably landed him in trouble at times but in at least one area it proved a remarkable success: Northern Ireland. Prior to becoming Taoiseach, Reynolds had given no indication that he would spend much, if any, time on the Northern Ireland problem. He was a typical Fianna Fáil politician in that he subscribed to the lofty goals of unification which gave the Party a certain intellectual coherence but which very few in the Party actually paid any heed to. On his becoming Taoiseach it was widely assumed that this would be the case with Reynolds as well. Not only had he made no grave pronouncements about Northern Ireland but he was also roundly considered as a man for whom economic success was how political success was defined.

Moreover Northern Ireland had rarely been either an electoral asset or indeed a liability in Irish politics since Fianna Fáil had first taken power in 1932. Even in the grim and dark days of the early troubles and the Arms Crisis in the late 1960s and early 1970s, Northern Ireland held little sway at the ballot box for Irish voters. This was the case in 1973 when the electorate ushered Fianna Fáil out after sixteen years in office and would again be the case four years later in 1977, in Reynolds's first election, when Fianna Fáil returned with a huge electoral landslide, taking over 50 per cent of the vote and gaining a majority of 20 seats. But for Reynolds none of this mattered. What mattered was that he discerned a scenario where on becoming Taoiseach he could persuade the IRA to declare a ceasefire, cajole the British and the representatives of Ulster Unionism into a political deal, and convince the Americans to support it. Basically he envisaged peace in our time. Not everyone would sign up to it but for Reynolds, if he could not use the power of the office of Taoiseach to chart forward a strategy for peace, well, what was the point in being in office at all? Continuing the secret negotiations with Sinn Féin and the IRA that had begun with Charles Haughey, Reynolds set about, in what would be his short three-year career as Taoiseach, to build a secure peace in Northern Ireland. Whether he was up to being Taoiseach or not, and there is no doubt that temperamentally he certainly was not a very good coalition builder, there can be little doubt that Reynolds, in placing Northern Ireland at the heart of his government, did the Irish state and its people no little service.

Another coalition for Fianna Fáil

While O'Malley might not have considered Reynolds up to the job of being Taoiseach, although he did agree to serve with him, one person who also seemingly had no difficulty about the idea of working with Reynolds was Labour's Dick Spring. Having come out of the fiasco of the 1982–87 government barely clinging on to its political life, Labour, under Spring, had rebuilt and revitalised itself in its five years in opposition to a point whereby, when the 1992 election campaign began, it look destined to receive its highest ever vote share and number of seats. Running on a platform of social democratic economics and moral liberalism, Labour's relative popularity was based primarily on the back of Spring lambasting Fianna Fáil, Haughey and Reynolds while in opposition. A second key factor was a go-it-alone political strategy by Labour whereby the Party argued during the campaign that if there was no overall majority Fianna Fáil and Fine Gael should go into coalition government. With that cunning strategy of distancing itself from its normal coalition partner of Fine Gael, Labour had put itself at the vanguard of those criticising the economic orthodoxy of Fianna Fáil, Fine Gael and the PDs, all of whom were offering traditional conservative market-oriented solutions to the country's continuing economic woes, particularly that of unemployment, which remained stubbornly high (O'Leary, 1993: 403). This strategy would prove enormously successful as Labour recorded its highest ever percentage of the first preference vote and gained its largest ever number of seats.

Once the votes were counted, Dick Spring changed his anti-Fianna Fáil and anti-coalition tune. The 1992 election saw the electorate repudiate once more Fianna Fáil's attempts for a single-party government. In fact from the beginning of the campaign no sane analyst of Irish politics considered it a likely possibility. The outcome of the campaign resulted in yet another first in Irish politics as this time a party in power continued in office after a general election but with a new coalition partner. While Fianna Fáil's dance with the PDs might have ended in failure after a very long courtship, it quickly found a new partner in Labour.

Initially there seemed no prospect at all that Fianna Fáil could form another coalition. For the first time in its history the Party had gone below 40 per cent of the first preference vote and had lost 9 seats to fall to 68. Moreover, since Reynolds could not make coalition with the PDs work, there seemed little chance of him making a successful coalition with anyone else. In fact, given the way the election numbers stacked up, there was only one possible alternative coalition for Fianna Fáil and that was with Labour with its 33 seats and 19 per cent of the vote. But no rational observer of the Irish political scene felt this was likely given the antipathy shown by Spring to Fianna Fáil in the course of the previous Dáil and the widely expressed view that Reynolds could not work within a coalition format.

The big problem, however, in relation to an alternative government was that Fine Gael, the obvious party to lead a non-Fianna Fáil government, had itself done spectacularly badly, losing 10 seats to fall to 45 and dropping 4.5 percentage points of its vote to fall to 24.5 per cent. This was a massive 25

seats and 14 per cent of the vote less than it had achieved in 1982 under
Garret FitzGerald. It had made no advance electorally under John Bruton.
The normal alternative coalition government of Fine Gael and Labour did
not have the numbers to form a government and could do so only with the
help either of the PDs, who in the circumstances had polled reasonably well,
winning 10 seats, up from 6, or of the new Democratic Left Party, founded
out of a split in the old Workers' Party and which had been in existence for
only eight months, winning 4 seats. A Fine Gael–Labour–Democratic Left
government would not even have a majority in the Dáil and would be relying
on independent support, while a Fine Gael–Labour–PD government would
have a small but workable majority (Rafter, 2011a: 152). Ideology has never
been much of an issue in Irish politics but it certainly raised its head in this
period. Simply put, Labour and the PDs were at ideological loggerheads.
Labour favoured increased government involvement in the macroeconomic
affairs of the state while the PDs viewed such intervention as ruinous to the
development of a prosperous market-driven economy and society. Fine Gael,
for its part, seemed to simply assume that Labour would come into line and
agree to such a coalition. As Spring's chief adviser, Fergus Finlay, put it:
'John Bruton had annoyed everyone in the Labour party by seeming to take
our participation in his choice of rainbow for granted … he was almost tri-
umphalist, still operating on the assumption that he would be the next Taoiseach – and that we would do the decent thing' (Finlay, 1998: 132).

Both Fine Gael and the PDs had already dismissed the idea of Democratic
Left being in government on ideological grounds, and while they were prepared for tough negotiations they could see no alternative beyond the so-
called rainbow coalition. Dick Spring's view, voiced during the election
campaign, of the possibility of a rotating Taoiseach was dismissed out of hand
by Fine Gael. Fine Gael had got the most seats of this alternative coalition
government and thus would lead the coalition. As Brian Farrell pointed out:
'this public attempt to lay down conditions was not the best basis for negotiations with a Labour party which had just secured an historic electoral victory'
(Farrell, 1993: 150). This was even more the case since an alternative coalition of Fianna Fáil and Labour was all the time within plain sight, although
no one within Fine Gael or the PDs could see it. Some exploratory talks were
held but Labour with its massive seat and vote increase had no intention of
going into government with the PDs in any circumstances. The talks were a
sham, with the PDs complaining later of being surprised by the insulting way
they were treated by Labour (Collins, 2005: 145). When it finally dawned on
Fine Gael and the PDs that Labour had another alternative and was actively
going to pursue it, O'Malley tried to warn Spring of the dangers of working
with Reynolds. This cut no ice with Spring, who dismissed it as petulance
on O'Malley's part. This was to prove a serious error by the Labour leader,

who then proceeded to lead the largest ever number of Labour deputies into a coalition government with Fianna Fáil. The idea of the rotating Taoiseach was dropped and instead Spring got an enhanced Office of the Tánaiste, which had somewhat dodgy constitutional legality. While he was pleased with the outcome, the public reacted with no little bemusement as the last thing most first-time (and clearly last-time as well) Labour voters expected was for the Party to go into government with Fianna Fáil. This was echoed by one of Spring's chief advisers, the lawyer John Rogers, who, at a meeting of Spring's inner circle to discuss the possibility of coalition with Fianna Fáil, 'spoke first and passionately. He emphasised the fact that Albert Reynolds as Taoiseach did not appear to be the result anticipated by the electorate. We had campaigned for change – how could we find ourselves supporting the same Taoiseach' (Finlay, 1998: 140). But the prospect of Fianna Fáil as a willing coalition partner in a government of equals was too much for Spring to turn down. Like Haughey and O'Malley, he too crossed his own personal Rubicon by agreeing to take the risk. He was soon to find out that the Albert Reynolds of coalition promising was a very different political animal indeed from the Albert Reynolds of decisive government leadership, of tribal support for his own party, and for ignoring his coalition partners. Meanwhile a very lonely air descended on Fine Gael and John Bruton. who could not quite believe that Labour had decided to embrace Fianna Fáil. As Ivan Yates puts it: 'Total despair descended on Fine Gael. Our traditional alliance party had forsaken us and done the unthinkable. Initially we didn't know whether to attack or befriend Labour knowing that we would never get into government without them' (Yates, 2014: 130). That proved to be a very prescient point. The Fianna Fáil–Labour government with a massive majority of 18, the coalition that was expected to go two full terms and last a decade, was done and dusted within two years.

As with much else in Irish politics the reasons for its demise are pretty simple on one hand but fiendishly complex on the other. At its heart, lack of trust between Reynolds and Spring was the main issue in the failure of this government to even get half-way into its term. A number of self-serving accounts from both the Fianna Fáil and Labour camps have been subsequently published in which each side naturally blames the other. On the Labour side, memoirs by Spring's chief adviser, Fergus Finlay, and one of his senior ministers, Ruairi Quinn, firmly lay the blame at the door of the not-to-be-trusted Fianna Fáil, which of course raises the question why Labour would enter coalition with it in the first place. For their part the two most senior politicians in Fianna Fáil, Albert Reynolds and Bertie Ahern, are in no doubt that the fault lay with Labour, which failed to come to terms with its momentous decision to enter government with Fianna Fáil and seemed keen to end the coalition as swiftly as possible. Spring was variously seen by

Fianna Fáil as moody, prickly, easy to take umbrage, and when he wasn't offended Finlay would happily take offence for him (Duignan, 1995: 86–7).

The 1993 tax amnesty was the first sign of trouble between the pair and remains 'one of the great mysteries of Irish political life' (Clifford and Coleman, 2009: 202), with seemingly everyone in public life, including all the cabinet, opposing it with the crucial exception of Reynolds. Also opposed to the amnesty were the Revenue Commissioners, whose investigations unit was seemingly on the brink of nabbing many of the evaders who owed up to potentially £100 million, the Department of Finance and the Attorney General's office, who doubted the constitutionality of the proposal (Clifford and Coleman, 2009: 205). A previous amnesty issued only five years earlier had rather stringent terms attached to it where the tax evaders, or applicants as they were officially called, would be required to pay all tax and thus avoid interest and penalties. Now yet another amnesty was in train, this one with much easier terms of a payment of only 15 per cent of the moneys due. Having it so soon after the previous amnesty obviously raised the question of when the next one would come. It essentially seems to be a no-brainer that a party which had made glorious political capital in opposition by excoriating Fianna Fáil for low standards could not possibly agree to such an amnesty. But that is what Labour did, and bizarrely blamed Fianna Fáil, or more specifically Bertie Ahern, for leading it astray. Not willing for whatever reason to simply tell Reynolds that Labour could not stand by such an amnesty, Spring attempted to hide behind Bertie Ahern who, it was mooted, was as Minister for Finance implacably opposed to the amnesty. Finlay argues that Spring wanted the amnesty quietly buried and that there was no need to expend political capital on a confrontation with the Taoiseach in opposing it, particularly when the Minister for Finance was so trenchantly opposed and there was a majority in cabinet who felt the same way (Finlay, 1998: 171). Reynolds, for his part was fairly smitten with the idea but gives it just barely a page in his memoir where, in defending it as bringing in a significant level of much-needed revenue for infrastructural development, he bluntly states: 'it would also bring business investment back into the country and everyone would gain' (Reynolds, 2009: 227). That is, everyone with the possible exception of all those who surely wondered why they were paying their full tax liabilities. The long-standing Fianna Fáil backbencher John O'Leary in a recent valuable account of his life in Irish politics lays the blame at the feet of the Minister for Finance, stating 'Ahern told us it was necessary; he said there was a lot of money in accounts overseas and we needed the tax revenue' (O'Leary, 2015: 271). The Finlay memoir is extraordinary in its telling of the decision by the cabinet to agree to the amnesty: he again puts the blame squarely on Ahern and seems to see the Labour ministers as innocent bystanders enduring a badly timed bout of stage fright: 'As far as I know, no arguments were put forward on behalf of the Department of Finance, and none of the Labour Ministers insisted on a point of principle. None of us knew what had happened. But the amnesty that the Minister for Finance opposed was put into effect a few weeks later by the Minster who opposed it' (Finlay, 1998: 172). Why the Labour ministers and their leader Spring did not object when Ahern changed his mind is curiously left unsaid.

As for Bertie Ahern, he paints a completely different picture, noting to two early sympathetic biographers that when the discussion of an amnesty was taking place in April and May of 1993 he was fighting a lonely battle in cabinet with no Dick Spring or Ruairi Quinn to help him out. He does, however, throw the Labour Party a figleaf of sorts, noting that 'in earlier meetings Dick Spring and Ruairi Quinn had reservations but in the end they reluctantly voted for the amnesty' (Whelan and Masterson, 1998: 121). Rather extraordinarily, Ruairi Quinn's memoir written in 2005 does not mention the tax amnesty at all. Ultimately, Ahern insists that, although he was opposed to the proposal, he eventually introduced it and then thought of resigning over it as he was the only one fighting for the little people against the expediency of getting the money in that permeated everyone else in cabinet. Out of this miasma of confusion Ahern in the end thought it better to stay at cabinet and fight for those self-same little people from within the confines of power. As he ultimately puts it in his own memoir, Labour failed to support him. He states that he 'tried talking to Ruairi, but he was non-committal when I raised it with him'. On the day of the fateful cabinet meeting the Labour ministers kept mum and 'just sat on their hands looking sheepish. I don't know if Albert had done a deal with Dick.' And poor Bertie Ahern, the devoted champion of the poor and the law-abiding taxpayers alike, was completely isolated. He notes that he was 'furious and I let Quinn know it'(Ahern, 2010: 153). The normally verbose Quinn stayed silent and continued that monastic vow when it came to writing his own memoir over a decade later. As for Ahern, as two more sceptical chroniclers of his career point out: 'the most cunning, the most devious of them all actually considered resigning on a measure that he himself had proposed to cabinet. Strange indeed' (Clifford and Coleman, 2009: 207). A few months into the new government such mistrust as is evident from these contradictory accounts boded ill for the government. The report of the Beef Tribunal was to provide it with its next honesty test.

By the summer of 1994 it had become known in political circles that Justice Liam Hamilton was in the throes of finishing up his report into the beef industry. The tribunal had faced all sorts of difficulties during its tortuous three-year existence in the form of legal challenge and, as we have seen, in the testimony of O'Malley and Reynolds a casuistry of language that could be best interpreted as he said, he said. One of the gravest hindrances to the tribunal was the decision by the Supreme Court to uphold a challenge by the then Attorney General, Harry Whelehan, to the ruling made by the tribunal with regard to its right to inquire into discussions at the Cabinet. As Hamilton in his introduction to the report made clear: 'By virtue of the ruling of the Supreme Court on the question of absolute privilege from disclosure of discussions which took place at meetings of the Cabinet, the Tribunal was prohibited from inquiring as to such discussions and members of the Cabinet were equally precluded from giving evidence with regard thereto' (Hamilton, 1994: 11). The Attorney General's appeal related to a decision passed down by Judge Rory O'Hanlon in July 1992 where, in a defence of the right of the tribunal to delve into discussions taken at cabinet, he declared with remarkable candour that 'it has not been unknown in the history of government in other countries for totally corrupt governments, and for members, to enrich themselves dishonestly at the cost of the public purse' (*Irish Times*, 11 July 1992). O'Hanlon was of the view that an absolute ban on disclosure of what had transpired at government meetings would not have due regard to the public interest and to the rights of the individual as guaranteed by the Constitution. If an absolute blanket of confidentiality had been intended in contradistinction to the legal situation in so many other democratic communities, he would have expected it to be spelled out in clear terms in the Constitution. As it was not, O'Hanlon upheld Hamilton's view that it was in the public interest and fundamental to his inquiry that he be able to inquire into cabinet decisions. If O'Hanlon was to take an alternative view then the effect of the Attorney General's submissions would be to prevent any tribunal of inquiry from obtaining the information it needed to establish guilt where guilt existed (O'Toole, 1995: 280–1). In essence the Attorney General's opinion, acting, as the Supreme Court on hearing the appeal made clear, with at least the tacit support of the Reynolds government, was that cabinet confidentiality was a golden rule of Irish government set down in the Constitution and no public interest defence could counteract it. Reynolds reacted to O'Hanlon's decision with typical fury. As the government press secretary, Seán Duignan, paints it, 'Taoiseach had been predicting that it would go against the government. That still did not prevent him from going ballistic when he heard it confirmed. No way can he run a government without cabinet confidentiality. I have drunk enough to say to him that we have no judicial, political, media or public support on the issue' (Duignan, 1995: 44). The Attorney General's immediate appeal to the Supreme Court showed that this was not quite an accurate picture, as the court in a 3–2 decision took the view that cabinet confidentiality was indeed sacrosanct and that the public interest in essence ranked secondary to the government's interest.

Most commentators assumed that Reynolds must have put Whelehan up to appealing to the Supreme Court, but given later events there can be little doubt that the Attorney General took the decision himself. Nevertheless

Reynolds was tarred with the appeals brush, with the opposition braying that he pushed the Attorney General into appealing against the decision in order to frustrate the work of the tribunal and protect himself. There can be little doubt but that the decision of the Supreme Court came as a massive relief to Reynolds in terms of the ultimate outcome of the tribunal. As the most perceptive analyst of the tribunal, Fintan O'Toole, points out, the decision ultimately had the result of keeping the people in the dark as to why the government took the decisions it did in relation to export credit insurance of the Irish beef industry, particularly when it came to Larry Goodman: 'No one – not the houses of parliament which commissioned the report, not the President of the High Court who conducted the inquiry, not, above all, the public in whose "national interest" the decisions were made – can ever know why the whole thing happened' (O'Toole, 1995: 281).

When the Beef Tribunal report was published on Friday 29 July 1994 – the Friday of a long weekend – it presaged the beginning of the end for the Reynolds–Spring coalition. Reynolds points out that the tribunal report was issued in the normal manner to the minister in charge of the area being investigated, Agriculture in this instance, and that Joe Walsh, the then minister, passed it on to him as Taoiseach. Then Reynolds let his team of advisers go at it as he paced around his office certain that he would be vindicated. And his advisers indeed came up with the expected vindication, telling him that apart from criticising some of his decisions the report left him in essence in the clear. Reynolds, showing the impetuosity that made him clearly unsuited to be Taoiseach of a coalition government, insisted that the media be instantly alerted, telling Duignan: 'I've taken this shit long enough. I'm not taking another minute of it. Tell the pol corrs I'm vindicated' (Duignan 1995: 113). Saner voices in Reynolds's camp told him there was no need to go this path without at least telling his coalition partners. But Reynolds was having none of it and insisted on 'his day in the sun'. It was a curious and certainly unstatesmanlike reaction. Labour was convinced it had a deal that once the report was published there would be no immediate comment from the government. Reynolds denied that there was any such deal. More to the point, the Labour part of the government had serious difficulty getting to see the report at all. Finlay's memoirs offer an unintentionally hilarious account of the obfuscation that Fianna Fáil went to that night in order to have the report to itself for as long as possible. Finlay tells of not being able to get into the Taoiseach's private offices, of the Taoiseach refusing to take the Tánaiste's calls, of locked doors and secret knocking codes. He is described by Duignan as being 'this old testament whirlwind of wrath, biblical beard quivering, like Moses about to smite the idolators of the Golden Calf, and he's thundering that Albert is refusing to talk to Dick, that his staff are saying he's gone when he knows damn well that he is sulking down there in his office. Repent,

repent!' (Duignan, 1995: 114). Finlay, while denying the metaphor of the biblical figure full of wrath, was certainly angry and tense and clearly had his reasons to be in such condemnatory mood. After all, with his boss out of Dublin it fell on him to get the Labour view across and to stop Reynolds pulling a proverbial Fianna Fáil stroke. He failed. But then again he could hardly have succeeded. Reynolds was determined to tell his side of the story first, no matter the consequences. As Finlay points out, one of the puzzling things about that fateful night was that even though Reynolds and his team had the report for a couple of hours before anyone else 'it was an amazing achievement that they were able to find so quickly, in the nine hundred pages of the report a couple of key sentences, pages apart, on which the Taoiseach was able to base his claim of vindication' (Finlay, 1998: 235). The Beef Tribunal report was a bit like the evidence presented to it; long, opaque and turgid. Amongst other things it discovered a three-year sustained relationship between a government and a private company unparalleled in the history of the Irish state. In the course of that relationship the government clearly broke the law and asked little as to the private practices of the company which all the time was 'abusing public funds on a large scale and contriving to cheat the public of taxes' (O'Toole, 1995: 281).

What it did not discover was any sort of collusion between Albert Reynolds and Larry Goodman, noting that there was no evidence that Reynolds was close to Goodman or that Goodman had any political association with him. In that context Reynolds was certainly entitled to his view of vindication in relation to his personal integrity and that all the decisions he took were in the national interest. The trouble was that he seemed to have an extraordinarily narrow view of what the national interest was, and it certainly seemed to be different to the public interest. Moreover the tribunal itself unfortunately never defined what it understood the national interest to mean (Byrne, 2012: 120). In any event politically there was no need for Reynolds's petulant behaviour in issuing an extraordinarily selective view of what the tribunal said about him. Once the public became aware of the nature of the issuing of the report, the view stuck that by releasing their own interpretation Fianna Fáil, and Reynolds in particular, were attempting to mislead both the media and the public as to what the report actually said and, in essence, to misrepresent its findings. It was a hopeless display of political leadership and marked the beginning of the end of Reynolds's time as Taoiseach. It is best summed up by Reynolds's bizarre recounting of his eventual conversation with Spring in the early hours of the morning where he states that the Tánaiste called 'to express his anger that I had pre-empted the government's perusal of the verdict. Not a word of congratulations, you're in the clear, only more dire warnings and threats. "Would you deny me my hour in the sun, Dick?" I asked him' (Reynolds, 2009: 381). Written fifteen years after the publication of the report, no finer an example of narcissism and lack of self-awareness can be found in modern Irish politics. And all for nought. Two weeks after the report was published an opinion poll in the *Irish Times* found that, though many voters were critical of the actions of senior politicians, most had limited knowledge of the contents of the report. In making findings of fact as distinct from allocating blame the tribunal had in essence copperfastened a view taking hold within the public that golden circles did indeed exist in public life, and more importantly that they were beyond any legal, political or even moral reproach or sanction. As the noted scholar of political corruption in Ireland Elaine Byrne points out, the report ultimately was 'a futile exercise in ambiguity, facilitating such moral uncertainty about political responsibilities that terminology like consequence was absent from any discussion on the Tribunal findings. In effect, the implicit licence to act without impunity was now established explicitly' (Byrne, 2012: 131). Notwithstanding the fact that the Beef Tribunal failed to deliver a head in terms of blame or even mandate a significant change in public policy, the tribunal of inquiry was to be used again three times in quick succession to investigate payments to politicians and land re-zonings in Dublin, with startling results but little change in how Irish people voted.

A government collapses

In the meantime the Fianna Fáil–Labour government was entering into its final stage of collapse, with the central player being neither Reynolds nor Spring but an obscure lawyer named Harry Whelehan. Described by Reynolds in his biography as his 'nemesis' (Reynolds, 2009: 382), Whelehan was a pernickety, letter-of-the-law Attorney General with an inadvertent nose for trouble. Reynolds had barely taken up the office of Taoiseach when Whelehan, who had been in office since September 1991, posed him with his first problem by seeking and then securing an injunction to prevent a pregnant fourteen-year-old-girl, who had been the victim of rape, from travelling to England for an abortion. In this instance Whelehan had acted independently of the government, and seemingly without consulting any minister in that government. He was later vindicated by the Supreme Court as having acted properly and appropriately within the meaning of his office. His view was that in the meaning of the eighth amendment to the Constitution there was an unborn child with a constitutional right to life with nobody to advocate the right of that child to be born other than the Attorney General, hence his action seeking an injunction to prevent the abortion. He had then strongly argued the government's case on cabinet confidentiality in the Supreme Court while acting rather narrowly in what he believed to be the state's interest, rather than in the wider public interest. Again he considered this to be in the scope of his constitutional position. Attorneys General the world over who have to make controversial decisions are nothing new, and notwithstanding the abortion crisis, known as the X case, and his travails at the Beef Tribunal Whelehan was generally considered to be a good legalistic Attorney General albeit one with no political nous whatsoever. His refusal to turn a blind eye in the X case, while in many ways admirable, summed up his relative political naivety and he was widely seen as 'an innocent abroad in the cut-throat atmosphere of Leinster House' (Collins, 2001: 277).

Albert Reynolds himself was a staunch Catholic who held relatively conservative religious views but on abortion he decided on taking the office of Taoiseach that it was a subject best left alone. The X case decided by the Supreme Court in March 1992 quickly put a stop to that. There was also a legacy issue from the Haughey government to deal with. In the summer of 1991, Haughey and his Minister for Foreign Affairs, Gerard Collins, were convinced by anti-abortion activists that Ireland needed a special protocol on abortion within the Maastricht Treaty on European Union, which was due for ratification the following year. The argument presented to the Fianna Fáil–PD government was that without such a protocol there was a fear that opponents of abortion in Ireland would oppose the Maastricht Treaty. Given the recorded mobilising power of these groups in both the 1983 abortion referendum and the 1986 divorce referendum, this was not a threat to be taken lightly. In December 1991 Collins persuaded his European colleagues to take the protocol on board. It was a decision that, like the 1983 abortion referendum itself, had come about through the efforts of the pro-life lobby alone (O'Reilly, 1992: 139). Once the Supreme Court, however, famously adjudicated that abortion was in fact permissible in Ireland under the eighth amendment to the Constitution, if a mother's life was at risk including through suicide, pressure from groups lobbying to overturn this decision became intense, leaving Reynolds to feel that he had little choice but to sanction another round of referendums to be held in November 1992 on the same day as the general election. The abortion referendums of 1992 on the so-called substantive issue, the right to travel, and the right to information, were very different from the 1983 referendum in that Fianna Fáil under Reynolds took a much more hardline position in relation to the pressure exerted on it by the pro-life groups, withstood the wording offered by them, and pushed forward with its own wording. Indeed the Reynolds government adopted a significantly tougher stance than Haughey's government of only a few months earlier when it came to dealing with such lobbying. This can be ascribed to the personal belief of Reynolds that it was the duty of government and indeed all political parties, rather than sectional interest groups, to offer leadership in such sensitive social areas. In any event the electorate rejected the government's proposal on the substantive issue while affirming the right of all Irish citizens to travel and information. The abortion question then played little role as Reynolds and Spring struck their coalition deal in the aftermath of the referendum and general election.

While being Attorney General inevitably involves lawyers immersing themselves in political life as the chief legal advisers to the government, being a High Court judge and particularly being president of the High Court has no real political connotations. Judges issue decisions and that tends to be irrespective of any political consequences those decisions might well have – as can be seen for instance in Justice Hamilton's Beef Tribunal report. In September 1994 a vacancy arose for the position of president of the High Court, when the then incumbent Hamilton was nominated for the vacant position of Chief Justice of the Supreme Court. Whelehan had lobbied both sides of the political divide for the position, having mentioned earlier to Dick Spring that he would be interested in it should it become vacant and also having sought and received support from a number of Fianna Fáil TDs. No one in Fianna Fáil was overly enamoured with Whelehan but no one either could think of a reason why he should not get the position. He had not impressed anyone with his handling of the X case, but by the time the presidency of the High Court vacancy arose he had come to be respected by certain figures in Fianna Fáil (Garry, 1995: 194). Ultimately he was to get the support of the one man who really mattered; Albert Reynolds. As with much else in Reynolds's political career, his judgement and decision-making in the Whelehan affair showed the stubborn streak which had brought him to the zenith of Irish politics but would very quickly bring him to a nadir that he himself could never have imagined; resignation as Taoiseach and leader of Fianna Fáil in a matter of months. And all because he could not countenance any perceived climb-down on his part. Abiding by a convention that a serving Attorney General had first option on senior judicial vacancies, Reynolds, despite knowing of Spring's downright opposition, gave Whelehan his word that he would support him if and when the presidency of the High Court became available. Reynolds was never a man to be bound by convention, so the presence of precedent as the singular reason to appoint Whelehan makes very little sense. Fergus Finlay's warning to Seán Duignan that if Reynolds 'tries to force Harry on us, we will make the Beef Tribunal row look like a storm in a teacup' (Duignan, 1995: 117) was airily dismissed by Reynolds. Following a late-night meeting between Reynolds and Spring where as much seems to have been left unsaid as was said, there does seem to have been some implicit understanding that Whelehan would be appointed President of the High Court and Reynolds considered that he had in effect won this battle of political wills (Collins, 2001: 279). The Attorney General's office, of which Whelehan was naturally head, however, would within the week come in for stringent criticism for its delay of some seven months in issuing a response to an extradition request from the RUC in Northern Ireland relating to a paedophile priest named Brendan Smyth. Spring lost no time in reiterating his opposition to the Whelehan appointment, with the result that in a colossal display of hubris and impatience Reynolds insisted on railroading the appointment through cabinet. Spring and his Labour ministers walked out, leaving a stunned though outwardly calm Reynolds pondering his options. Rather unbelievably with the fate of his second coalition hanging by the proverbial thread, Reynolds, with his Minister for Justice, Máire Geoghegan Quinn, set off for Áras an Uachtaráin – the President's residence – for the swearing in of their new High Court president. In his memoir Reynolds seems to imply that there was an enormous hurry to make the appointment: he describes a call coming through from the Áras that the President, Mary Robinson, was going away for the long weekend but that if he and his team could get over there – a short trip of no more than twenty minutes or so – the formal appointment could be made immediately (Reynolds, 2009: 391–2). Instead of using this opportunity to delay the appointment, given that his government was in imminent danger of collapse, Reynolds stubbornly pushed ahead. As Stephen Collins recounts it: 'The atmosphere in the Áras was cold and unreal with everybody, apart from a beaming Whelehan, conscious that they were in the middle of a major political crisis. The President was glacial and even the new Attorney General, Eoghan Fitzsimons, who was there to get his seal of office, looked grim. "Extraordinary haste," muttered the President's special advisor, Bride Rosney' (Collins, 2001: 281). To make matters worse, all this was going on in the midst of extremely long, complex and difficult negotiations about the Northern Ireland peace process.

And with that appointment of Harry Whelehan, Albert Reynolds to all intents and purposes brought down his second coalition government and signed his own political death warrant. His chief adviser, Martin Mansergh, summed it up thus: 'the Taoiseach was engaged in a power play that went hideously wrong – what he wanted, he had to have, and that was the end of the matter' (Finlay, 1998: 264). There were some frantic efforts to resuscitate the coalition over the next three days, including an admission by Reynolds that he was wrong to appoint Whelehan against the opposition of Labour, which raises the question as to why he did it in the first place. Reynolds, on Monday 14 November 1994, had gone so far, through his intermediary, the Attorney General, Eoghan Fitzsimons, as to ask Whelehan to resign in a bid to save the peace process on the grounds that the collapse of the government could threaten the fragile peace in Northern Ireland, but Whelehan had simply refused. As far as Labour was aware this was Reynolds acting alone and without input from any other senior Fianna Fáil minister. All rescue bids were eventually scuppered on the emergence of yet another delayed extradition case in the Attorney General's office – the so-called Duggan case – and an

inadvertent misleading of the Dáil by Reynolds about the timelines involved
as to when he was told about this particular case. Once Labour became aware
of this, it went to Reynolds to famously look for a head. As Reynolds recalls
it, Ruairi Quinn stated, 'Labour had come for a head, Harry's or yours; it
doesn't look like we're getting Harry's'. Quinn's memory is more blunt,
noting that in the middle of the meeting, with the clock ticking on the resump-
tion of the Dáil, he basically got fed up with Reynolds, forcibly telling him:
'it is very fucking simple: we either have your head or Harry Whelehan's'
(Quinn, 2005: 316; Reynolds, 2009: 402). Notwithstanding Quinn's pompos-
ity, they did indeed get the head of Albert Reynolds, who resigned as leader
of Fianna Fáil. His resignation was quickly followed by Harry Whelehan,
who decided that he could not work as President of the High Court as he had
not the full support of the government and of the Attorney General, Eoghan
Fitzsimons, who resigned after holding his position for only thirty-four days.
It was bloodletting on an extraordinary scale. And Albert Reynolds, the self-
made man of Irish politics, the man who had reached the pinnacle of Irish
politics just fifteen years after being first elected, the man who had placed
Northern Ireland centre stage in politics of the Irish Republic, the man who
brought an entrepreneurial zeal, hitherto unknown, to policy–making, ended
up as one of the great tragic figures of Irish politics: a Shakespearean hero
who brought himself down simply because he did not know how to
compromise.

A new coalition for Ireland

And yet notwithstanding all this political and legal carnage there seemed
every chance that Labour would serenely decide to stay on in government
with the new Fianna Fáil leader, Bertie Ahern. A couple of weeks of pre-
dictable and desultory meetings about a piously named charter of renewal
took place, but pretty much every significant political figure in both Labour
and Fianna Fáil was of the view that the messy Reynolds–Whelehan resignation affairs should be consigned to the dustbin of history and treated with
political amnesia just to be sure. The lone dissenter to this view was once
again Spring's chief adviser, John Rogers, who argued that 'you just never
knew where you stood with Fianna Fáil' (Finlay, 1998: 267). In fact such
was the giddy excitement in both parties about going back into government
that, when the Fine Gael leader, John Bruton, made the not unreasonable
point on RTÉ radio that, given the extraordinary events of the previous few
weeks, Dick Spring should not simply and blithely go back into government
with Fianna Fáil, it was later described by Fergus Finlay with a complete
lack of self-awareness as basically 'sore losing' (Finlay, 1998: 270). Finlay
did have one significant point in his favour, and that was that the public

seemed generally very positive about a continuance of the Fianna Fáil–Labour government, with a poll showing 63 per cent of the people favouring that option on the election of Bertie Ahern as leader of Fianna Fáil and very little support for any alternative coalition option (Girvin, 1999: 16). Yet the following day Spring, Finlay and the rest of their Labour colleagues had a Pauline conversion about that perennial loser in Irish politics, John Bruton, when the *Irish Times* reported that they had pretty much been deceived all along not simply by Reynolds but by other ministers in Fianna Fáil over the Smyth affair.

The story the *Irish Times* published on 5 December 1994 was basically that when Fitzsimons, on Reynolds's behalf, went to ask Whelehan to resign on the Monday night in question, 14 November, this was not on the basis of the Northern Ireland peace process, as Labour had been told was the case. It was in fact on the basis of the precedent of the Duggan case which was known not only to Reynolds but to other Fianna Fáil ministers as well. Labour believed that Bertie Ahern and his negotiation team had been acting in bad faith. They demanded a report from the Attorney General, Fitzsimons, who eventually corroborated the fact that, yes indeed, other senior Fianna Fáil ministers besides Reynolds had known of the Duggan affair. Albert Reynolds had gone into the Dáil on the Tuesday after the Fitzsimons–Whelehan meeting and had basically been accused of withholding information and in the process lost the confidence of the Labour part of his government. Now three weeks later the *Irish Times* was revealing that other ministers in Fianna Fáil had this information. Not even Labour could stomach such a situation whereby Reynolds would be succeeded by Ahern who had as much knowledge as Reynolds did about the whole affair. What would have been the point of Reynolds resigning at all if that was the case? In that context Labour broke off the negotiations with Ahern and Fianna Fáil.

Fianna Fáil for its part saw the collapse of the government as the natural outcome of Labour never really wanting to be in power with Fianna Fáil and doing everything in its power to bring about such an outcome, which raises yet another question of why they ever signed up for an agreement with Labour at all. In any event it viewed the reasons for pulling down the coalition as entirely spurious and duplicitous. After all, Fianna Fáil pointed out, did not Máire Geoghegan Quinn, the Minister for Justice, allude to the fact in an earlier Dáil speech that Fianna Fáil ministers did in fact know of the Duggan case? Why then the extraordinary volte-face by Labour when the *Irish Times* published a story that had been in effect part of the Dáil record for a few weeks? To Fianna Fáil this was as clear as day. To Labour it was a heavily coded speech full of obfuscation. In any event the ultimate fall of the Fianna Fáil–Labour government must be attributed to the man whose job it was to keep it together: Albert Reynolds. The blunt reality was that Reynolds acted in both his coalition governments as if he was leading a single-party govern-ment. He could not seem to grasp the fact that coalitions required compro-mise. The electorate had denied Fianna Fáil an overall majority and, given that Fianna Fáil had chosen coalition, it was incumbent on the leader of that government to make it work. Labour members were not innocents abroad in the fall of the coalition, but to ascribe a malevolent intent to bring down the government is to see a conspiracy where none existed. Labour wanted to be in government, liked the spoils of office, felt it was doing a good job, and glimpsed the possibility not only of a second term with Fianna Fáil but of being in government perennially. It could coalesce with Fianna Fáil or Fine Gael; putative kingmakers rewarded with major ministries and input into policy formulation. The idea of Labour pulling down the government in a fit of pique over Fianna Fáil chicanery does not add up. What does is what simply happened. Labour's trust in Fianna Fáil had eroded to the point of collapse. It was not willing to serve under Ahern if Fianna Fáil continued to ignore its fears, and thus decided to end the relationship.

The Dáil ultimately in its wisdom decided to set up a committee to inquire into the circumstances of how the government fell. It was, as is commonly the case with such committees, a pointlessly partisan affair. Fianna Fáil gave its side, Labour gave its, and the committee, which split amongst tribal party lines, eventually decided that no one was at fault. Any blame that was ascribed was for a hapless official in the Attorney General's office who had sat on a file for seven months without doing much if anything about it, and for Eoghan Fitzsimons, who was criticised for 'his inexperience of the polit-ical environment', as if that was the chief role of an Attorney General (Dáil Debates, vol. 451, col. 1066, 4 April 1995). Blaming official bureau-crats was the quintessential Irish way for absolving politicians of any culpa-bility and allowed both political parties to avoid losing face and claim vindication.

While this inquiry was going on Labour had, however, turned its increas-ingly lonely eyes to John Bruton and Fine Gael, and lost no time in putting together an alternative government which included Democratic Left. The electorate of 1992 had given the politicians various options and now it was time to try another one of them. John Bruton, scarred by the experiences of being spurned by Dick Spring in 1992, was not going to risk the same thing happening again and readily agreed both to the participation of Democratic Left and to a programme for government that was essentially the same as that of the Fianna Fáil–Labour government. The colour of the coalition had changed. The policies had not. Bruton, so determinedly hostile to Democratic Left just a few years earlier, could now hardly contain his excitement about working with it. If anything summed up the non-ideological nature of Irish politics it was that.

As this new rainbow coalition government settled into office it continued a broad consensus on Northern Ireland, the economy and social welfare. Fine Gael, which in opposition had been critical of social partnership as operating outside of parliamentary scrutiny and oversight, quickly lost any interest in actually putting an end to that structure of devising and implementing macroeconomic policy, or, as some of its more hostile critics understood it, a cosy cartel of chicanery capitalism. Instead it began to espouse the benefits of social partnership as being central to the economic success of the country, which was seen in the fact that in December 1994 the public finances were in surplus for the first time since 1967. Fine Gael in fact became zealous converts to social partnership, actively promoting Partnership 2000, agreed in 1997, as the continuing basis for the consensual development of the economy, as this agreement copperfastened the corporatist arrangements whereby the unions, business groups and farmers all had central roles in the development of the macroeconomy. Moreover there was a maintenance of social welfare levels and the promise of a significant degree of redistribution. As Brian Girvin points out, this 'astonishing volte-face seems to have been a product of Bruton's experience of government and his conviction that the Christian Democratic dimension of Fine Gael should be given prominence over the neoliberal strain' (Girvin, 1999: 23). It seemed that the policies pursued by successive Fianna Fáil governments of different hues had not only brought significant economic successes but had persuaded Fine Gael to continue them in government. Fianna Fáil, however, due to the petulance of Albert Reynolds, was now in opposition, leaving a different coalition to run the ship of state.

Of morality and corruption

Despite the strong economic indicators that it had inherited, the new triple-pronged coalition had two major difficulties which it had to work through: those old Irish perennials of morality and corruption. After the defeat of the 1986 divorce referendum, Fine Gael and Labour resolved to have another go at removing the prohibition of divorce from the 1937 Constitution once the rainbow coalition was formed. At a fundamental level the original defeated amendment had for the first time placed the issue of marital breakdown firmly on the political agenda and in particular the need for the state to develop a humane response to such breakdown whilst providing for adequate financial and material provisions for those in family separation cases. Although it was the anti-divorce campaign which had proved successful in mobilising opinion against the amendment, nevertheless the political debate after the referendum concentrated on reforming family policies, and the policy process reverted to routine procedure in the Department of Justice, with various women's interest groups lobbying on equality-focused issues. Eventually in 1989 the then Fianna Fáil minority government adopted the Fine Gael deputy Alan Shatter's judicial separation initiative, first introduced as a Private Member's Bill in the Dáil in 1987, and passed the Judicial Separation and Family Law Reform Act (Galligan, 1998: 103). To the extent that this statute broadened the grounds for judicial separation to include a 'no fault' provision and more explicit measures on financial settlements and protection for children, it set the scene for a rerun of the divorce referendum. After the 1992 election, the Fianna Fáil–Labour government in its programme for government explicitly committed itself to 'a major programme of family law reform, culminating in a referendum on divorce in 1994' (Fianna Fáil–Labour, Partnership for Government, 1993). This was renewed by the new coalition, which resolved to hold the referendum within its first year in office.

The referendum was eventually held in November of 1995 and the campaign was primarily fought by concerned interest groups as the government deliberately pursued a low-key approach, with one minister claiming that by doing so the hysteria associated with the 1986 divorce campaign would be avoided (Girvin, 1996: 179). Given the nature of the various moral campaigns of abortion and divorce in the 1980s and early 1990s, it is hardly credible that any campaign on a moral issue in Ireland could not be without elements of hysteria. Although the reasoning of the government could be considered suspect, the fact that it took a back seat let the various interest groups involved come to the fore in the debate, and ultimately the campaign, about removing the Constitutional ban on divorce. The forces of moral conservatism had shown themselves to be far better skilled in modern pressure-group techniques than their opponents in the abortion and divorce referendums of the 1980s. By the 1995 divorce referendum, however, those groups in favour of the amendment such as the Divorce Action Group and the Right to Remarry Group had proved themselves to be efficient operators in the game of pressure politics. In the words of one journalist who followed the campaign closely: 'without the efforts of members of voluntary organisations with direct experience of marriage breakdown who … felt it was necessary to campaign for divorce independently of the Government, the amendment would have been lost' (*Irish Times*, 27 November 1995).

In fact the proposal was barely carried. Polls taken just four months before the referendum showed that 69 per cent of those questioned favoured changing the Constitution to allow for divorce (Girvin, 1996: 175). That there was a margin of just a half of a percentage point, and over nine thousand votes in favour, of the proposal once the votes were counted can be attributed to the professional strategy of those involved in the No campaign who associated traditional Irish and Catholic values to their cause. Indeed the No Divorce campaign had established a steering committee in December of 1994 which from then on had worked on a 'comprehensive and professional plan to defeat the referendum' (*Irish Times*, 29 November 1995). Another anti-amendment group, the Anti-Divorce Campaign, was formed in the months prior to the campaign and consisted of a core group who had steered through the 1983 abortion amendment and formed the anti-divorce campaign of 1986. Nevertheless the government had managed to achieve a significant social achievement in persuading the people to remove the divorce ban from the Constitution. In an Ireland which was still quite conservative in its thinking this was no mean feat.

After the farrago of the Beef Tribunal it seemed that politicians had had enough of tribunals of inquiry but only two years later yet another one, the McCracken Tribunal was established. The main remit of the McCracken Tribunal was to inquire into the so-called 'Dunnes Payments' episode. The immediate origin of both the McCracken and the subsequent Moriarty Tribunal into payments to politicians lay in a rather mysterious and often squalid family dispute about control of the most famous supermarket group in Ireland, the billionaire retail outfit Dunnes Stores. This arose after the chairman of the company, Ben Dunne, was arrested in Florida in July 1992 on allegations of possessing cocaine, having been found by local police in a hotel room with quantities of the drug and in the company of a local prostitute. It was also reported, though subsequently denied by Dunne, that he had tried to commit suicide by jumping from a seventeenth-floor balcony. Following this dramatic episode involving one of Ireland's leading businessmen and most public figures, there came into the public domain a dispute, which had been going on in private for some years, between Dunne and his sister Margaret Heffernan, over ownership of the Dunnes Stores group (Smyth, 1997). During this often rancorous dispute it emerged that a whole host of payments had been made to a variety of politicians. In the light of this, the Oireachtas established the tribunal in February 1997 as the best way both to establish the facts of these payments and to command public confidence in terms of openness and accountability in the political process. It would be extremely successful in both endeavours as it uncovered some extraordinarily jaw-dropping facts about payments to politicians and finished all its work in six months.

The McCracken Tribunal dealt with the initial flurry of allegations about financial links between the Dunnes Stores group and two senior politicians, the former Taoiseach and leader of Fianna Fáil, Charles Haughey, and the former Fine Gael minister Michael Lowry. The Tribunal proved remarkably successful in eliciting information from both Irish and offshore financial institutions in its search for secret payments. It uncovered a host of payments from Ben Dunne to politicians of various parties. Haughey's opulent lifestyle, long a source of wonder all across Ireland, was exposed as existing largely on the donations of wealthy businessmen. He at first denied before the Tribunal that he had received any financial contributions from Dunnes Stores. However, when faced with hard documentary evidence that £1.3 million from Dunnes had found its way to him while Taoiseach between 1987 and 1991, he belatedly acknowledged its receipt. It also emerged that, practically throughout his political career, Haughey's financial and tax affairs had been handled by a close friend and practising accountant, Des Traynor. The latter controlled the so-called Ansbacher accounts, a complex and extensive tax-avoidance system, traces of which the tribunal, and a separate investigation by the Department of Enterprise, Trade and Employment into the Dunnes Stores group, had uncovered. Of this, some £40 million was held in a Cayman Islands bank. The Tribunal also discovered that a commercial firm, Celtic Helicopters, run by one of Haughey's sons, had benefited from funds in these accounts (Keena, 2001: 235–44).

For his part, Michael Lowry, appointed as Minister for Transport, Energy and Communications by John Bruton, was disgraced when it emerged during the course of the McCracken proceedings that his refrigeration company had had only one real customer: Dunnes Stores. After resigning from ministerial office in December 1996, but crucially before the end of the McCracken Tribunal, he made a personal statement to the Dáil, stridently denying that he had done anything wrong, engaged in any abuse of office or held any offshore bank accounts. Following the appearance of the Tribunal's report, in September 1997, showing quite clearly that he had several such accounts, he had to offer this rather surreal apology:

> With the benefit of hindsight I now accept that the words I used and the example I gave were most unfortunate and conveyed a misleading impression. I fully accept responsibility for that. However, I categorically assure this House that it was not my intention to mislead. I offer my full and sincere apologies to the Ceann Comhairle and to all Members of the House then and now for having misled them in any way. (Dáil Debates, vol. 480, col. 615, 10 September 1997)

The importance of the McCracken Tribunal lay in its clarity, efficiency and unequivocal conclusions about payments to both Haughey and Lowry. It also cast much new light on the performance of the Revenue Commissioners in relation to tax avoidance, specifically with regard to the Ansbacher accounts. Both general and political reaction to the tribunal was positive, with the then Tánaiste, Mary Harney, declaring that her faith in tribunals had been restored by McCracken. In that context, Fianna Fáil felt obliged to agree to a further tribunal into the affairs of Haughey and Lowry after the June 1997 general election, which saw it enter into coalition with the PDs led by Harney. The decision to initiate new tribunals into payments to politicians, and the planning industry, was one that would have significant and extremely long-lasting implications for the Irish political system but would ultimately leave the vast majority of Irish voters strangely unmoved when it came to the ballot box.

Prior to this, however, and rather bizarrely, the major political parties agreed that it would be improper to determine who else held money in the secret Ansbacher accounts, even though these were patently illegal and implied large-scale tax evasion (O'Halpin and Connolly, 1998: 141). Nevertheless, only a few months later, on a tide of rising public anger, the Fianna Fáil–PD government set up an official investigation into the Ansbacher accounts. This initially took the form of the Tánaiste, Mary Harney, announcing that she was appointing Gerard Ryan, an accountant and senior civil servant from her own Department of Enterprise, Trade and Employment, to investigate possible breaches of company law by Celtic Helicopters in the wake of details contained in the McCracken Report. This was later expanded into a full Revenue Commissioner investigation, when evidence linking a host of wealthy individuals to the Ansbacher accounts emerged at the Moriarty Tribunal hearings into payments to politicians. The final Ansbacher report issued in July 2002 revealed that some of those who hid their money in the Cayman Islands had been appointed to state boards to serve the public interest. The names listed included former directors of Aer Lingus and Bord Fáilte, the author of the influential Culliton Report on industrial policy and a former director of the Central Bank (Keena, 2003).

The McCracken Tribunal was clearly very successful in tracking down payments to Michael Lowry and Charles Haughey from Dunne. Nevertheless, its conclusion that 'there was no political impropriety' on the part of Lowry and that 'there appear[ed] in fact to have been no political impropriety' on the part of Haughey (McCracken, 1997: 70, 73) seemed to imply that the covert payments to both individuals had had no effect on their political behaviour. This was despite the fact that the Tribunal castigated Haughey, stating that it was 'quite unbelievable' that he would not have known of the illegal off-shore accounts and consequent tax evasion, and that much of his evidence was 'unacceptable and untrue'. Moreover, it stated quite bluntly that no Taoiseach 'should be supported in his personal lifestyle by gifts made in secret to him' (McCracken, 1997: 52, 72–3).

The conclusions of the McCracken Tribunal did, however, force the Oireachtas to establish a further tribunal (the Moriarty Tribunal) to examine whether business interests might have secured favourable policy decisions from Lowry or Haughey during their respective ministerial careers. No one knew it at the time but this tribunal and another into the re-zoning of land (Flood/Mahon Tribunal) would take over fourteen years to complete and coincide with another long period of Fianna Fáil power in Ireland. Going to the polls in June 1997, the electorate would give the outgoing government little credit either for passing the divorce referendum or for facing up to Ireland's complex problem of corrupt influence in public life. The ultimate result was Fianna Fáil political hegemony for close on fourteen years, aided and abetted by a large dollop of PD neoliberalism.

4

Tribunals of inquiry and the politics of corrupt influence

At no time during our meeting were any favours sought or given.

Ray Burke, 15 September 1997

Payments for no political response

Fianna Fáil was the big winner in the 1997 general election, returning with 77 seats, an impressive gain of 9 on its 1992 showing, albeit on a similar overall percentage of the vote at 39.3 per cent. With the 4 seats won by the PDs, the two parties negotiated a programme for government and were supported by a number of independents. Bertie Ahern, so cruelly in his own mind, deprived of the position of Taoiseach in 1994 when Dick Spring jilted him for John Bruton, had finally reached the pinnacle of Irish politics. He would have an astonishing political career as Taoiseach. He won three general elections in a row, proved a crucial figure in the Northern Ireland peace process, oversaw a booming economy, albeit one which ultimately headed for disaster, and finally become embroiled in a squalid dispute with the Planning Tribunal which would see his career end in significant public ridicule. His beginning and end were bookmarked by tribunals of inquiry which stalked both the twenty-eighth Dáil and indeed Ahern's career like Banquo's ghost at Macbeth's table.

On becoming Taoiseach, Ahern appointed his fellow northside Dubliner Ray Burke as Minister for Foreign Affairs. It was in many ways a rather odd and ill-fated appointment. Long a controversial figure, Burke's tenure was to last barely four months as on 7 October 1997 he resigned his ministerial position. Burke had become embroiled in allegations about controversial re-zoning of land in North County Dublin and since his appointment as minister had been constantly dismissing reports that he had received £30,000 in political donations during the 1989 general election campaign. However, in September 1997, Burke finally admitted having received such a figure in cash during the 1989 general election at a meeting in his home with two property development figures, one of whom he had never previously met. He maintained that there was nothing unusual or sinister in this and that the money received was simply an election contribution of which he passed on £10,000 to Fianna Fáil headquarters. Burke had played the classic payment-for-no-political-response card, as he insisted that 'at no time during our meeting were any favours sought or given' and he remained as minister (Dáil Debates, vol. 480, col. 617–18, 15 September 1997).

In the light of Burke's revelation, the Oireachtas set up a tribunal of inquiry to examine some of the more contentious planning re-zoning decisions in Dublin. However, it was clear his position was becoming increasingly untenable. In early October the *Irish Times* revealed that Burke played a key role in the granting of eleven Irish passports to a Saudi Arabian banker and his family in 1990 in return for investment under the passports-for-sale scheme. Burke had had enough. He resigned as both a minister and a TD. He took the step, he said, because the 'ongoing public controversy' was preventing him giving his full attention to the Northern Ireland talks and ongoing developments in the European sphere'. In his resignation statement Burke made clear that in his view he had been wronged: 'I want to clearly restate that I have done nothing wrong'. The following day in the Dáil, the Taoiseach defended Burke, stating that he was an honourable man who had been hounded out of office by John Bruton and his likes: 'I hope he is proud of his handiwork, that he never comes to a similar untimely political end and that all his actions as a Government member would survive the intense scrutiny as Mr. Burke' (Dáil Debates, vol. 480, col. 330, 8 October 1997). The Taoiseach's inelegant language mirrored his anger. He had suffered a bitter defeat in having to accept the resignation of a senior minister so early into his government's tenure, which was accentuated when Fianna Fáil lost the subsequent by-election in Dublin North, held the following March, to Labour. Moreover Ahern had to establish a judicial tribunal into planning matters and the Burke payment. It had not been a good start to his administration (Cullen, 2002: 102; Murphy, 2003: 3).

Just under three years later in July 2000 while campaigning in another by-election, this time in Tipperary South, Ahern himself continued the payments-for-no-political-response defence. He maintained that the 'vast majority of donations to Fianna Fáil are not made in expectation of either favours or special access' (Murphy, 2006a: 94). However, when asked by the chairman of the Planning Tribunal, Feargus Flood, in May 2003 why land developers were giving councillors money, the long-time Fianna Fáil local councillor and then Senator Don Lydon was forced to admit: 'I believe that they hoped to influence (them). That's my firm belief. They did it then, they did it before, they do it now' (*Sunday Tribune*, 18 May 2003).

Both the Flood and Moriarty tribunals enjoyed spectacular success in uncovering complex networks of covert financial payments to politicians and government officials, and if they did not prove definitively that money bought public policy favours at local or national level they increasingly posed the question of why else businessmen would contribute so lavishly and so discreetly to certain individuals. From the off, both tribunals came under sustained attack from the political, media and academic worlds. In their early years they were criticised as exercises in futility, with the noted journalist and tribunal veteran Paul Cullen complaining in the *Irish Times* in November 1999 that 'Flood's exercise in futility begins again' (*Irish Times*, 22 November 1999). They were also dismissed as expensive wastes of time and public money, and in the rarefied air of political sociology as being purveyors of a false consciousness and of a renewed illusion of public accountability in an inherently unreformed and undemocratic polity (Corcoran and White, 2000; O'Halpin, 2000). Yet both the Hamilton Tribunal of Inquiry into the beef processing industry and the McCracken Tribunal of Inquiry into payments to politicians revealed that certain large businesses regularly made substantial contributions, particularly at election time, to political parties that they considered sympathetic to them. And before Lydon's appearance at the Flood Tribunal, no politician of any hue would have admitted that those who funded the political process did so in the expectation of a return on their investment.

The Flood Tribunal had its terms of reference widened in June 1998 following the disclosure of a further payment of another £30,000 to Burke in 1989. The tribunal was also empowered to investigate all improper payments made to politicians in connection with the planning process. Throughout 1998 and 1999 it seemed that the Flood Tribunal was becoming somewhat of a redundant exercise amidst a number of conflicting stories and evidence. Yet the tribunal team pushed and literally had its day in court when in April 2000 the political lobbyist, and former government press secretary, Frank Dunlop told the tribunal that fifteen Dublin county councillors received payments totalling £112,000 in connection with the re-zoning of a giant shopping centre in west Dublin at the time of the local government elections in 1991. Dunlop had initially been a reluctant witness and, in the earlier part of his evidence, had strongly denied ever making cash payments to councillors in return for votes on re-zoning issues. However, the Tribunal's discovery of a bank account in his name, from which £250,000 had been paid out at around the time of the Quarryvale re-zoning, led to a reassessment of Dunlop's evidence. Cautioned by Justice Flood to reflect on his previous testimony in the light of the existence of this account, Dunlop bared his soul in a momentous day's evidence.

Both the Taoiseach, Bertie Ahern, and the leader of Fine Gael, John Bruton, announced that they were appointing high-ranking committees to ascertain whether any party members received illicit payments while serving as county councillors. Those who had would face sanctions, including possible expulsion, from their respective parties. Fianna Fáil announced that its Standards in Public Life Committee, put in place as part of the Party's code of ethics agreed at its 1999 Ard Fheis, would be convened to establish whether any of its members were affected by Dunlop's allegations. Fine Gael, for its part, announced a three-person internal party inquiry and vowed that any person against whom allegations of corruption were proved would be expelled from the Party (Murphy, 2000: 194).

Meanwhile Dunlop continued to give more sensational evidence, reaching a climax in May 2000 when he identified a further £75,000 he paid to politicians in return for their support on re-zonings. Moreover it transpired that a further £250,000, which flowed through Dunlop's myriad bank accounts, remained unaccounted for and was thought to have been paid to politicians throughout the 1990s. This evidence resulted in Fianna Fáil extending its internal inquiry into whether any of its elected representatives accepted money for planning favours up to and including the Dunlop evidence.

Fine Gael was the first to conclude its internal review, on 12 May 2000. Chaired by Senior Counsel James Nugent, the report revealed that Fine Gael's deputy leader, Nora Owen, chief whip, Seán Barrett, two other deputies, Michael Joe Cosgrave and Olivia Mitchell, and two senators, Therese Ridge and Liam Cosgrave, had received donations from Frank Dunlop. The six Fine Gael Oireachtas members told the Party inquiry that the donations were political contributions and had not influenced their votes. In the case of Senator Cosgrave and Councillors Cathal Boland and Anne Devitt, the then leader of the Fine Gael group on Dublin County Council at the time of the Dunlop payments, the committee was unable to come to definitive conclusions in relation to payments made to them. This resulted in John Bruton stating that he would seek to prevent all three politicians from standing for the Party in any future Dáil election unless they provided more information on donations they had received from builders, developers or their agents (Murphy, 2006a: 97). Amidst threats of legal action from the councillors and vehement denials of any impropriety, the report led to little, and at the 2002 general election both Cosgrave and Boland stood without success. Yet most bizarre of all was John Bruton's olive branch to Michael Lowry in early June 2000 when he held out the prospect of a return to the Fine Gael fold for Lowry, since to exclude him permanently when he had paid the appropriate penalties would be 'unchristian'. Lowry, appointed Minister for Transport, Energy and Communications when the Fine Gael–Labour–Democratic Left government had assumed office in November 1994, had been forced to resign his ministerial position in November 1996 after the McCracken Tribunal revealed substantial payments to him from the businessman Ben Dunne on which he had avoided tax. This unheralded absolution by Bruton in the midst of the Moriarty Tribunal's investigation into Lowry's affairs caused deep resentment within Fine Gael itself and not a little public criticism of an appearance of double standards (Murphy, 2003: 10).

Fianna Fáil issued its report on 7 June 2000. The committee, chaired by the parliamentary party chairman, Dr Rory O'Hanlon, interviewed Fianna Fáil members of Dublin County Council during the period from 1985 to 1991 and the period from 1991 to the local elections of 1999. Running to two hundred pages, the report revealed a whole host of payments to a variety of members but focused primarily on the Dublin West TD Liam Lawlor (Cullen, 2002: 140–68). It accused him of being uncooperative and contradictory with respect to a series of payments made to him over a number of years by a variety of individuals.

Lawlor had received between £12,000 and £14,000 in donations before the early 1990s, and £38,000 in consultancy fees from Dunlop in 1994 and 1995. The report stated that during questioning Lawlor had given conflicting accounts of dealings that a Czech-based company – The Irish Consortium *SRO* – in which he owned a one third share had had with Frank Dunlop. Later Lawlor revealed in the annual register of members of the Dáil that he was also a non-executive director of a company called Zatecka 14 SRO, based in Prague. Lawlor, who had been embroiled in numerous planning controversies over a long career, resigned from Fianna Fáil, claiming he had done so because he did not want to distract from the workings of the government. The Dublin North TD, G. V. Wright, also came under scrutiny as the report revealed he had received £20,000 in donations, including £10,000 from Frank Dunlop, over a period from late 1991 to early 1994, when he had been the party whip on Dublin County Council. Wright insisted to the inquiry that all the donations he had received had been unsolicited. However, the property developer Owen O'Callaghan directly contradicted this claim when he issued a statement to the effect that he had given £5,000 to Wright only after having been asked for an electoral contribution (*Irish Times*, 8 June 2000). The Fianna Fáil report ultimately declared that any councillor convicted of a corruption offence should be banned from holding public office for life, and maintained that councillors should not be allowed to act as consultants to property developers while serving on a local authority (Murphy, 2000: 195–6). Wright, however, suffered no penalty and was indeed comfortably re-elected as TD for Dublin North in 2002. For his part Lawlor found himself increasingly at odds with the Flood Tribunal and was jailed for contempt on no fewer than three occasions in the thirteen months between January 2001 and February 2002. He would sadly pass away in 2005 as a result of injuries he suffered in a car crash just outside Moscow, proclaiming his innocence of corruption charges to the last.

In any event, during the presentation of a variety of items of witness evidence at the Flood Tribunal in the spring of 2003, it emerged that both these party reports were little short of cosmetic window-dressing. The Tribunal showed that the Fianna Fáil councillors Tony Foxe and Don Lydon, and Fine Gael's Liam Cosgrave, son and grandson of two former leaders of the Irish state, failed to disclose full information both to the tribunal and to their respective party inquiries. Lydon suggested that the Fianna Fáil inquiry into political payments had ignored its own terms of reference by concentrating only on allegations relating to Frank Dunlop. He further maintained that the inquiry had not carried out a complete trawl when interviewing councillors. When questioned at the tribunal about why he had failed to disclose a number of political contributions to the inquiry set up to investigate payments to councillors by Frank Dunlop and/or developers, Lydon stated that members of the committee had told him the inquiry was only dealing with 'two or three things' and was not 'a general trawl' (*Irish Times*, 3 May 2003).

The Flood Tribunal also showed quite clearly that Liam Cosgrave misled the Fine Gael inquiry about the size and number of donations he had received from Frank Dunlop. Cosgrave admitted to the Tribunal that he that he had received almost £8,000 in election expenses from Dunlop, not the £3,000 he had declared to the Fine Gael inquiry. He maintained he had simply forgotten or underestimated the donations, again insisting that all payments he had received were legitimate political donations and had had nothing to do with the various re-zoning controversies that the Flood Tribunal was investigating. He went on to castigate the Fine Gael inquiry as 'sloppy' and 'sinister'. The Fine Gael inquiry said it was unable to come to a definitive decision in relation to the payments Cosgrave had received, something he described as the 'the worst thing that has ever happened to me' (*Irish Times*, 4 April 2003). Dunlop had named Cosgrave as one of nine county councillors who allegedly took bribes in return for their votes on the re-zoning of land at Carrickmines in south Dublin, maintaining he gave Cosgrave £20,000 in payments, some of which were legitimate political contributions and some basically bribes. Cosgrave, who had complained bitterly about both the Fine Gael inquiry and the Flood Tribunal, was ultimately caught in a web of his own deceit. Having complained that both inquiries were sloppy, he relied on his own shoddy memory, a memory shown to have been seriously deficient in its recollection of moneys given to him.

The Flood Tribunal and Ray Burke

In September 2002, the Flood Tribunal issued its second interim report, dealing mostly with Ray Burke. The question of political donations first came to haunt the Fianna Fáil–PD coalition government when Burke resigned. Burke had been involved in various planning controversies since as early as 1974, and had at one stage been interviewed by the Gardai (police) about a planning development at Mountgorry, County Dublin. Moreover, in the mid 1980s, he had been chairman of Dublin County Council, which carried out numerous re-zonings, usually against the advice of its own planning officials. No charges were ever brought against Burke in relation to any re-zoning questions. Still given his controversial past it is a bit of a wonder why Bertie Ahern appointed him at all to the crucial position of Minister for Foreign Affairs in 1997, particularly when the peace process in Northern Ireland had not been bedded down.

After his resignation Burke was embroiled in countless battles with the Flood Tribunal. He gave his first evidence in July 1999, and most of the second interim report, running to over 150 pages of text with another 250 pages of appendices, was devoted to him. After sifting through some at times turgid and evasive evidence from Burke, Mr Justice Flood ruled that Burke had indeed received corrupt payments from a succession of builders, including Michael Bailey, Tom Brennan and Joseph McGowan. He also ruled that Burke, during his time as Minister for Communications in the late 1980s, had made decisions that were not in the public interest after receiving payments from Century Radio's main backer, Oliver Barry. This related to the establishment of Ireland's first national commercial radio station, Century Radio. Century was the victor in a national competition amongst four groups to provide this new commercial service; a service basically established to compete with the state broadcaster, RTÉ. The decision was made in January 1989 by the ten members of the Independent Radio and Television Commission set up by the Minister for Communications, Burke, some four months earlier. It was dubbed Radio Fianna Fáil by some because of its connections in high places (Cullen, 2002: 170). In May 1989, four months after Century had won the commercial radio licence, its main backer, the impresario Oliver Barry, gave £35,000 in cash to Burke at one of his departmental offices.

After it won the commercial radio licence, Century benefited to an extraordinary degree from direct interventions by Burke. He initially reduced the transmission fee payable by Century to RTÉ for the use of its transmissions mast, thereby saving Century some £636,000 over seven years. Not content with doing this once, Burke again reduced the fee, saving Century around £500,000 a year. Moreover he capped RTÉ's advertising and attempted to introduce a host of other measures that would have seriously diminished RTÉ's ability to keep the huge audiences it had built up, to the benefit of Century (Cullen, 2002: 203–4). In the end none of this mattered as Century collapsed, but that was no fault of Burke, who seems to have done everything humanly possible to ensure its success. This was too much for Justice Flood. In a devastating critique of the Century episode, he ruled that Barry's payment of £35,000 to Burke had had the effect of ensuring that decisions made by Burke, and no one else, in his capacity as Minister for Communications would reflect favourably on those paying him:

> The Tribunal is satisfied that Mr Burke's decisions ... were all motivated by a desire on his part to benefit those who had paid monies to him, and that proposals on such issues would not have been advanced by Mr Burke at that time were it not for the fact that he had been paid £35,000. In all the circumstances the Tribunal concludes that the payment made to Mr Burke was a corrupt payment. (Flood, 2002: 65)

After these findings, the Flood Tribunal report became an instant best-seller, with eager queues forming at the government publications office. It was to remain at the top of the best-seller charts for weeks. But this public display of approval would ultimately prove to have little long-term impact as the tribunal would last for another decade.

Besides Burke, Mr Justice Flood found that Tom Brennan, Michael and Tom Bailey, Tom Bailey's wife, Caroline, Joseph Murphy junior, and Joseph Murphy senior, Oliver Barry, James Stafford, Joseph McGowan, John Finnegan, Roger Copsey, Frank Reynolds, Tim O'Keeffe and John Bates had all obstructed the Tribunal's work. Its report was subsequently sent to the Director of Public Prosecutions, the Garda Commissioner, the Criminal Assets Bureau, the Revenue Commissioners and the Office of the Director of Corporate Enforcement. Burke rejected the tribunal's findings but his reputation was in tatters and he became the first former minister to be jailed on foot of investigations undertaken by a statutory tribunal of inquiry when in 2005 he pleaded guilty to two counts of lodging false tax returns and was sentenced to six months, imprisonment, of which he served just over four and a half. He later made a settlement of €600,000 with the Criminal Assets Bureau (Byrne, 2012: 172).

And then close to a decade later an extraordinary thing happened, which made one wonder what the whole tribunal era in Irish politics had been about at all and whether it had been worth it. In January 2015 the Planning Tribunal, later known as the Mahon Tribunal, after Judge Alan Mahon who took over with two other colleagues from Justice Flood in 2003, apologised to Ray Burke and a number of businessmen for finding that they had hindered and obstructed its work. In that context the tribunal stated that all findings of hindrance and obstruction made against individuals in its second and third interim reports would be removed and Burke and others would be entitled to claim full legal costs for their appearances at the tribunal (*Irish Times*, 15 January 2015).

The tribunal's decision to reverse its finding arose from a Supreme Court decision in July of 2014 when, in a case taken against the tribunal by Joseph Murphy Structural Engineers, the judges of the tribunal raised a number of concerns about the way the allegations made by the tribunal's key witness, James Gogarty, against Mr Burke and a number of other people had been handled.

The Supreme Court found, and the tribunal accepted, that important material described by one of the judges as 'potentially explosive' and which was relevant to the credibility of Gogarty, was wrongly withheld. The material included allegations made by Gogarty, who died in 2005, against a politician and a law officer (*Irish Times*, 15 January 2015). In light of the tribunal having conceded in the JMSE case that the material should not have been withheld, its findings of corruption against the former Dublin city assistant manager George Redmond were reversed. The tribunal had originally been spectacularly successful in showing that Redmond, the most important planning official in Dublin for over a quarter of a century, was literally in the pockets of a number of wealthy builders. 'I was the Council; I had the powers', he rather magisterially declared when he first entered the witness box in September 1999 (Proceedings of the Flood Tribunal from 20 September 1999).

He was soon humbled by the tribunal lawyers, and by Justice Flood, who warned him to reflect on the credibility of his claim that his opulent lifestyle was funded from his civil servant's salary. When threatened with up to two years in jail for misleading the tribunal, he finally admitted that he had received huge amounts of money from a variety of builders and landowners. Perhaps most famously, Redmond was arrested at Dublin Airport in March 1999 by the Criminal Assets Bureau and was found to be carrying £300,000 in cash and money drafts. The second interim report of the Flood Tribunal had found that for close on three decades since the 1960s he had been in receipt of regular and substantial payments from builders and developers in the Dublin area, 'the equivalent of receiving one substantial house per annum free' (Byrne, 2012: 173; Flood, 2002: 8). He was subsequently convicted on two counts of corruption in 2003 arising out of the payment of a £10,000 bribe, but these were overturned when new evidence of bank accounts became available. The court of criminal appeal ultimately decided that, had these accounts been available to the original jury, a different verdict might well have been found and hence the conviction was unsafe. Two further cases were taken against Redmond by the state: he was found not guilty in one while the jury could not reach a verdict in the other. In 2008 the state announced that it would not press any other charges against Redmond, who had faced investigations by the Gardai, the Revenue Commissioners, the Criminal Assets Bureau and the tribunal. Nevertheless the reputation of this at one time obscure public official was ruined and he faded off the public scene. The announcement in December 2014 that all findings of corruption made against him were reversed was met with a weary collective shrug by the Irish population, who struggled to remember who exactly George Redmond was.

The Moriarty Tribunal

For its part the Moriarty Tribunal had been most effective in uncovering a whole host of payments to Charles Haughey. This had been ongoing while Haughey himself was facing criminal charges arising from his alleged obstruction of the McCracken Tribunal. Following a variety of comments, most notably by the Tánaiste, Mary Harney, that Haughey 'should be convicted' and 'spend time in prison', an indefinite stay was put on the trial by Justice Kevin Haugh in June 2000 on the grounds that Haughey could not get a fair trial, and ultimately no trial was held (*Irish Independent*, 27 May 2000). The Moriarty Tribunal proved remarkably successful in tracking down a complicated money trail leading to Haughey, and estimated that he had received £8.5 million in donations over a sixteen-year period. But these revelations were not the only source of controversy for Fianna Fáil at the Moriarty Tribunal. In late June 2000, the Party became embroiled in a dispute with the tribunal over whether or not Party members had co-operated fully with it. This related to a list of donors given by the Party to the tribunal and whether or not there was a second list or extract containing other donors. Fianna Fáil blamed the tribunal for causing the controversy with the then Minister for Defence, Michael Smith, stating that it had given all its documents to the tribunal and 'anything they missed was their fault' (*Irish Times*, 29 June 2000). The dispute, however, led to the appearance of the Taoiseach, Bertie Ahern, at the tribunal. He tried to explain how a complaint from a donor, Mark Kavanagh, that he had not been given a receipt for a donation of £100,000 to Charles Haughey in 1989, had been withheld from the tribunal. Fianna Fáil had not told the tribunal about this payment, even though irregularities in its documentation had led to an internal party investigation in 1996. The Taoiseach, Bertie Ahern, had previously been caught up in controversy over revelations at the tribunal that he had pre-signed all the cheques on the Fianna Fáil leader's allowance account in the period 1984–92 (*Irish Times*, 16 October 1999). Some of these cheques, the tribunal discovered, had been made out to exclusive restaurants in Dublin and the expensive Charvet shirt shop in Paris.

It was also learned that John Ellis, Fianna Fáil TD for Sligo–Leitrim, was saved from bankruptcy twice by Haughey in 1989 and 1990, using money taken from the state-funded party leader's allowance. Meanwhile, and in rather surreal fashion, a member of the Dáil's Public Accounts Committee, the Fianna Fáil TD for North Kerry, Denis Foley, charged with investigating off-shore tax evasion, was himself found to be the holder of an Ansbacher account. Foley's punishment turned out to be a fourteen-day paid suspension from the Dáil. The Minister for State, Ned O'Keeffe, and the backbench TD Beverly Cooper-Flynn were others to find themselves in difficulties during the course of the 1997–2002 twenty-eighth Dáil. O'Keeffe was forced to resign as minister in February 2001 for a breach of the Ethics in Public Office Act. Cooper-Flynn was expelled from her parliamentary party in 1999 after she voted against an amendment calling on her father, the EU Commissioner Pádraig Flynn, to respond to claims that he was paid £50,000 by the developer Tom Gilmartin.

On the other side of the political fence, the Moriarty Tribunal became bogged down in investigating the award of the country's second mobile phone licence to Esat Digifone in 1995, during the rainbow government of Fine Gael, Labour and Democratic Left. A payment of $50,000 to Fine Gael from the winning consortium was the subject of a detailed tribunal investigation. The payment occurred while Michael Lowry, Minister for Communications at the time the licence was granted, was a trustee of the Party. The tribunal uncovered a vast array of complex financial transactions, and wildly different accounts of what happened. Both Lowry and his civil servants making the decision had always strenuously denied any impropriety in the awarding of the contract.

In the middle of the Fianna Fáil–PD government of 1997–2002 a major political scandal developed which brought the issue of cronyism in Irish public life to the fore: the so-called Sheedy affair. This concerned the unorthodox early release in November 1998 of Philip Sheedy, a prisoner convicted of dangerous driving causing death two years earlier. An inquiry by the Chief Justice led to the resignation of two judges, one of them the Supreme Court Justice Hugh O'Flaherty, and a court official (Collins and O'Shea, 2003: 177). The Fianna Fáil–PD coalition came under enormous strain when it then appointed O'Flaherty to the position of Vice-President of the European Investment Bank on a salary of £147,000 in May 2000. O'Flaherty, long associated with Fianna Fáil, had, in 1999, been forced to resign from the Supreme Court on threat of impeachment by the government over his role in the Sheedy affair. Bertie Ahern was also involved when it was alleged he had made representations on Sheedy's behalf to the Minister for Justice, John O'Donoghue, to obtain day-release for Sheedy. Nevertheless, the government had ridden out this particular storm until its shock decision to appoint O'Flaherty, a man without any banking experience whatsoever, to the EIB post brought the Sheedy case back into the open. Serious divisions emerged between the coalition partners, with the Minister for State at Foreign Affairs,

PD TD Liz O'Donnell, being most critical of the decision. PD Senator Helen Keogh was also deeply disturbed by the appointment and ultimately defected to Fine Gael. The problems this appointment created for the government were seen to most dramatic effect in the Tipperary South by-election of 23 June 2000. The left-wing independent candidate, Seamus Healy, won the election, with Fianna Fáil being relegated to third place – only the second time in the history of the state that this had happened at a by-election – with a dismal showing of 22 per cent of the first preference vote. It was an eloquent state-ment of dissatisfaction with the government, and was reinforced by the government's poor opinion poll showings. The government's satisfaction rating fell to below 50 per cent for the first time since the 1997 general elec-tion in an IMS poll on 15 June 2000, while an *Irish Times*/MRBI opinion poll suggested that 68 per cent of voters believed the government had been wrong to nominate O'Flaherty as Vice-President of the EIB (*Irish Independ-ent*, 15 June 2000; *Irish Times*, 16 June 2000). Nevertheless, with anything up to two years to a general election and with no evidence that any of the revelations at the various tribunals were having much of an effect on the government's popularity, the result of this by-election was likely to have little long-term significance for the government come a general election (Murphy, 2003: 11–12). And sure enough, when the resultant general election of 2002 took place, this sorry tale of cronyism had long been forgotten by the voters.

In essence the scandals that surrounded the 1997–2002 Fianna Fáil–PD government had very little impact in terms of public behaviour when it came to election time. The Fianna Fáil–PD government became the first in over thirty years to be re-elected, and Fianna Fáil, despite being the most tainted with corruption and cronyism, came extremely close to achieving an overall majority. Corruption rarely surfaced as an issue at the May 2002 general election. In contrast to the media coverage of the various tribunals, which focused heavily on the sleaze being uncovered, Fianna Fáil's internal research findings showed that the public was in no way antagonistic to the Party, and had in fact little interest in these tribunal investigations (Collins, 2003: 23). Public corruption has been defined as 'the breaking, for the sake of financial or political gain, of the rules of conduct in public affairs prevailing in a society in the period under consideration' (Tanzi, 1998). Justices Flood and Moriarty in their initial findings most certainly showed that such rules were broken in the Ireland of the 1990s. From Charles Haughey's Charvet shirts to Ray Burke's sale, for €4.8 million, of a house he received from its builders for free, the words of Edmund Burke, that corrupt influence is itself the per-ennial source of all prodigality, hold true. These scandals and the corruption underlying them proved extremely useful as a means of highlighting abuses of power but in reality they had very little impact in how either politics in Ireland was conducted or how Irish citizens voted.

The travails of Bertie Ahern

The pattern of political corruption and cronyism having no impact at election time continued into the election cycle of 2007 when the Fianna Fáil–PD government faced the electorate after five years of various political controversies but more significantly dramatic economic growth. Bertie Ahern called the election on Sunday 29 April 2007 for polling on 24 May, a three-and-a-half-week campaign. Announcing the election, the Taoiseach said that, once again, the moment had arrived for the people to decide Ireland's future: 'No one knows what the outcome of this election will be. The people have a real choice and two very different alternatives before them. That choice will frame Ireland's future and the consequences of this election will be felt for many years to come' (*Irish Times*, 30 April 2007). Ahern's admission that there was a clear choice between voters and that there was an alternative government on offer with a chance of winning the election betrayed the nervousness within government as to the outcome of the election. It was all remarkably different from the astonishingly confident launching of the 'showtime' 2002 general election (Murphy, 2003: 18).

There was speculation that the timing of the Taoiseach's decision to dissolve the Dáil, and his refusal to answer questions on announcing the election, were connected with the fact that the Mahon Tribunal, which at that stage had been investigating certain planning matters and payments for nigh on ten years, was due to open its public inquiry on Monday 30 April 2007 into the so-called Quarryvale affair. The tribunal announced before Easter that it would begin its public session on Quarryvale and would continue to sit in public until two weeks before the election. Ahern, his former partner Celia Larkin and those known to have given him money in 1993/94 were listed as witnesses at the tribunal.

Bertie Ahern had delivered on his promise made back in 2002 to serve a full five years as Taoiseach. Unlike five years earlier, however, the outcome of this general election would be in doubt until right up to polling day. Ahern's Fianna Fáil–PD government had indeed lasted the full five years but would face an opposition that offered an alternative government to an electorate which, after ten years of Ahern with his unique style of consensual government, might have been in the mood for change. Moreover by the time Ahern actually called the election, discussion of his personal finances had been a significant political news story ever since the *Irish Times* revealed in September 2006 that as Minister for Finance in 1993 and 1994 he had accepted payments of between €50,000 and €100,000 from a variety of business people and that the matter was being investigated by the Mahon Tribunal (*Irish Times*, 21 September 2006). The inquiries into Ahern's finances began after allegations were made about supposed payments to him by property developer Owen O'Callaghan in relation to the Quarryvale development in west Dublin. Both Ahern and O'Callaghan stated publicly that no such payments were made. On the day the election was called, a spokesperson for Ahern was forced to reiterate this point, stating that the 'Taoiseach did not seek any monies, he received no monies, nor was he offered any monies from Mr O'Callaghan or by anybody connected with him ... He never received money in connection with any tax designation for Quarryvale or anywhere else' (*Irish Times*, 30 April 2007). The odd nature of Ahern's finances – while Minister for Finance in the first half of the 1990s he had had no bank account and had kept large amounts of cash in his office safe – would dominate the first half of the election campaign and cause significant difficulties that the PDs in particular would not be able to shake off. Michael McDowell had become leader of the PDs, and Tánaiste, in September 2006, and within two weeks, with the *Irish Times* revelation about the Taoiseach's finances, would be thrown head-first into the most sensational controversy in Irish politics in the ten years of Bertie Ahern as Taoiseach.

The political controversy that followed these revelations lasted for more than two weeks, and for a brief period it looked as if Michael McDowell might pull the PDs out of government. Fianna Fáil let it be known that if this did happen it would carry on in government anyway and it came out strongly in defence of the Taoiseach, with senior figures robustly defending him in a variety of media outlets. The turning point in the controversy came when Ahern gave a long television interview to RTÉ's Bryan Dobson on 26 September which was broadcast in full on the Six One news and in which he gave details of payments totalling £39,000 made to him from friends during difficult personal circumstances in the early 1990s when he was Minister for Finance. Ahern also revealed that he had received a further payment of £8,000 after a personal trip to Manchester to watch his beloved Manchester United and attend a dinner. He explained that the payments were in effect a 'dig out' from friends during a period of personal difficulty for him in relation to the breakup of his marriage. This went down well with the general public, and in the first opinion poll after the controversy there was a dramatic rise in support for Fianna Fáil, which went up a massive 8 points to 38 per cent of those who expressed a preference. There was also a slight increase in popularity for the Taoiseach himself, who saw his rating improve by a single percentage point to 53 per cent. Rather contradictorily, 64 per cent of those polled thought that he was wrong to take the money. The startling result of this poll, which also saw Fine Gael down 2 to 26 per cent and Labour down 4 to 11 per cent, while the PDs saw a slight increase of 1 to 3 per cent, seemed to settle any frayed nerves in government, and both parties settled down to prepare for a pre-election budget. This poll would also have the consequence of making Fine Gael and Labour very wary of raising the issue of the

Taoiseach's finances during the election campaign itself. The lure of power, it seems, was too much for McDowell to walk out on. He salved his own conscience by announcing that he had secured an agreement from the Taoiseach that an ethics bill would be drafted to cover the issue of gifts or loans from friends in the future, and on that basis he stayed in government, ready to fight an election looking for a third Fianna Fáil–PD coalition in a row (Murphy, 2008: 17).

Notwithstanding the furore surrounding his finances, Bertie Ahern proved to be the Teflon Taoiseach during the 2007 general election campaign. While questions of his peculiar financial arrangements dogged him at every turn and obsessed journalists, they proved of little consequence with the one group that truly mattered: the voters. As the campaign progressed, Fianna Fáil became more energised when it became clear that the electorate seemed bothered neither about Ahern's finances nor about any other perception of corruption or cronyism surrounding the Party. The week before the election Ahern was widely seen to have won his one-on-one television debate with Fine Gael's Enda Kenny, and the last polls of the campaign saw Fianna Fáil surge to over 40 per cent. By polling day it was no surprise that Fianna Fáil was heading back into power, and ultimately it won 77 seats on 41.6 per cent of the vote, a similar vote share to that it had received in 2002. With the PDs enduring a disastrous election, returning just 2 seats, with its leader Michael McDowell losing his seat, Ahern moved swiftly to form a new coalition to include the barely functioning PDs and a new partner in the Greens. While the Greens were unhappy with the inclusion of the PDs in Bertie Ahern's calculations for government stability, they could do nothing about it.

With 86 seats between them, Fianna Fáil, the PDs and the Greens negotiated a programme for government and seemed to have a pretty secure majority. Despite some opposition to the very idea of going into government with Fianna Fáil, with one Green TD, Ciaran Cuffe, writing after the election that 'a deal with Fianna Fáil would be a deal with the devil', the Greens agreed at a special convention on 13 June 2007 to enter government (Minihan, 2011: 32; O'Malley, 2008a: 209). This did not, however, stop Cuffe from accepting a junior ministry a number of years later. In a masterpiece of Jesuitical thinking, the Green leader, Trevor Sargent, made it clear that, while he would not lead the Greens in a government with Fianna Fáil, he would be happy for a different leader to do so and he also had no qualms accepting a junior ministry in government. Bertie Ahern himself wryly noted that Sargent 'tied himself in knots over that, resigning the leadership, refusing a seat in cabinet, but then joining the government as a junior minister. I'm sure there was a point of principle in there somewhere, although it was lost on me' (Ahern, 2010: 324). One of Sargent's own colleagues, the newly elected deputy for Dublin

Mid West, Paul Gogarty, also criticised him, complaining about the stupidity of the 'morally tangled' decision (Minihan, 2011: 24). In any event Sargent did step down as leader and was replaced in July by the newly appointed Minister for the Environment, John Gormley, who defeated a vocal critic of the coalition, and former Party MEP, Patricia McKenna by a margin of two to one. Gormley, who had led the programme for government negotiations with Fianna Fáil, declared himself happy with Ahern's finances and settled down to the business of government.

The business of government, however, was to prove quite difficult due to the thorny issue of Ahern's finances, which made a spectacular comeback just a few months later in September 2007 when the Taoiseach gave public evidence at the Mahon Tribunal. The rationale behind these public hearings was to give Ahern the opportunity to explain apparent discrepancies between his accounts to the tribunal of various payments he received and the evidence from banking records that the tribunal's legal team had uncovered in the course of its investigations. The crux of the inconsistency was a bank lodgement by Ahern of £24,838.49 on 11 October 1994 which he claimed was made up of the proceeds of two dig-outs from friends and acquaintances, one of which he received at a dinner following a football game in Manchester. The bank record for the day, however, showed that the lodgement was probably £25,000 sterling. If the tribunal judges accepted this as accurate, then all sorts of awkward queries relating to how Ahern had come to obtain £25,000 in sterling would have to be answered (Clifford and Coleman, 2009: 321–2). Moreover it would also have the effect of bringing into doubt everything Ahern had told both the tribunal in private session, and in public pronouncements to the media, including whether he had received any other payments.

After four days in the witness box and ever increasingly odd explanations as to the sources of his money, the carefully painted picture by Ahern's spin doctors of him having 'bent over backwards to co-operate with the tribunal was ruined' when it had emerged that he signed an affidavit in 2005 that omitted vital information that he had transferred £50,000 from his account to that of his then partner Celia Larkin (Clifford and Coleman, 2009: 324). Most of Ahern's answers as to the sources of his money were opaque, not backed up by any documentary evidence, and consisted of explanations from the Taoiseach that were different from his previous enunciations on the matter of his finances. Finally Ahern was reduced to telling the deeply sceptical tribunal judges that he could not remember a number of crucial events central to the controversy, most particularly the buying of £30,000 sterling in the early 1990s which he stated might have been done in instalments or by somebody else, whom he could not name, on his behalf (*Irish Times*, 21 September 2007).

The sheer oddness of Ahern's evidence emboldened the opposition to act. The Labour leader, Eamon Gilmore, upped the ante considerably by calling on the Taoiseach to resign in the light of his evidence while Fine Gael called for a vote of no confidence in Ahern when the Dáil resumed after its summer break. Enda Kenny preceded this no confidence motion by declaring in a television interview that through his rambling and incoherent answers Ahern had adopted the motto of 'Louis the Sun King: "L'Etat c'est moi" – I am the State' (*Irish Independent*, 24 September 2007). This was a particularly damning criticism since Ahern had long claimed that he had been thirty years in politics and had no interest in personal enrichment. Indeed he had told the tribunal that 'he endeavoured to serve the country to my utmost. I have no interest in personal gain or benefit and never had' (Clifford and Coleman, 2009: 323). The accusation also of course brought to mind visions of the former Fianna Fáil leader Charles Haughey's own woes in relation to financial donations, his resignation statement from the Dáil quoting Othello that he had done the state some service, and his penchant for expensive Parisian shirts. Ahern's attempts to distance Fianna Fáil from this era were crumbling around him in the light of his evidence to the Mahon Tribunal. The vitriolic nature of the debate in the Dáil was highlighted by Enda Kenny bluntly declaring that Ahern had not told the truth to the Irish people, and by Eamon Gilmore claiming Ahern's story was 'cock and bull'. For its part Fianna Fáil, in the guise of Tánaiste Brian Cowen, accused the opposition of hypocrisy. John Gormley rather nervously and with much unease told the Dáil that the Greens were not the moral custodians of Fianna Fáil and would wait for the outcome of the tribunal (*Irish Times*; *Irish Independent*, 27 September 2007). With that the government won the vote by 81 to 76. An opinion poll just over five weeks later at the beginning of November, however, found that three-quarters of voters indicated that they did not believe that Ahern had provided full disclosure about his personal finances to the Mahon Tribunal (*Irish Times*, 3 November 2007). The writing was on the wall.

Ahern bows out

In November 2007 the Mahon Tribunal began to dig further into two large deposits to Bertie Ahern's accounts in December 1993 and September 1994 of just under £50,000. These investigations were ultimately to lead to Ahern's resignation as Taoiseach and leader of Fianna Fáil in May 2008. Two months earlier the final political unravelling of Ahern's glittering political career began to play out. Grainne Carruth, his secretary for a period in the mid-1990s, gave evidence to the tribunal that she had in effect lodged sterling sums of money to Ahern's account at the Drumcondra branch of the Irish Permanent Building Society. Ahern had claimed that moneys lodged for him by Carruth were from his salary cheques, and Carruth maintained this line. However, when the tribunal showed unequivocally that documentary evidence pointed clearly to the fact Carruth had made a number of sterling lodgements, she stated: 'I have to accept as a matter of probability in my dealings here yesterday that it was sterling' (Clifford and Coleman, 2009: 356). This evidence was the beginning of the end for Ahern. While there had long been doubt as to how Ahern had come into significantly large amounts of money, this was the first time that there was indisputable and inescapable conflict between his version of events and what the tribunal had clearly established to be the facts. Equally as damaging was the perception that Ahern had left his former secretary dangling by herself in front of the unforgiving gaze of the tribunal. For Ahern the matter was somewhat more simple: he declared it 'real lowlife stuff, picking on an ordinary mother of three who by bad luck had found herself right in the middle of a massive story and dealing with issues from fourteen years earlier relating to a job she had long left' (Ahern, 2010: 329). He did not, however, try to reconcile her evidence with his, thus leaving the inescapable conclusion that her appearance at the tribunal was really down to him and no one else. No omissions or casuistry of language could avoid that fact.

Ahern's political support ebbed away as both the Greens and PDs urged him to clear up the contradiction between his evidence and Carruth's. Seemingly unable to do so and with increasing disquiet within Fianna Fáil, Ahern on 2 April 2008 announced his decision to resign as Taoiseach and leader of Fianna Fáil on 6 May 2008. He had had an extraordinary career and stated that, like everything else he did in his political life, his decision was based solely on what was best for the country: 'I have served the country and the people I have had the honour to represent in Dáil Éireann honestly … I know in my heart of hearts that I have done no wrong and wronged no one' (Clifford and Coleman, 2009: 360). Ahern would spend the next month on a type of valedictory tour, the highlight of which was an address to the United States Congress on 30 April 2008, before he stepped out of the political limelight. His woes at the Mahon Tribunal would last beyond his exit from the political stage as he found himself the subject of much public ridicule after an appearance at the tribunal in June 2008 where he told the astonished judges that he had won an amount of money on a horse (*Irish Times*, 5 June 2008).

The Mahon Tribunal eventually published its final report in March 2012, devoting some 265 pages to Ahern. At its heart the tribunal investigated Ahern's finances in order to establish whether he directly or indirectly received substantial sums of money from Owen O'Callaghan. The tribunal had been told by one of its witnesses, the developer Tom Gilmartin, that O'Callaghan had paid a total of £80,000 to Ahern while the latter was a government minister. He further alleged that O'Callaghan paid £50,000 to

Ahern in 1989 when he was Minister for Labour, and another £30,000 was paid to Ahern at a later date, when he was Minister for Finance. The relevance of these payments was bound up with the tribunal's substantive inquiry into the payment of money to politicians relating to the re-zoning of lands at Quarryvale (Mahon, 2012: 1267). For their parts both Ahern and O'Callaghan strongly denied that there were any payments. O'Callaghan flatly denied that he told Gilmartin at any time that he had paid any moneys to Ahern while Ahern rejected any possibility that moneys had been given to him by O'Callaghan. It was a simple matter of which testimony the tribunal wanted to believe. Ultimately the tribunal was unable to identify what it called the 'true sources of the funds in question' and thus it could not 'determine whether or not the payment to Mr Ahern of all or any of the funds in question were in fact made by or initiated or arranged, directly or indirectly, by Mr O'Callaghan, or, indeed by any other identifiable third party' (Mahon, 2012: 1473).

Yet, in a damning indictment of his evidence, the tribunal found that 'much of the explanation provided by Mr Ahern as to the source of the substantial funds identified and inquired into in the course of the Tribunal's public hearings was deemed by the Tribunal to have been untrue' (Mahon, 2012: 1473). It was a simple yet devastating critique of the man responsible for signing off on the establishment of the tribunal in the first place. Importantly for Ahern and his defenders, the tribunal did not make a finding of corruption against him, and he quickly and publically stated that he had never received a corrupt payment in his life and had always told the truth to the tribunal. Unfortunately for him the tribunal and indeed most of Irish public chose not to believe him.

Most importantly Fianna Fáil itself, the party that he had served all his adult life, the party whom he had led to a historic three election victories in a row, chose not to believe him. In its own instant response to the publication of the report, Fianna Fáil, now under the leadership of Ahern's own protégé Micheál Martin, accused him of 'conduct unbecoming' and said it would move to expel him from the Party. For Fianna Fáil, although the central allegation against Ahern had not been sustained, the receipt by a senior office-holder of large amounts of money which a sworn tribunal held was of unclear origins, and the failure to give any credible explanation, required an unequivocal response. It noted that 'no matter how high a member rises within the party and in elected office, they still carry a duty of trust for the members of Fianna Fáil and for the people who elected them'. In that context Martin maintained that it was a matter of

> profound personal and professional regret to see the extent to which Bertie Ahern fell short of the standard of personal behaviour which was expected of

the holders of high office. In the manner in which he received this money while holding high office and in the giving of rejected evidence to a sworn tribunal Bertie Ahern betrayed the trust placed in him by this country and this party. (Martin, 2012)

It was hard-hitting stuff, and ended with the following blunt and in many ways shocking decision by its then leader, a man whom Ahern had first appointed to ministerial office in 1997 and reappointed in 2002 and 2007 and a man who had unquestioningly said he believed Ahern's evidence before the tribunal:

> I, together with the party's officers with whom I have met and consulted, believe the conduct of Bertie Ahern as outlined in the evidence made public through the Tribunal and the findings of the Tribunal constitute conduct unbecoming a member of Fianna Fáil. Accordingly, I will propose a motion to expel him as a member of Fianna Fáil at the special meeting of National Executive. We are writing to Mr Ahern to inform him of this decision. (Martin, 2012)

Ahern was not about to go through the torture of facing expulsion from the party that had basically been his life, and instead resigned his membership of Fianna Fáil. He maintained that he been a victim of a 'serious breach of constitutional justice' by the tribunal and that its findings were both incredible and a grave injustice to him personally. He described his resignation from Fianna Fáil as a 'political decision' taken in the best interests of serving the Party and was not to be construed as an admission of wrongdoing in any form (*Sunday Independent*, 25 March 2012). He subsequently described leaving Fianna Fáil as a 'real emotional wrench. The party has been an integral part of my life for 40 years. I always worked hard and did my level best for Fianna Fáil and for the wider public' (*Irish Times*, 26 March 2012). Ahern also attacked the tribunal itself, not only insisting that it had done him a grave disservice and wounded him deeply by finding that he had given untrue evidence but also noting that 'after spending over a decade of inquiries and countless millions of euros, the tribunal has not made – nor could it make – a finding to support the scurrilous and untrue allegation that I had been given a corrupt payment by Mr Owen O'Callaghan' (*Sunday Independent*, 25 March 2012). This was in essence pandering to the widespread notion that the tribunals were basically one big waste of time. But there is no doubt that the conduct unbecoming phrase deeply wounded Bertie Ahern. The same phrase had been used against Des O'Malley when he was expelled from Fianna Fáil in 1985, and led to the deep division within Fianna Fáil in that miserable decade. Ahern, on becoming leader of Fianna Fáil in 1994 and Taoiseach in 1997, had done everything in his power to ensure that his Fianna Fáil would be a united party and that his coalitions with the PDs would be unified governments. He had achieved both but was ultimately brought down by his own evasive conduct at the tribunals. It was the ultimate irony that one of his first acts as Taoiseach was to set up the tribunal which would essentially bring him down.

The tribunal also found that the former minister Pádraig Flynn had wrongfully and corruptly sought a payment of £50,000 from the developer Tom Gilmartin, and that once the money had been handed over to him he then 'proceeded to utilise the money for his personal benefit' (Mahon, 2012: 2458). For Fianna Fáil it was wholly inappropriate for any person to give a minister a payment of £50,000 and that it was 'reprehensible that Pádraig Flynn should have taken it for his own use. That behaviour on his part was a disgrace and betrayed the trust that the Irish electorate had placed in him' (Martin, 2012). This was also conduct unbecoming, and Fianna Fáil took the same action with Flynn as it did with Ahern, proposing to expel him from the party. The same result ensued, with Flynn also falling on his party sword by resigning his membership.

The tribunal balance sheet

For its part the Moriarty Tribunal had published its final report the previous year in March 2011, just a month after the general election which saw the Fianna Fáil vote collapse and Fine Gael come close to gaining an overall majority. It had originally published a report in 2006 and then produced its second report in two volumes five years later. Overall it had lasted for thirteen years and six months, ran to some 2,348 pages, and cost an estimated €50 million. And to what purpose? Its main finding was that Michael Lowry was the recipient of direct financial contributions, as was his party, Fine Gael, from a businessman, Denis O'Brien, who benefited from a decision made by Lowry's Department of Transport, Energy and Communications, namely the awarding of the Irish state's second mobile phone licence to O'Brien's company, Esat Digifone. The tribunal found that a 'cocktail of irregularities' within the evaluation process was complemented by the 'insidious and pervasive influence' of Lowry (Byrne, 2012: 165–6; Moriarty, 2011: 1050). As the leading scholar of political corruption in Ireland, Elaine Byrne, pithily notes, Justice Moriarty's findings can be reduced to this one paragraph in his report:

> Lowry displayed an appreciable interest in the substantive process, had irregular interactions with interested parties at its most sensitive stages, sought and received substantive information on emerging trends, made his preferences as between the leading candidates known, conveyed his views on how the financial weakness of Esat Digifone should be countered, ultimately brought a guillotine down on the work of the Project Group, proceeded to bypass consideration by his Cabinet colleagues, and thereby not only influenced, but delivered, the result ... (Byrne, 2012: 166; Moriarty, 2011: 1050)

The tribunal was excoriated by both O'Brien and Lowry, who rejected its findings as biased, selective and not substantiated by evidence or fact, and furthermore implied that Justice Moriarty had 'gone rogue and become obsessed with destroying Ireland's international reputation' (Byrne, 2012: 167). Destroying Ireland's international reputation in what it might well be asked? Moriarty made no definitive finding of corruption against Lowry. In fact the word 'corrupt' is used only once in an accusatory manner throughout all three volumes and 2,384 pages of the report, when Moriarty notes that the relationship between Ben Dunne and Lowry was 'profoundly corrupt to a degree that was nothing short of breathtaking' (Moriarty, 2011: 419).

But the tribunal report had little impact at all on either the ordinary citizens of the Irish state or their elected representatives. In welcoming the publication of the report and accepting its finding, the newly installed Taoiseach, Enda Kenny, stated it was another 'report, reeking of fanatical greed, obsessive attachment to power, and breathtaking attempts to acquire, use and access privilege' and was 'enough for the people of Ireland as they watch their own lives imploding and the future they had planned disappearing'. He went on to declare resoundingly that 'for the sake of our democracy, and in the context of the national misery caused by weak and reckless administration and corrupt, self-serving politicians: we must return both government and parliament to the people. We must rehabilitate the idea of civic virtue – the idea of the duty and nobility of public service. We must. And we will' (Dáil Debates, vol. 728, col. 6, 29 March 2011). Very fine words indeed; and yet seven months later Denis O'Brien – who had unmercifully attacked the tribunal since its report was issued, rejected all its findings, set up a website solely dedicated to discrediting the tribunal and insisted that the sole chairperson of the tribunal was in effect trying to ruin Ireland's international reputation – was a guest of the Kenny-led government at the Global Ireland Economic Forum, where he was lauded by a government source as one 'who was involved in many important Irish businesses and charities and had an important contribution to make to the forum' (*Irish Times*, 6 October 2011). This was not just a Fine Gael approach to the tribunal. Its coalition partners, Labour, in the guise of former leader and then Minister for Communications Pat Rabbitte, insisted he had no concerns about the invitation extended to O'Brien to attend the subsequent Global Irish Economic Forum in 2013 and stated that the government's aim in the forum was to nurture economic development and attract investment in Ireland (*Irish Times*, 28 August 2013). This is the classic 'the tribunal is in the past' defence and pretty neatly sums up the attitude of the modern Irish state to the tribunals, their reports and ultimately their consequences.

Michael Lowry topped the poll as an independent in the general elections of 1997, 2002, 2007 and 2011, polling over 29 per cent of the first preference vote in three of those elections. All were held after the revelations of the McCracken Tribunal that he had literally been in the deep pockets of Ben Dunne. Denis O'Brien, although a tax exile from Ireland, remains one of the country's most influential citizens, having a controlling influence in Ireland's only independent national radio stations, Newstalk and Today FM, while being the largest shareholder in Independent News and Media, the publishers of Ireland's most widely read newspaper the *Irish Independent* and the influential *Sunday Independent*. He also owns a controlling share in a wealth of other media outlets. Fianna Fáil's election meltdown in 2011 owed nothing to any perceptions of corruption associated with the Party but was the result of the economic tsunami that hit the country due to pretty pathetic economic mismanagement. Tribunals of inquiry were of no practical relevance to the voters in any Irish election since 1987.

So how we can categorise tribunals of inquiry? Were they star chambers and the 'Frankenstein of modern Irish society', as the taxing master James Flynn described them as far back as March 2000 or were they necessary instruments which allowed our democratic and administrative systems to be rebuilt as 'the exhumed cadavers of corrupt decisions are first subjected to a thorough post-mortem' as the historian Eunan O'Halpin argued? (O'Halpin, 2000: 191). Where now stands the balance sheet of tribunals of inquiry in Ireland? From the Hamilton Report into the beef industry, through McCracken and Moriarty into payments to politicians, to Flood/Mahon into planning corruption in Dublin, these tribunals of inquiry have uncovered vast, secret and complex payments to politicians. Having heard copious amounts of evidence, the judges in each case rejected evidence given by certain politicians but crucially did not find politicians to have acted corruptly. They did find that an insidious nexus of builders, developers and politicians was at work which led to an unhealthy and at times corrupt interlinking of business, private and public interests in Ireland. But beyond these findings not much has changed. Since the final reports of the Moriarty and Mahon tribunals in 2011 and 2012 a type of collective amnesia has befallen Irish society. The Fine Gael–Labour government has done nothing about either report, notwithstanding the Taoiseach Enda Kenny's soaring rhetoric after the publication of the final Moriarty Report. The unravelling of the early stages of the planning tribunal's findings into George Redmond and Ray Burke clearly now raises the question as to whether there was any point to these tribunals at all. Can they now be summarily dismissed as the ultimate in national navel gazing? Can we reduce them to an examination of the Irish psyche which found that Ireland was a place where politicians were on the take but that no one really did anything wrong; a place where tribunal decisions are accepted but nothing is done about them; a place where the political landscape changes because of economics not the tawdry fumbling in a greasy till that inflicted the political and administrative landscape of the modern Irish state? Tribunals did some good; of that there can be little doubt. The rumours and innuendo that passed for political gossip and tittle-tattle in polite Irish society for decades were shown to have actual substance. A raft of legislation, most notably the Ethics in Public Office Acts of 1995 and 2000, the introduction of legislation covering electoral donations and campaign spending and the creation of the Standards in Public Office Commission Ireland, have resulted in a scenario where Ireland is clearly now a society where political corruption in planning and payments to politicians will not be accepted. But it is also a society where the past is indeed a foreign country; a foreign country where citizens bemoaned the private influence that riddled the public policy process but did very little about it.

5

Fianna Fáil and the politics of hubris

We still retain very substantial freedom to control our political and economic destiny.

Mary Harney, 21 July 2000

Sitting on the sidelines, cribbing and moaning is a lost opportunity. I don't know how people who engage in that don't commit suicide.

Bertie Ahern, 4 July 2007

Fianna Fáil economics

Members of the Irish electorate were nothing if not sanguine about the nature of corrupt influence in its politics. Far more concerning to them was their economic fortunes. Notwithstanding the fact that the 1994–97 Fine Gael–Labour–Democratic Left government was overseeing several robust economic indicators, the voters decided it was not doing enough and instead opted for a Fianna Fáil–PD alliance elected on a broad tax-cutting programme. The new Taoiseach, Bertie Ahern, made one of the crucial appointments of modern Irish history by choosing the irascible Kildare TD Charlie McCreevy as his Minister for Finance. McCreevy, opposition spokesman since Ahern was elected Fianna Fáil leader, was as complex as Fianna Fáil itself. Classically populist Fianna Fáil was able to garner support from all corners of Irish society by presenting itself as different things to different sections to the electorate. To those who considered the national question the most important issue in Irish politics, Fianna Fáil was the party of the fourth green field; the party who under Eamon de Valera always had a plan for unification; the party which wasn't Fine Gael. There was a particular and peculiar strain which ran through parts of Fianna Fáil which viewed Fine Gael, and by extension those who supported it, as being somehow less than Irish.

On the economy Fianna Fáil's chameleon nature was even more pronounced. It offered itself as the party of the developer class; of the ruthless entrepreneurial class on the make; of the ambitious middle class who saw Dublin as the place to make their fortunes. Yet it also presented itself as the champion of both the urban and rural poor. Rural Ireland according to itself was safe in Fianna Fáil's hands. Not the rural Ireland of the Fine Gaelers on tractors that Fianna Fáil was so contemptuous of but the rural Ireland of the small farmer, the labourer, the party of the plain people of Ireland who had their dinner in the middle of the day. And then there was the poor of urban Ireland and Fianna Fáil's rather American view of the class system that there was in fact no need for a working class. Fianna Fáil always viewed itself as the real Labour party; the party of social and economic progress, the party of free secondary education, the party which copperfastened economic sovereignty by engaging with Europe when it realised that self-sufficiency had had its day. It was the party which in essence offered the people of Ireland hope, the party which made it possible for their lives to be better, and for their children to have more opportunities than they had. The party which offered the people a safety net through social welfare when they needed it. That's what Fianna Fáil in essence stood for since its famous foundation in the La Scala Theatre in May 1926.

All this changed under Bertie Ahern and his finance ministers, Charlie McCreevy and Brian Cowen. Fianna Fáil discarded its careful reputation as a party that could be trusted to keep a close eye on the economic tiller for one which effectively adopted an 'If I have it I spend it' philosophy. Married to this was a political hubris which was dismissive of any warning voices from within Ireland or beyond. Truly Icarus in the guise of Fianna Fáil had flown too close to the sun. The result was a scarring burn not just across the Party but across all of Irish society, with the loss of economic sovereignty.

The beginnings of this Icarusan flight of fancy can be traced to Charlie McCreevy. McCreevy was not without guts, having been to the forefront of the heaves against Ahern's mentor Charles Haughey that span Fianna Fáil into torment in the early 1980s. He went so far as to put down a motion of no confidence in October 1982 which didn't please anyone, particularly those who were opposed to Haughey, with Des O'Malley accusing him of going on a solo run and calling the whole thing 'a self-indulgent act' (O'Malley, 2014: 135). When Haughey saw off his challengers, McCreevy seethed on the backbenches, and according to Ahern seemed happy to tend to his accountancy practice (Ahern, 2010: 171). But accountancy was never McCreevy's passion. That was politics, and in particular Fianna Fáil politics. It had been assumed by many that McCreevy would join the PDs when Des O'Malley established that most ideological of all Irish parties in 1985. After all, the PDs were made in McCreevy's image: economically and socially radical, pro-enterprise, hostile to excessive public spending and generally suspicious of too much government interference in all aspects of Irish society. But

McCreevy did not leave Fianna Fáil. Rather he stayed and attempted to change it from within. He was frozen out during the Haughey era but was eventually rewarded when appointed Minister for Social Welfare by Albert Reynolds in 1992. It was here that McCreevy impressed Ahern with his ability 'as a straight guy, not prepared to be rolled over and always ready to face down challenges' (Ahern, 2010: 171). McCreevy epitomised the Fianna Fáil of the Celtic Tiger era. He put in place the conditions for the rapid expansion of the economy and did so while generally having a good time. He was a regular Gaelic Athletic Association and horse racing aficionado, as much at home in Croke Park and Cheltenham as he was in the corridors of Leinster House. Having spent a very long apprenticeship, he finally attained the Ministry of Finance in the summer of 1997. The accountant from Kildare was about to radically alter the tax base of the Irish economy to bring in a type of Irish trickle-down economics which would have the dual purpose of putting more money in people's pockets whilst still enabling Fianna Fáil to keep an eye on those who traditionally relied on the Party to ensure they wouldn't starve: the urban poor.

In McCreevy's first budget as Minister for Finance, introduced on 3 December 1997 to much fanfare, the top and standard income tax rates were reduced by 2 per cent and capital gains tax was cut from 40 to 20 per cent. This determination to favour business and the better-off would run through all his budgets. Corporation tax, for instance, would be lowered from 36 to 12.5 per cent over the course of the government's tenure of office. Yet, in McCreevy's first budget, more than £100 million was also spent on increasing social welfare payments. Greater emphasis was always placed on cutting tax rates rather than increasing allowances or widening bands, which resulted in most benefits being channelled to those on higher incomes (Hardiman, 2000: 305–6). The beginning of 1998 saw the Irish economy 'in the black' for the first time in thirty years with the exchequer able to meet day-to-day spending without borrowing. By the end of the year unemployment was at 6 per cent – down from 10 per cent when the government took office in mid-1997. In light of this the rise of the so-called Celtic Tiger would become intrinsically linked in the public's mind with the government and throughout 1998 its satisfaction rating remained high, hovering between 68 and 73 per cent. A highlight of the government's economic strategy was the privatisation of Telecom Éireann, piloted by the Minister for Public Enterprise, Mary O'Rourke, when the communications company was floated on the stock market in July 1999 with well over half the adult population of the state buying shares in the new entity called Eircom.

Privatisation came much later to Ireland than other Western European countries. This was not terribly surprising in a country where the need to look to the state was much stronger than in continental Europe. This should not be confused with socialism. The Irish state encouraged a patrician view of what it could provide its citizens. This was particularly the case when Fianna Fáil was in government, as that party was always comfortable with monopolising transport and energy utilities, deciding that it was better for the state to provide its citizens with their energy and telecommunications needs. This led to the farcical situation where getting a telephone in modern Ireland proved to be something of a Herculean task for most householders. In the 1970s for instance, when use of the telephone was the norm for most Western European households, there was a two-year waiting list in Ireland. In reality the wait for installation was much longer and there was an even more bizarre two-tier system of getting on the list at all which depended on one's occupation. In supposedly classless Ireland, doctors and lawyers got preferential treatment when it came to getting a telephone installed by the state. Albert Reynolds, when he became Minister for Industry and Commerce, took it upon himself to do something about this ludicrous situation and managed to lead the Irish state out of its archaic telecommunications structure by committing over £1 billion of public money to revolutionise the telephone system. He in essence used an entrepreneurial model of bonuses for state workers to do their job more effectively (Reynolds, 2009: 89–93). It was the classic Irish solution to an Irish problem whereby state workers, in secure pensionable positions and supposedly providing a service for the population, had to all intents and purposes to be bribed by the self-same Irish state to do that job.

Two decades later the culmination of loosening the statist strings in the telecommunications market resulted in the floatation of Eircom shares and a type of general mania in the population, who had seen numerous privatisations in Britain but had never tasted such exotic fruits in Ireland. In the Eircom share fiasco we can see the first signs of hubris that would engulf the Irish population and bring the country to the edge of ruin within a decade. Those who bought shares in Eircom seemed to weirdly neglect that age-old adage of shares that their value can go down as well as up. After a strong start the share price began to collapse and with it the Irish appetite for privatisation. But not, however, before one of the most bizarre election gimmicks of any functioning modern democracy raised its ugly head when Fine Gael, in its election manifesto for the 2002 general election, actually included a proposal to compensate individuals who had lost money by investing in Eircom shares. How this was to work was never fully explained. Neither was it explained why anyone within Fine Gael thought that this was a good idea. And finally it was never really explained where the money to compensate these speculators, for that is what they were, would come from. In pithy but rather pointless language the Fine Gael 2002 manifesto pointed out simply that individual investors in Eircom would be allowed to offset their losses against income tax. What the half of the country's citizens who did not buy

Eircom shares in the first place were to think of this scheme was something that did not apparently dawn on Fine Gael. The weird scheme was dreamt up by one of Fine Gael's heavyweights, Jim Mitchell, its deputy leader, who with Michael Noonan had been behind the push to oust John Bruton as leader of the Party in 2001 (Rafter, 2011b: 38–40). There was some irony in this position as Mitchell had been to the forefront of pioneering aviation competition as Minister for Transport in the early 1980s in authorising routes for private carriers, including Ryanair amongst others, to fly between Ireland and Britain, providing important choice for consumers beyond the state-owned national carrier Aer Lingus. The Eircom compensation scheme fiasco was in essence a desperate gimmick included in the manifesto by an equally desperate party which was facing into its worst ever election result. The Eircom fiasco did have one other main political casualty when Mary O'Rourke, the public face behind the Eircom share launch, and not only Minister for Public Enterprise but also deputy leader of Fianna Fáil, lost her once thought impregnable seat at the subsequent general election. She blamed this on internal party machinations which carved up her constituency to her own detriment, saying 'I knew there was an agenda to put me out and put him in' (O'Rourke, 2012: 149). The 'he' referred to Senator Donie Cassidy, a long-standing Fianna Fáil constituency rival. O'Rourke in her memoir castigates Ahern for his evasive behaviour during this episode, while he in his own autobiography characteristically does not mention it at all. In any event Ahern would have his general election victory based on Fianna Fáil's supervision of a booming economy.

For all the government's problems with tribunals and alleged political corruption, by the close of the twenty-eighth Dáil it could point to a mass of statistical evidence showing that it had presided over an economic boom. While both Fianna Fáil and the PDs would run as independent parties, it was clear that both would campaign on the government's economic record. It was certainly a record that could easily be sold in an election campaign. The most startling indicator of the government's economic success was the huge increase in Gross Domestic Product (GDP). Ireland's economy as measured by real GDP grew at an annual average rate of 8.5 per cent over the period 1996–2000, compared to an EU annual average rate of 2.3 per cent. Moreover relative GDP per capita in purchasing power parity terms saw Ireland grow from 75.7 in 1991 to a staggering 111.0 in 1999. This compared favourably to other generally considered underdeveloped countries such as Spain, for which figures went from 79.8 to 80.2, Greece which went from 61.2 to 68.7 and Portugal which went from 64.7 to 74.1 in the same period (Bradley, 2000: 21).

Such growth in the economy was mirrored by the rapid fall in unemployment during the government's tenure. The unemployment rate, which had stood at almost 10 per cent in 1997, was halved to 5 per cent by the end of 1999 (O'Connell, 2000: 63). The huge decrease in unemployment and the consequential increase in job growth, with an estimated 370,000 new jobs created since 1997, was understandably trumpeted continuously by the government. This was all the more so as the bulk of the employment created was in the private sector (FitzGerald, 2000: 44). Furthermore the reduction in the rates of personal taxation at both the higher and lower levels to 42 and 20 per cent respectively was put forward by the government as both a cause and an effect of the economic boom.

Warnings from Europe about government spending and the state of the public finances found no real outlet amongst the opposition parties and were summarily dismissed by the government and by McCreevy in particular. This is best summed up by the government's attitude towards the first Treaty of Nice referendum campaign. The Treaty of Nice was agreed by the member states of the European Union in December 2000, and the government decided to hold a referendum on its ratification on 7 June 2001. There had been much controversy over European issues throughout the Fianna Fáil–PD government's tenure. In October 1999 the cabinet decided that Ireland would join the NATO-led Partnership for Peace organisation despite a Fianna Fáil 1997 manifesto promise that a referendum would be held on any such move. While this might have been seen as a pro-European move, and one that brought Ireland into the mainstream of EU countries when it came to matter of defence, things were much different in the economic sphere. In September 2000 the Minister for Arts, Heritage, Gaeltacht and the Islands, Síle de Valera, delivered a broadside against the whole European project wherein she questioned Ireland's role within the EU, argued against closer European integration and asserted that Ireland had more in common with the United States than with the EU. This mirrored a speech given by the Tánaiste, Mary Harney, a few months earlier at a meeting of the American bar association in Dublin which also struck a Eurosceptic tinge and in which Harney claimed she believed in a Europe of independent states, not a United States of Europe, and that spiritually Irish people were much closer to Boston than Berlin (O'Malley, 2011a: 194).

In the meantime a number of scrapes between the Minister for Finance, Charlie McCreevy, and the European Commission culminated with McCreevy asserting that he wouldn't let government fiscal policy be run from Brussels after EU economic and finance ministers had censured his 2001 budget for basically pump-priming the economy too much. A distinct Eurosceptic tinge ran through the coalition, with McCreevy, de Valera, Attorney General Michael McDowell and ministers of state Éamon Ó Cuív and Willie O'Dea all voicing public reservations as to the future development of the EU (O'Mahony, 2001: 210). With regard to Nice the Attorney General advised the government that a referendum was necessary, and the government held it in conjunction with two other referendums: one to abolish the death penalty and another to ratify the establishment of a permanent International Criminal Court under the United Nations. It was the Nice Treaty, however, that engendered the most debate.

The Treaty of Nice was in essence a device to reform the institutional structure of the European Union to deal with the Union's eastward expansion. However, as with almost all EU treaties in Ireland, the subsequent referendum debate was dominated by issues that were tangential at best to the treaty. While all the main political parties and sectional interest groups advocated a Yes vote, Sinn Féin and the Greens sought a No vote, and it was generally agreed that the No campaign with its lurid and controversial poster 'You will lose! Power, Money, Freedom' won the campaign. It was also to win the day. The lacklustre nature of the campaign was mirrored in the turnout of just 35 per cent, the lowest ever recorded for a European referendum, and the treaty was rejected, with 54 per cent voting against. Among the No voters, as he subsequently admitted, was minister of state Éamon Ó Cuív, who, although he campaigned for a Yes vote, rather bizarrely claimed that he was voting against the elite, not seeming to realise that he was a card-carrying member of that self-same elite. While the Nice defeat caused some consternation in Europe, domestically it was a victory for the smaller parties and one they would strive to hammer home in the general election. Rather more worrying for the government was the attitude of McCreevy, who proclaimed that the result was a sign of a healthy democracy and a remarkably healthy development whilst going on to note that the rejection of the treaty was a wake-up call for all 'democratic governments of Europe that what they are possibly pursuing in a number of areas is not in line with the wishes of their own peoples and that should be borne in mind by us all' (*Irish Times*, 27 June 2001). This rather vague phrase in fact neatly summed up the Irish attitude to the EU under Ahern and McCreevy: leave us be to run our country in the way we see fit. That of course is what happened, with remarkably grim results for the Irish state and its population over the course of the next decade. But in 2001 and 2002 this was all in the future. As the election of 2002 loomed, the single most important fact for the government was that it had presided over the greatest boom in the country's history and electorally this is what would be stressed during the election campaign. It was to be Fianna Fáil's trump card, and one that the opposition found impossible to counter. And with that impossibility the Fianna Fáil–PD minority coalition became the first government in over thirty years to be re-elected. Not all in Fianna Fáil were happy with the economics that drove this electoral support. Ray MacSharry, who as Minister for Finance in the 1987–89 government had done so much to rein in the rampant public expenditure of the 1980s, was recently scathing of this approach:

> I have always maintained that Charlie McCreevy, as Minister for Finance, was short-sighted in the scale of the expenditure he sanctioned. Brian Lenihan was left to pick up the can for the 'when the money's there we'll spend it' philosophy, which in my view was never strategically sensible. The focus of that Fianna Fáil–PD government was all wrong. They were concentrating on expenditure and where they could profitably spend money and not enough attention was being paid to the sustainability of the revenue stream. The Government felt that they could afford both massive increases in public pay and huge reductions in income tax because of the enormous revenues that property-related taxes were bringing in. The culture of the time seemed to be to spend this revenue without giving a second thought as to whether this level of revenue would be available the following year. When I suggested this was a mistake, McCreevy was far from happy. In one conversation, he said to me 'I have two billion of a surplus. Do you think I should leave that there?' I replied, 'yes I do,' but he just laughed at me. (MacSharry, 2014: 105–6)

But that was a lonely voice in the wilderness and it certainly was not in the public domain at the time. Fianna Fáil had public money to spend, and not only did it spend it but the public overwhelmingly supported it in this strategy.

The woes of opposition

The 2002 election was nothing short of a catastrophic disaster for Fine Gael. It won just over 22 per cent of the vote, down over 5 percentage points on its 1997 showing, but lost 23 seats, leaving it with only 31 deputies in a parliamentary cull that saw many high-profile members lose their seats. By teatime on the day of the count the Fine Gael leader, Michael Noonan, announced his resignation, stating on RTÉ television that the election result was 'beyond our expectations and beyond our worst fears. It's been a seriously bad election for our party' (Kennedy, 2002: 103). In the light of this result Fine Gael's position as the second party of the state was in jeopardy. Its reaction to the election over the course of the next Dáil could see it either rejuvenate itself or potentially collapse into irrelevance. The irony of Noonan's resignation after only sixteen months in the job was not lost on his predecessor, John Bruton, or on all those who both engineered a leadership change and voted for Noonan as the man to revive Fine Gael.

In February 1994 John Bruton survived a challenge to his leadership of Fine Gael and was elected Taoiseach ten months later when the Fianna Fáil–Labour government imploded in mid-Dáil and was replaced by the rainbow coalition. He was not to be so lucky seven years later. In November 2000

Bruton faced an unexpected motion of no confidence placed against him by the maverick Waterford TD Austin Deasy. Bruton had on the whole failed to improve his party's position since its rather unexpected defeat in the 1997 general election. Fine Gael did manage to win the Cork South-Central by-election in October 1998 and came a close second in Tipperary South in June 2000, but its results in the European and local government elections were uninspiring. Moreover its poll ratings were continuously poor. Bruton's main opponents in the Party were taken by surprise by Deasy's motion and did not support it, so it was defeated by a margin variously claimed to be 3:1 or 5:1 (Gallagher and Marsh, 2002: 37). There was, however, to be no respite for Bruton's leadership. On 21–2 January 2001 an MRBI poll showed that Fine Gael support was at 11 per cent in Dublin and that only 37 per cent of voters were satisfied with Bruton's performance as party leader. This led Michael Noonan and Jim Mitchell to announce that they were putting down a motion of no confidence in Bruton, and that they were doing so in response to pressure from ordinary party members. Bruton stood up to the challenge but it was clear that he was fighting a losing battle. Despite a number of combative media performances, he was unable to stop the seepage of support and lost the motion by 39 votes to 33. It was the first time that any Fine Gael leader had been voted out of office. Once Bruton had lost the confidence motion it quickly became clear that Michael Noonan was the preferred choice of the parliamentary party to take over the reins of leadership. A former Minister for Justice and for Health and the then spokesperson on Finance, Noonan defeated the Mayo TD Enda Kenny 44–28 in a contest that roughly divided along the pro- and anti-Bruton line of the confidence vote. Noonan became Fine Gael's eighth leader, and at fifty-seven was the oldest person ever to become leader of the Party (Gallagher and Marsh, 2002: 37–9).

With a general election being predicted by most pundits for some time in 2001, Noonan did not have long to prove himself. He was widely perceived to have performed well in his role as finance spokesperson marking Charlie McCreevy, most particularly in relation to McCreevy's 1999 plans to individualise the tax system, where Noonan forced the minister to make belated concessions to stay-at-home wives. Noonan did, however, have one very major skeleton in his closet from which he was never to escape: the fact that he was Minister for Health during the Hepatitis C scandal in which the state, as he himself subsequently acknowledged, had treated one of the victims, Brigid McCole, with extreme insensitivity, hiding behind the politically explosive defence of legal advice. It was something that Noonan had apologised for on numerous occasions but was never able to escape from. His leadership, however, was almost doomed from the beginning as he was immediately plunged into controversies over the past funding of the Party and tax-free under-the-counter payments to staff (even though he had no responsibility for these, and upon becoming leader had initiated an immediate ban on corporate donations to Fine Gael), and a renewal of media interest in the McCole case (Rafter, 2011b: 50–1). The cumulative result was that there was to be no kick-start to Noonan's leadership, and Fine Gael continued to languish in the polls. Its position was never to get better right up to the calling of the election at pretty much the latest possible date by Bertie Ahern.

Michael Noonan's resignation on election count night presented Fine Gael with a clean opportunity to elect a new leader. Fine Gael party rules dictated that, following the resignation of the party leader, a successor was to be elected within thirty days. The electoral body was limited to members of the Fine Gael parliamentary party, and in the summer of 2002 that meant forty-nine individuals: the depleted Dáil group, members of the outgoing Seanad, and members of the European Parliament. Despite some rumblings about the electoral system, with a view expressed by some members that the Party would be better to wait until the autumn, the opposite view best expressed by the outgoing senator Maurice Manning prevailed: 'This is going to be the most competitive opposition in the history of the State. If Fine Gael is a bystander with no leader during the early formative life of this Dáil then we would risk having permanent damage inflicted upon us' (*Irish Times*, 5 June 2002). Four names ended up on the ballot paper: Enda Kenny, a minister in the 1994–97 rainbow coalition and a TD for Mayo since 1975; Richard Bruton, also a minister in the rainbow government and a TD for Dublin North-Central since 1982; Gay Mitchell, a junior minister in the rainbow government and a TD for Dublin South-Central since 1981; and Phil Hogan, briefly a junior minister in the rainbow government and a TD for Carlow–Kilkenny since 1989. During the campaign there was a deliberate attempt to ensure that there would be no public bloodletting as there had been in the upheaval that ended John Bruton's tenure as leader in January 2001. The main focus of all four candidates was on the necessity to rebuild the Fine Gael organisation and rejuvenate the morale of the Party faithful after its crushing election defeat. Gay Mitchell was the only candidate to spell out his message in any clear ideological way, placing Fine Gael firmly in the European Christian Democratic tradition. This, however, did not go down too well with the parliamentary party constituency, which wanted a promise of better electoral days ahead. In many ways this summed up modern Irish politics perfectly. Any politician in either Fianna Fáil or Fine Gael who tried to articulate a genuine ideological political philosophy was treated with suspicion. Enda Kenny, in the Dáil for over quarter of a century without ever having done very much, seemed a far safer bet for electoral success and thus the Fine Gael electorate went for the Mayo TD who would, according to one of his proposers, fellow Mayo man Michael Ring, 'look well on posters and had a nice fresh face' (*Irish Times*, 6 June 2002). The results were not made public, although it was reported that Kenny was ahead on the first count and after the elimination of Hogan and Mitchell, he easily saw off the challenge of Richard Bruton (Rafter, 2003: 114). Kenny, who had previously lost out to Noonan, was fifty-one years of age on his election, and was faced not only with a decimated political party but with having to oppose a Taoiseach who had just led a government to re-election for the first time since 1969 and was reckoned to be the most popular politician of his generation. In these circumstances Kenny faced a gargantuan task to make Fine Gael relevant.

The 2002 election was no better for the Labour Party. Five years earlier Labour felt completely hard done by with the result of the 1997 general election. An ungrateful electorate had decided to bring Labour back down to earth after its stunning breakthrough in 1992. From the heights of 19.3 per cent of the vote and 33 TDs in 1992, Labour was reduced to 17 seats from 10.4 per cent of the vote. The voters had patiently waited in the long grass for Labour and, despite the fact that the government was presiding over a strong and improving economy, it lost the election. One of the main reasons for this was that the people had their minds made up from an early stage that Labour had in essence sold them a pig in a poke at the 1992 general election by promising mainly that they would remove Fianna Fáil from office. Notwithstanding the change of government in 1994, the public were not prepared to forgive Labour for committing the mortal sin of actually going into power with Fianna Fáil after the historic 1992 breakthrough. The defeat in the 1997 election hit Labour hard and left it pondering its future. The same could be said of Democratic Left, who polled just 2.5 per cent of the vote, winning 4 seats.

From its outset Democratic Left had contained a sizeable minority who had argued that there was no place for a new party to the left of Labour (Dunphy, 1998: 57). Now, with its failure to expand its vote in 1997 after a period in government, these voices began to grow loud once again. By mid-April of 1998 it emerged that a study group established by the Democratic Left leader, Proinsias De Rossa, and Ruairi Quinn, who had been elected as leader of the Labour Party once Dick Spring resigned after the 1997 election, was identifying common ground on policy issues, although a statement emphasising the distinctive role of both parties seemed to dampen any thoughts of an early merger. Yet there was a realisation particularly within Democratic Left that it had little future as a separate party. According to Eamon Gilmore: 'There was a sense that when it [the 1997 general election] was over the game was up ... It was very much a sense of the two Labour parties working together' (Rafter, 2011a: 285).

In May of 1998 Democratic Left campaigned for a Yes vote in the Amsterdam Treaty on the grounds that it would be good for social cohesion in the European Union. The Amsterdam Treaty amended the Maastricht Treaty of 1992 by attempting to strengthen the rights of EU citizens by placing a stronger emphasis on citizenship in areas such as employment, security and justice. Notoriously Eurosceptic from a left-wing perspective up to this point, Democratic Left's position now further removed a point of difference between itself and the Labour Party. A week after the Amsterdam Treaty referendum, Democratic Left first proposed the creation of a new political formation with the Labour Party which would not only transform left-wing politics in the country but bring about, from the left's perspective, the long-cherished realignment of Irish politics. This was treated with much scepticism by members of the media, all other political parties and most other seasoned political observers. Yet momentum continued apace and in early July Democratic Left and Labour signalled their intention to establish a left-wing policy think-tank which would operate irrespective of the merger talks (Rafter, 2011a: 319). It was, however, yet another sign that the merger was growing closer. By the late summer much of the negotiations for a new political force had been completed. In early August it was reported that the parties had finished the first stage of talks on a possible merger, and a 'mission statement' for a new left force in Irish politics had been drawn up (*Irish Times*, 4 August 1998). In mid-September Quinn came out strongly in favour of a new formation that could win between 30 and 40 seats, though some opposition was voiced within Labour over possible constituency clashes. Events moved quickly and both parties' ruling councils instructed their negotiating teams to draw up final documents. Finally on 20 November 1998 Quinn and De Rossa agreed to a merger of their parties. The final stages were not without their difficulties. De Rossa was in many ways the main stumbling block, actively seeking alternatives including bringing the Greens into a wider political force on the left. He was rebuffed by the Greens, an even smaller party than his own, and, as it became clear that the driving intellectual forces behind the merger proposal, Eamon Gilmore and Pat Rabbitte, had emotionally crossed the Rubicon, De Rossa finally gave his own personal approval to the merger, plaintively telling the historian of the Party Kevin Rafter that 'if you cannot discern a significant difference between what you're saying and the other main Left party, then it makes sense to work together rather than against each other. So that was the way I came to it' (Rafter, 2011a: 325).

The ultimate result was the cumbersomely titled *Agreement on the Union of The Labour Party and Democratic Left*, which was finally signed by both party leaderships in December 1998. Its aims were understandably broad, with the document boldly declaring that it intended to construct a 'radical, participatory political movement in Ireland which will aim to lead a Government of Reform'. It aimed, however, to do this through normal capitalist means, leading Rafter to pithily note that 'there was little by way of the language or sentiment of the radical Left' in the final document (Rafter, 2011a: 329). And perhaps that is why nothing really happened for the new political force. It was no more radical than in many ways Fianna Fáil was. The individual parties hadn't really done anything terribly radical while in government between 1994 and 1997. And the voters, when given their chance to re-elect that government, said no thanks.

Nevertheless there was significant optimism in the air when the merger finally launched in January 1999, after a special joint conference saw Democratic Left members support the agreement in a secret ballot with a Yes vote of 89 per cent, while Labour overwhelmingly supported the deal on a show of hands at a special delegate conference. Whether this new political force – still called the Labour Party – would be able to realign Irish politics remained to be seen. Labour for one thought that it had indeed brought about such a realignment back in 1992, only to be proved spectacularly wrong in 1997 (Girvin, 1999: 4). The 2002 election proved the fallacy of this realignment aspiration. Hopes within the left that the newly strengthened party would transform the fortunes of left-wing politics in Ireland were dashed by the reality of the 2002 election when there was little change in Labour's strength. Some criticised Labour for failing to offer the electorate an alternative government by more firmly committing itself to a coalition with Fine Gael. Given Fine Gael's meltdown, such criticism was probably somewhat unwarranted. And in any event the whole idea of the new Labour Party was that it wanted to lead a government of the left. It did not want to have to prop up yet another right-wing Fine Gael government with Labour reduced to protecting social welfare rates, and not much else, while all the time piously declaring that things would be much worse if Fine Gael was in government on its own. In that context it had no real choice but to offer itself to the electorate in 2002 as a party ready to lead a government of the left. The voters were having none of it, however, and gave Labour 10.8 per cent of the seats, enabling it to win 20 seats. There was a drop of 2 percentage points on both Labour and Democratic Left's performance in 1997 and the loss of a seat. Dick Spring, who must have thought that he had begun the realignment of Irish politics with Labour's great breakthrough in 1992, suffered the ignominy of losing his seat in Kerry North as the party abjectly watched on helplessly as the voters quite happily re-elected the Fianna Fáil–PD coalition. This ultimately left the new Labour Party to wallow in the fact that it had basically held its own vote while being unable to persuade any floating voters as to its aims and ambitions for Ireland.

That failure led to the end of Ruairi Quinn's leadership and yet another bout of introspection for Ireland's oldest party. The glory days of just a decade earlier had dissipated, to be replaced by a return to the party's core vote of just over a tenth of the electorate. Still Labour had no shortage of candidates to take Quinn's place. This was particularly the case since the merger. Ultimately there were four candidates for the leadership: Brendan Howlin, the

Party's deputy leader from Wexford who had served in government between 1992 and 1997 and had lost out to Quinn for the leadership in 1997; Róisín Shortall, first elected in Dublin North-West in the Spring tide of 1992 and without ministerial experience; and two former Democratic Left members, Eamon Gilmore of Dun Laoghaire and Pat Rabbitte of Dublin South-West. All four were pretty much agreed on policy issues but differed significantly in regard to political tactics. Shortall was the most hostile to coalition, advocating that the Party remain outside government until it had a minimum of 40 seats. Given that in its history Labour had never even once reached this figure, such a stance might well result in its never entering government again. Howlin and Gilmore expressed their opposition to Fianna Fáil but did not rule out the possibility of going into government with it. Rabbitte was more clear-cut in opposing coalition with Fianna Fáil and was widely seen as a critic of the Quinn–Howlin electoral strategy of keeping this option open. There was a view within the Party that Rabbitte's background in Democratic Left might lessen his appeal among long-standing Labour Party members as there were only approximately 250 former Democratic Left members in the total electorate of 3,942. However, his declaration prior to the general election that he would not serve as a Labour minister in a government involving Fianna Fáil gave him the status of challenger to the status quo within the Party and the candidate for change (Fitzgerald et al., 2004: 231). This 'anti-Fianna Fáilism' was one of the key distinguishing factors between Rabbitte and Howlin, who quickly emerged as the front runners.

Ultimately Rabbitte was comfortably elected, having been over five hundred votes ahead of Howlin on the first count. Another former Democratic Left member, Liz McManus from Wicklow, was elected deputy leader, leaving some in Labour wondering whether they had been the victims of a reverse Democratic Left takeover. On his election as leader Rabbitte pledged that his aim was to make Labour the great national voice of popular opposition to the government and ultimately lead a new government of the left. A more realistic aim was perhaps to get Labour into government after the next general election, a task that would not be easy considering the popularity of Fianna Fáil – the real Labour party as Bertie Ahern liked to call his Soldiers of Destiny (Ahern, 2010: 209).

Another self-styled labour party in that it considered itself a defender of the working class, although in this case with a distinct green tinge, was Sinn Féin, which won 5 seats in the 2002 election on 6.5 per cent of the vote. Its vote could partly be explained as being due to the success of the Northern Irish peace process in which it was, of course, intimately involved. Sinn Féin had won its first seat in an Irish general election since 1957 in 1997, when Caoimhghín Ó Caoláin was elected for the Party in Cavan–Monaghan. The following year saw one of Fianna Fáil's great political triumphs when the

Good Friday Agreement was signed on 10 April 1998. The contribution he played in ending violence in Northern Ireland is widely and rightly seen as Bertie Ahern's finest political achievement. Fianna Fáil's relationship with Northern Ireland was always somewhat ambiguous. The ambition of a united Ireland was explicitly inserted into the 1937 Constitution by Eamon de Valera, and the reunification of the country was a central tenet of its very existence. But it was an aim which the Party did very little about, not least because in reality there was very little it could do. Moreover public opinion in the Republic rarely concerned itself with problems in Northern Ireland. While the outbreak of the troubles and the arms crisis of 1969–70 posed serious questions for the Irish state, for Fianna Fáil and indeed for the Irish people, the reality was that Northern Ireland was indeed a foreign country. The hunger strikes of 1981 brought mass mobilisation and protest, and the election of two anti-H-Block candidates, Paddy Agnew and Kieran Doherty, in the June election of that year. Doherty would die on hunger strike after having been a TD for less than two months. The support for the hunger strikers, although limited, did persuade Sinn Féin to look seriously at contesting elections in the Republic. But once the hunger strikes ended and Northern Ireland continued as a relatively low-level sectarian conflict, people in the Republic got on with their lives and Ireland's political parties settled into a position of rousing themselves every now and again to think about contributing to a solution to the conflict. This led to the 1985 Anglo-Irish Agreement signed by the then Fine Gael Labour government and trenchantly opposed by Fianna Fáil, which then went on in its own inimitable fashion to implement it when returned to power in 1987. First in a covert way under Charles Haughey's minority government, then more explicitly under Albert Reynolds and finally and most successfully under Bertie Ahern, Fianna Fáil, and its leaders, expounded significant energy and managed to engineer a process whereby, although there was little electoral gain to be had, finding a solution to the Northern Ireland troubles became central to the Party's strategic aims in government.

Fianna Fáil's commitment under the leadership of Ahern to finding a solution to the Northern Ireland problem was evident throughout its period in office with the PDs from 1997. In the slow trajectory initially from the vortex of violence to the Good Friday Agreement and to the later creation, collapse and restoration of the governing Northern Ireland Assembly, one of the constant facets of Irish politics was the commitment of Fianna Fáil to finding a political solution to Northern Ireland. In this the party of the fourth green field abandoned its own form of tribalism best exemplified by Charles Haughey's irredentist approach, and replaced it with the consensual efforts of at first Albert Reynolds, and then Bertie Ahern. In this approach both Fianna Fáil leaders benefited from a continuous bipartisan approach taken by their democratic political opponents in the south, something which Fianna Fáil itself was always reluctant to adopt in opposition. There was virtual unanimity in the Dáil on the Taoiseach's handling of the Northern Ireland multi-party peace talks that eventually led to the Good Friday Agreement of 10 April 1998. Six weeks later on 22 May a referendum was put to the electorate in Northern Ireland on the ratification of the Good Friday Agreement, which essentially outlined the framework and procedural safeguards for a process devised to institute a new form of governance in Northern Ireland (Tonge, 2005: 34–5). One proviso of this was that the Irish government should hold a referendum on the same day, proposing the amendment of Articles 2 and 3 of the Constitution, to be replaced by articles enshrining the 'principle of consent'. This proposal was backed by all the main political parties in the Republic and was presented to the electorate as supporting the shoring up of peace in Northern Ireland and helping to provide a lasting settlement. It was overwhelmingly endorsed by the people with a Yes vote of close to 95 per cent. Yet the referendum also left large numbers of the population apathetic, as the turnout for one of the most significant changes to the Irish Constitution since its inception over sixty years earlier was only 56.26 per cent; a figure which showed that, for all its emotive appeal, Northern Ireland and its troubles left a significant number of Irish people strangely unmoved.

This was then the difficulty for Sinn Féin: how to advance electorally in the Republic when its whole raison d'être of a united Ireland meant little for vast swathes of the Irish voter. And for those to whom it did matter there was always Fianna Fáil to vote for. In that context Sinn Féin began the long march to political relevance in the Republic of Ireland by organising in disadvantaged communities and presenting itself as a left-wing force which would not, unlike Labour, be seduced into coalescing with a right-wing party. But it did consider itself as having a potential coalition relationship with Fianna Fáil, despite advocating social and economic positions that were far to the left of Fianna Fáil (Ó Broin, 2009: 281). In 2002 Sinn Féin's generally leftist position was enough to win it 5 seats; a significant breakthrough by any standards, contributing, along with the Greens who won 6 seats and independents who won 14 seats, to return an opposition in the Dáil that was more fragmented than it had been in well over half a century (Mitchell, 2003: 220). This electoral success for Sinn Féin would continue in the local and European elections in the summer of 2004. Mary Lou McDonald had a startling victory in Dublin, where she polled over 14 per cent of the first preference vote, taking in excess of sixty thousand first preference votes to win a seat in the European Parliament. At local level this trend continued as Sinn Féin gained 33 seats, bringing its total to 54. Moreover its share of the vote in Dublin, at 18 per cent, seemed to presage great things for the Party come the next general election.

Ideological politics Irish style

But in 2002, notwithstanding various political machinations on the opposition benches, the reality was that the Irish voters, motivated mainly by the moneys in their pockets, were quite happy to say to the coalition: off you go again. The new government was quickly established after the election despite the then Attorney General and PD candidate Michael McDowell's bitter denunciation of the dangers of single-party Fianna Fáil government during the 2002 campaign when he complained that Fianna Fáil's plan for a national stadium, the so-called 'Bertie Bowl', had echoes of the Ceauşescu regime in Romania. The campaign saw McDowell climb a tree pole in Ranelagh to warn of the dangers of Fianna Fáil being allowed to govern on its own by hosting a placard boldly asking the question 'One-Party Government?' and giving the answer 'No Thanks' and thus providing one of the most iconic images of modern Irish politics. The PDs had originally gone into the election in poor spirits. Just two weeks before the calling of the election, minister of state Bobby Molloy resigned after improper contact was made on his behalf with a judge in the Central Criminal Court in relation to the sentencing of the brother of one of his constituents (Murphy, 2003: 17). Yet in an extraordinary turnaround the PDs had an excellent campaign, having decided to throw their lot in with McDowell's view that the only way they were going to survive was through launching a series of blistering attacks on their partners in government. The big gamble here was whether Fianna Fáil would take umbrage once the election was finished. But McDowell had rightly judged that the electorate would deny Fianna Fáil an overall majority and that the great consensus man of Irish politics, Bertie Ahern, would need the PDs as coalition partners and would thus quickly get over any emotional bruises from the campaign.

But if Ahern was the consensus man of Irish politics, the reality was that Ireland in 2002 was itself a hotbed of consensus politics. The manifestos of the main parties were not radically different beyond tone or nuance. The state of the health service was generally seen as the main problem facing the parties. Fianna Fáil imaginatively and with a straight face declared in its manifesto that it would permanently end waiting lists in hospitals within two years, although this pledge would mysteriously disappear in the programme for government agreed by Fianna Fáil with the PDs after the election. Fine Gael stated simply that it would end the two-tier system in the health service and that access to care in public hospitals would be based only on medical need. Labour promised a fair, high-quality health system with free GP care for all, while the PDs also promised to end waiting lists but did not set a timeframe. Health was also a priority for the smaller parties, with Sinn Féin declaring that the two-tier health system must be replaced with an equitable and efficient health service, while the Greens focused on community care which would be provided by local community health services. In essence all these manifestos were saying much the same thing, namely that there were problems with the health service that had to be fixed. The differences lay in the proposed remedies, but these were differences that did not excite the electorate. It was ever thus in terms of the Irish health service and the political class: a problem needed fixing but no one seemed to have a clue as to how to go about it other than simply throwing vast amounts of money at it.

Taxation was another issue on which there was broad agreement. While there were some minute differences in terms of corporate taxation, personal taxation was something that saw the parties in virtual agreement. Thus, for all the major parties, raising taxation for increased public spending or to cope with any possible downturn in the economy was not an option they were willing to endorse by putting into their manifestos. Bertie Ahern provided the best evidence of this overlap in terms of macroeconomic policy when he stated in a radio interview on RTÉ that there was nothing in the manifesto of either the PDs or Labour with which he fundamentally disagreed. While there was certainly something of a hedging of bets here, given the fact that there had been no majority government in twenty-five years, it also spoke to the essential non-ideological nature of Irish politics. Certainly the PDs had brought a touch of neoliberalism to Ireland and were staunch advocates of the limited state approach. Yet the Irish people themselves seemed much happier to support the aspirational centre much more associated with the chameleon Fianna Fáil electoral juggernaut.

And what a machine it was in 2002. Fianna Fáil had been preparing for this particular showtime since January 1999, when a group led by its Director of Elections, P. J. Mara, and the Party's general secretary, Martin Mackin, began weekly meetings to plan strategy and candidate selection for the election. By the time the election was called they had fine-tuned their campaign and based it on ideas used by the famous Millbank headquarters of New Labour in the British election of 2001 (Collins, 2003: 24). With Mara declaring the election campaign 'Showtime', Fianna Fáil played the card of economic success dealt by its other main electoral asset, its charismatic and popular leader, Bertie Ahern. Ahern, the ultimate symbol of consensus Ireland, had surpassed all expectations by leading his government to its full five years in office, becoming the second longest government in the history of the state, lasting 1,764 days. Not for him the self-destructive tendencies and distaste for coalition that fatally hampered his predecessors as leaders of Fianna Fáil, Charles Haughey and Albert Reynolds. For Ahern successful governments were long-lasting. He rightly surmised that the population had no appetite for unnecessary elections but was enthused by having to go to the polls every five years or so. In that context he resolved that his government would go the full term. He also enjoyed the cut and thrust of election campaigning and was much better at it than any of his rivals. Combined with the fact that he had a successful message to sell and a ruthless electoral machine behind him, it was no surprise that by the last week of the campaign the *Irish Independent* was declaring that it was 'all over bar the voting', after an IMS poll gave Fianna Fáil 49 per cent of the first preference vote (*Irish Independent*, 9 May 2002).

As it turned out, Fianna Fáil came agonisingly close to but did not get the elusive overall majority, winning 81 of the 166 seats. Ahern then quickly moved to establish a Fianna Fáil–PD government (Mitchell, 2003: 214–29). The PDs had, against all media predictions, won 8 seats, thereby doubling their representation and ensuring a comfortable majority for the incoming government. This was in contrast to the 1997–2002 coalition, which had relied on the support of four independents for its existence. The 2002–7 programme for government was negotiated without any great drama. The major commitments on the economy were to continue the budgetary and economic strategy that had delivered general prosperity while keeping the public finances in a relatively healthy state. Specific commitments were given to remove all those on the minimum wage from the tax net, to ensure that 80 per cent of all earners paid tax only at the standard rate and to increase the weekly state pension to €200 by 2007.

While the government's economic targets were broadly met, it did have a rather awkward start to its tenure as it emerged after the 2002 election that the economy was not in as good a shape as Fianna Fáil in particular had suggested during the campaign. In September 2002 a secret memorandum was exposed in which the Minister for Finance, Charlie McCreevy, shortly after the election, warned his cabinet colleagues of the need for major cutbacks and possible increases in taxation (*Sunday Tribune*, 22 September 2002). This led to calls for his resignation from the opposition, and accusations of deception proved rather difficult for the government to overcome. Bertie Ahern, in his own inimitable fashion, dismissed these charges at the time and later in his autobiography by stating, 'I knew this was rubbish and that decisive action in tightening up now would let the economy roar ahead again the following year. In the event, that is exactly what happened, but we made a mistake in not dealing with the media angle that we had misled people in the run-up to the general election' (Ahern, 2010: 260). This so-called economic roar was of course based on rampant property speculation, reckless lending and acceptance of cheap loans, and what can only charitably be described as pathetic political regulation of the financial sector.

In any event such charges of duplicity on the part of Fianna Fáil did initially stick and hung over the heads of both government parties for the first half of the Dáil. The failure of the government to complete other commitments over the course of its tenure – such as increasing the number of Gardaí to fourteen thousand as it had promised in its manifesto or the ludicrous and much-derided undertaking, voiced during the 2002 election campaign by the then Minister for Health, Micheál Martin, to end hospital waiting lists – also embarrassed the government. Perhaps most embarrassing of all was the plan unveiled in the 2004 budget to decentralise a number of government departments out of Dublin to end the so-called Dublin mind-set in policy formulation. This plan, entirely the idea of McCreevy, and only formally presented to his cabinet colleagues hours before the budget was to be delivered, had at its core an idea that 10,300 civil and public servants would move from Dublin to fifty-three locations in twenty-five counties, with such relocation to be accomplished voluntarily and without the paying of expenses. When the plan was finally shelved close to a decade later, barely a third of the targets had been achieved. But if this and other political initiatives were indeed half-baked, the reality for Irish citizens, however, was that quality of life issues, while important, were clearly secondary to the fundamental tenet of political life: namely that personal economic fulfilment trumped societal concerns during this period. This in many ways ran counter to the whole raison d'être of Fianna Fáil: that it in fact existed as a vehicle for the betterment of the nation.

This seemed to gnaw at something either in Bertie Ahern's conscience or in his renowned political antennae, as in September 2004 he presided over a pre-Dáil think-in in Inchydoney, West Cork, in which the star guest turned out to be a noted critic of Fianna Fáil's individualism-first philosophy, the priest Seán Healy, who was head of the Justice Desk at the Conference of Religious, before leaving to found and head up a new organisation called Social Justice Ireland. Healy had sharply criticised all of the government's budgets since Fianna Fáil and the PDs had taken office in 1997. While acknowledging that the economy had done very well, he pointed to the large number of individuals who he claimed had been left behind by the Celtic Tiger. He demanded that social welfare rates should rise, extra money should be spent on community employment schemes, all children should have medical cards and that tax credits should be refundable (*Irish Times*, 7 September 2004). The growing poverty gap was, according to Ahern, one of the paradoxes of Ireland's open competitive economy and he was keen that his party should remain focused on issues of social justice and social inclusion. In his memoir he rather touchingly revealed that he was genuinely pained and bothered a great deal by the fact that his government was presented as 'Thatcherite and uncaring' (Ahern, 2010: 285).

Father Healy's demands seemed to have a somewhat peculiar impact on Ahern in particular, as two months later he was declaring himself to be 'one of the few socialists left in Irish politics' (*Irish Times*, 13 November 2004).

Not an ideological socialist as he states in his memoir, fondly recalling that he might have said it tongue in cheek, but one who 'was genuinely interested in helping the poor and making sure that we redistributed wealth to help the low-paid and disadvantaged' (Ahern, 2010: 286). This seems suspiciously close to a proper definition of an ideological socialist but was well in keeping with Ahern's and indeed Fianna Fáil's capacity to present themselves as all things to all people.

Three weeks after the Inchydoney think-in, Ahern reshuffled his cabinet. Back in July of 2004 Ahern had announced that his Minister for Finance, Charlie McCreevy, would be Ireland's nominee to the European Commission. Despite protestations from both Ahern and McCreevy that they had agreed on this move as far back as September 2003, there were few who saw McCreevy's nomination as anything other than a demotion out of the Department of Finance for political reasons. In essence McCreevy had become the fall guy for Fianna Fáil's local and European electoral difficulties, with rumblings within the Party that its national electoral future could be salvaged only if McCreevy was moved and a new, more caring image adopted. Ahern's new cabinet, announced on 29 September, saw McCreevy replaced as Minister for Finance by Brian Cowen. After the reforming zeal of McCreevy, Cowen would initially prove to be a cautious minister whose aim would be to direct more resources towards the lower-paid and less well-off. His first budget would, for instance, see social welfare payments, tax bands and credits all significantly increased.

The catalyst for this new approach was the results of the local and European elections in June of 2004, where Fianna Fáil did spectacularly poorly. It was bad enough for Fianna Fáil that Fine Gael won a seat more than it did in the European elections, but the results in the local elections were nothing short of disastrous for Ireland's perpetual party of government, as it lost 80 seats and just held off Fine Gael as the largest party of councillors. Its share of the vote fell to just 32 per cent nationally and 24 per cent in Dublin. Overall the elections marked the lowest share of the vote that Fianna Fáil had won in a national election since its foundation in 1926. This in essence forced Ahern to act, and the new caring side of Fianna Fáil was put on display. These mid-term elections provided a boost to both Fine Gael and Labour, with Labour in Pat Rabbitte's first outing as leader doing well in the local elections, emerging as the largest party in Dublin, winning nearly 20 per cent of the vote and 34 of 130 seats. Fine Gael for its part had a very good European result and managed to increase its seats while holding its vote share in the local elections (Kavanagh, 2004; Quinlivan and Schon-Quinlivan, 2004).

What these mid-term election results did raise was the possibility of an alternative government of Fine Gael and Labour emerging to, at the very least, challenge the hegemony of Fianna Fáil and the PDs at the next general election. After the disappointment of the 2002 general election, that was some small consolation for Kenny and Rabbitte. As a consequence of those positive results both leaders decided that it was time to offer the voters a real alternative to the government. And so, while Bertie Ahern was refocusing Fianna Fáil in West Cork, Fine Gael and Labour took themselves to middle Ireland to publicly commit themselves to begin negotiations for an alternative government to be put before the people at the general election. Speaking at Belvedere House in Mullingar in County Westmeath, both Kenny and Rabbitte said that the message from the public after the local and European elections was that there should be such an alternative. In a joint statement, they welcomed what they called the 'Mullingar Accord'. They travelled to Mullingar to hail a power-sharing agreement between their parties on Westmeath County Council as 'a good indicator of how enhanced co-operation among the main opposition parties could produce a meaningful and decent alternative to the failed policies of the present Government' (*Irish Times*, 7 September 2004). The Mullingar pact was of little significance in itself. The two parties already co-operated with each other on a number of other councils, and both had also done similar deals with Fianna Fáil on other local authorities. However, the two leaders decided to use the Westmeath arrangement to build on the European and local election results to move towards presenting themselves jointly, perhaps together with the Greens, as an alternative government at the next general election. Indeed, Rabbitte said that the only reason the Green Party was not involved in the initial accord was that it had no councillors in Westmeath, which raises the question why they launched this initiative in Mullingar at all. In any event, while this was indeed the case, the Greens were happy to leave the traditional alternative coalition to Fianna Fáil to their own devices and would hold steadfast to an independent line all the way to the 2007 general election. Fine Gael and Labour also used the Mullingar Accord to launch a joint strategy on mental health, which, while worthy in itself, was not something that had ever exercised the minds of Irish voters and was unlikely to do so into the future. Ultimately, however, the Mullingar Accord gave both parties relevance and credibility and signalled from some distance out that the government could expect an alternative to be on offer to voters in the subsequent election, something which clearly was not the case just two years earlier. As much as anything else the Mullingar Accord gave Fine Gael the ability to create the impression of Kenny being a leader-in-waiting of an alternative government (Rafter, 2011b: 175).

Staying with Fianna Fáil

On the government side of the house, the removal of McCreevy had not only deprived the PDs of a valuable ally in government, it had also taken away the one senior cabinet member who in effect had straddled both coalition partners. At various times since Fianna Fáil and the PDs took office in 1997, the PD leader, Mary Harney, had made various half-hearted noises about the fact that the PDs had choices beyond Fianna Fáil and the larger government party could not take them for granted. Where they could go, however, was open to question. In April 2005 at their annual conference Harney declared that the PDs were not tied to a coalition with Fianna Fáil and would be willing to serve in government with Fine Gael and Labour, but not with the Greens, whose economic policies she described as 'crazy' (*Irish Times*, 11 April 2005).

Notwithstanding these warning shots across the bows of Fianna Fáil, the PDs were quite clearly a neoliberal political party with certainly very little in common with Labour and they were far more comfortable working with Fianna Fáil than with any other alternative. Research from expert surveys on party policy positions conducted in 1997, but before the election of that year, showed that, in terms of economic policy, the PDs were clearly on the right of the economic policy spectrum, and quite far away from any other party, including its coalition party after the election, Fianna Fáil. On a 1–20 scale, 20 being the most economically neoliberal, the PDs scored 17.27 (Laver, 1998: 162–3). Further expert survey research, based on 2002 data collected after the end of the first Fianna Fáil–PD coalition government, scored the PDs as 16.3 on a left–right survey and 17.4 on an economic survey, with 20 being the most right-wing (Benoit and Laver, 2005: 93). The PDs were clearly the most expressly neoliberal and right-wing party in Irish politics. Yet one scholar claimed that, while the PDs marked out the conservative edge in Irish politics, they were better described as centrist, arguing that 'Ireland does not seem to have any parties with extreme pro free market positions' (Gilland Lutz, 2003: 51). Yet the PDs clearly saw themselves as the prime movers in pursuing a liberal low-tax governmental economic policy, with Harney declaring in September 2004 that such a policy was the cornerstone of Ireland's economic success. She also claimed that the PDs had enjoyed a crucial influence on much of the economic policy devised by the Fianna Fáil Minister for Finance, Charlie McCreevy, since he took office in 1997, claiming that 'to a large extent many of the economic policies that he was able to implement were the policies espoused by the PDs' (*Irish Times*, 7 September 2004). Harney and McCreevy were ideologically aligned, and other Fianna Fáil members of the government, such as Martin Cullen and Seamus Brennan, were also widely perceived to be economic neoliberals, Cullen having been at one stage a member of the PDs (Murphy, 2006b: 301).

Moreover Fianna Fáil's grassroots were also comfortable with the PDs as coalition partners. Garry and Tilly, in an examination of the coalition preferences and policy priorities of Fianna Fáil activists prior to the 2002 election, noted that an overwhelming majority (85 per cent) of such activists favoured the PDs as their preferred coalition partner, although a clear majority (55 per cent) prioritised more spending on public services as the most important policy issue (Garry and Tilly, 2003: 85–7). Bertie Ahern, forever in tune with his party's grassroots, adopted a similar attitude and put any PD wobbles down to mid-term angst of a party constantly worried about its future existence.

In fact it was this worry about its continued future that led the PDs to an existential crisis as the government moved closer to a general election. In the summer of 2006, the Minister for Justice and party president, Michael McDowell, pressed Harney to honour what he perceived to be a long-standing commitment to step down as leader and, presumably, make way for him. McDowell, long seen as the leading intellectual force within the Party, had been appointed Minister for Justice, Equality and Law Reform on the government's formation in 2002 and had proved somewhat of a crusading minister, advancing a whole range of ideas, some more grounded in reality than others, including so-called Asbos for young offenders, café-style bars as replacement for traditional public houses and the creation of a Garda Reserve force. The first two ideas not surprisingly went nowhere, but the creation of the Garda Reserve force was driven through by McDowell in the teeth of opposition from Garda representative associations. He also tackled with enthusiasm the vexed question of overtime in the prison service and had successfully steered through the controversial citizenship referendum in June 2004 which tightened the citizenship rules for immigrants, ending the automatic right of citizenship to all children born on the island of Ireland. McDowell had to endure all sorts of allegations of racism during this referendum campaign, but the motion was overwhelmingly passed, with close to 80 per cent of the people voting Yes on a reasonably high referendum turnout of just under 60 per cent. If Bertie Ahern was the consensus man of Irish politics, then McDowell was its most polarising figure, notoriously once describing the Fine Gael grandee Richard Bruton as the Joseph Goebbels of Irish politics during a routine political spat about Garda numbers (*Irish Times*, 21 March 2006). The iron man of Irish politics did admit to an uneasy night's sleep and apologised the following day.

McDowell also played a crucial role as Minister for Justice in persuading the Democratic Unionist Party (DUP) to accept power-sharing in Northern Ireland by insisting that the ending of IRA criminality be central to any political deal. In an atmosphere in which Sinn Féin kept asserting that unless its own political view was adopted the peace process might collapse, this was no mean political feat by McDowell, in light of the Northern Bank robbery of 2004, the IRA murder of Robert McCartney in January 2005 and the ongoing and vigorously robust attempts by Sinn Féin to get the Fianna Fáil–

PD government to order the release of the IRA killers of Garda Jerry McCabe. Given the ambiguity of Fianna Fáil to much of these matters and the ambivalence of the British government of Tony Blair, McDowell insisted that the peace process could not be allowed to descend into a Kafkaesque show whereby criminality could be condoned on the grounds of the potential for more criminality. In this he was right, and his courage on this issue should not be underestimated.

Neither of course should that of Bertie Ahern. Throughout the course of his government's tenure the issue of Northern Ireland was constantly to the forefront of the Taoiseach's thinking. Ever since he became Taoiseach in 1997 he had striven to continue the legacy of Albert Reynolds and ensure political stability in Northern Ireland. And in the midst of a hectic election campaign in May 2007 where his personal finances were centre stage, he still managed to play a decisive role in bringing about a situation whereby the Northern Ireland Assembly, set up as part of the implementation of the Good Friday Agreement, but suspended by the British in 2002 leading to a return to direct rule, was restored as an agreement was finally reached between Northern Ireland's political parties to share power in a new government from 8 May 2007. Close to a decade after the Good Friday Agreement, which the DUP opposed, the four main parties in the north – the DUP, Sinn Féin, the Ulster Unionists and the SDLP – had for the first time agreed to govern collectively. This was in no small part due to the perseverance and political nous of Bertie Ahern. The following week at the invitation of the British Prime Minister Tony Blair he became the first Taoiseach to address both houses of the British Parliament. As he put it himself, it was 'an extraordinary honour and a first for a Taoiseach' (Ahern, 2010: 314). But typically, once it was done, Ahern was off back to Dublin and that night was canvassing on the Navan Road in his constituency. Northern Ireland was important to both Ahern and McDowell but in an electoral context it was rather irrelevant. In exit polls taken after the 2002 and 2007 general elections just 4 per cent in each election mentioned it as an issue influencing their vote (Marsh, 2008: 111).

Northern Ireland was not going to get the Fianna Fáil–PD government re-elected. The economy and the use to which public money could be spent were. In that context McDowell considered that the PDs would do better with him as leader and made it clear that he wanted to lead the Party into the election. Mary Harney was, however, reluctant to resign the leadership. She continued to resist any pressure to step aside for McDowell amid media reports that suggested that the residue of personal bitterness and enduring divisions between members of the parliamentary party was threatening the very survival of the PDs (*Irish Times*, 22 June 2006). Essentially the divisions within the Party had as much to do with a personality clash between Harney and McDowell as with anything else. There was also the fact that the Party's flagship policy, tax cuts for the middle class, had become to all intents and purposes redundant due to the steady lowering of all personal taxes over successive budgets. McDowell's ambition for the leadership of the Party was not to be denied, however, and he finally took the position on 11 September 2006, just four days after Harney had somewhat unexpectedly stepped down as leader, stating that she felt her decision was in the best interests of the Party. No other candidates emerged to challenge McDowell and he was elected unopposed as party leader and also became Tánaiste. The leadership seemed a poisoned chalice to McDowell when the travails of Bertie Ahern immediately came centre-stage and would dominate political discourse for the remainder of the government's tenure. In the lead up to the 2007 general election McDowell reiterated the PD stance of running without any pre-election agreement with Fianna Fáil. But there was something extraordinarily hollow about this, considering that McDowell had persuaded enough voters to return the PDs to power in 2002 as the junior coalition partner to, in essence, keep an eye on Fianna Fáil. McDowell's vacillation in September of 2006 about whether to pull the PDs out of government over Ahern's finances would eventually return to haunt him. The initial rise for the PDs in the polls was wiped out come election day when the Party was decimated by the voters, leading to McDowell losing his seat and resigning in a fit of pique on the night of the election. The PDs held just 2 of their 8 seats as Irish voters reverted to the two-and-a-half-party system that they had been used to since practically the foundation of the state. At the head of this system was Fianna Fáil. And it was to the Soldiers of Destiny and their complex chieftain Bertie Ahern that the Irish public went back to one last time in 2007. It was a decision which was to have grave consequences for the Irish state and for Fianna Fáil itself.

6

Fianna Fáil and the politics of nemesis

Even if we knew the banking crisis was coming I don't think we could have done anything.
> Bertie Ahern, in an interview broadcast on 18 October 2011

We carefully considered all available policy options.
> Brian Cowen on the arrival of the Troika, 28 November 2010

Perpetual Fianna Fáil government

Bertie Ahern was the man who made coalition and Fianna Fáil mutually compatible. With the party yet again polling over 40 per cent of the vote at the 2007 election, the prospect of perennial Fianna Fáil government in Ireland loomed. If Fianna Fáil could coalesce successfully with the PDs, and govern competently with Labour, then it could potentially coalesce with any smaller party and could certainly do a series of deals with independents. After the successful 2007 result for Fianna Fáil, Bertie Ahern decided to do both and put together a coalition with the Greens and the remaining two PDs while also doing a number of deals with independent TDs, all to make sure that his third coalition would prove to be as stable as his first two.

Fianna Fáil, the Greens and the PDs, with 86 seats between them, negotiated a programme for government and seemed to have a pretty secure majority. Bertie Ahern's paranoia about stability was somewhat reinforced when during the negotiations to form a government he agreed deals with the independents Jackie Healy Rae, Michael Lowry and Finian McGrath which mainly concerned the provision of resources to local amenities in their constituencies, thus repeating his trick from 1997 when he also agreed a number of deals with independents to ensure the stability of his first coalition. McGrath read parts of his deal into the Dáil record, though Fianna Fáil insisted that these were in reality non-deals as the projects would go ahead in any event (O'Malley, 2008a: 210–11). Ahern had been thinking about life beyond a two-party coalition with the PDs for some time. A year prior to the election the Taoiseach and his long-time Fianna Fáil compatriot Séamus Brennan had discussed the possibility of bringing the Greens into a future coalition, with Brennan telling Ahern that he thought the Greens would make good coalition partners and that they should nurture a relationship between the two parties. Ahern describes going into the coalition as a leap of faith as he could not tell how the Greens would do in government, saying moreover that he did not need their 6 seats but he wanted a government that would run for another historic full term, which would be the final piece of his legacy (Ahern, 2010: 324–5). Rather less plausibly, Ahern also reckoned that the Greens would bring new and interesting ideas to the public policy table, declaring government with them to be an exciting prospect.

For their part the Greens looked on coalition with their new partners with a mixture of trepidation and anticipation (Boyle, 2012). Having also won 6 seats in 2002, the 2007 election was a disappointment for the Greens as they returned to the Dáil with the same number of seats, notwithstanding their long stint in opposition railing against poor planning and development throughout the country. Nevertheless, the collapse of the PDs was a boon for the Greens as the Dáil arithmetic after 2007 left them at least in a position where an approach from Fianna Fáil to form a government was distinctly likely. However, as the Greens did not hold the position of 'kingmaker' in being able to threaten to leave government and form an alternative coalition, their ability to insist on a number of core principles was significantly reduced (Bolleyer, 2010: 615). Thus, when the approach from Fianna Fáil did indeed come, the Greens were dealing from a position of relative weakness. With no extra seats to dangle in front of Fianna Fáil, the Greens did not have a strong hand entering into negotiations and also had to put up with the fact that Brian Cowen was the senior negotiator for Fianna Fáil. Cowen's barnstorming performance in the second half of the 2007 election campaign had resurrected Fianna Fáil from its earlier doldrums, when Ahern initially announced the election at the rather bizarre hour of 8 a.m. on a Sunday morning amidst deepening public unease as to his own private finances. Cowen was described as having 'never betrayed any feelings of warmth towards the Greens' and of harbouring a 'hostile attitude to power-sharing with their party' (Minihan, 2011: 27). His attitude was a harbinger of much more serious disputes to come between Cowen and the Greens during the government's controversial tenure. Yet the Greens did choose to enter into coalition with Fianna Fáil and to 'pass along the enchanted way into government for the first time in their history' (Minihan, 2011: 20).

For the Greens, the economic principles of the PDs had led to rising inequality in Ireland. But the Greens could do nothing about the inclusion of the PDs in the new government. It was a sign of the weakness of both the Greens and the PDs that Bertie Ahern included them in his new coalition. The Greens did quite well when it came to the spoils of office, gaining 2 seats at cabinet: Gormley and Eamon Ryan became Minister for Environment and Minister for Communications, Energy and Natural Resources. They also received a junior ministry, the aforementioned Sargent, and two Seanad seats. In a later government reshuffle the Greens would also gain an extra junior minister. Government for the Greens, however, came with a very steep price, with the Party having to compromise on a number of not only important policy initiatives but also cherished holy grails, which turned out not to be that holy at all, including the use of Shannon airport by US troops, mostly on their way to Iraq, and the construction of a new motorway near the famous 'Hill of Tara', an area of immense cultural significance for many Green members (Bolleyer, 2010: 615). Their experience of government would prove to be bruising, ruin any reputation they had for economic competence and good governance and leave any future the Greens had in Irish politics in very grave doubt.

For their part, the other minority government party, the PDs after their disastrous election were barely in survival mode. The sensational and petulant resignation from public life on the night of the election by their leader, Michael McDowell, plunged them into a deep crisis made worse by their abysmal electoral performance. While the former leader, Mary Harney, was reappointed to the cabinet, continuing to take the Health portfolio, she was also forced into resuming the leadership of the Party, albeit in a caretaker capacity. With their only other deputy, Noel Grealish, a classic parish-pump politician from Galway, declaring no interest in leading the Party, the PDs were forced to look beyond their elected representatives for a fresh face to reinvigorate the Party's fortunes. After some internal wrangling a competition was eventually held between the party's two senators, Ciaran Cannon and Fiona O'Malley, both of whom owed their positions to being selected by Bertie Ahern as two of his nominees to the Seanad. Cannon eventually prevailed in April 2008, but the fact that he was never elected to any national position did not augur well for the Party's fortunes, nor did the fact that it had taken so long to fill the vacancy for leader. The end was in sight for the party that had broken the mould of Irish politics. The Party had ultimately been toyed with by the electorate. It had been saved in 1997 by Bertie Ahern doing a deal with their four elected deputies after the disaster of that election when the Party lost 5 of its 9 seats. After 2007 there was to be no such salvation. Cannon's election as party leader was greeted with indifference by the wider public. With little public support, a stagnant organisation and practically no funding beyond the state-granted leader's allowance, the four parliamentary party members, with the support of the former leader Des O'Malley, arranged for a special delegate conference to take place on 10 November 2008 to argue for the winding-up of the party. One of the documents submitted to that special conference was a letter from O'Malley calling on delegates to face electoral realism and to bring the Party to an end (O'Muineacháin, 2012: 126). The ultimate result was 201 votes to 161 to bring the PDs to an end. Over their twenty-three years in existence the PDs had had a rather remarkable impact on Irish politics, particular in the economic sphere, but they exited with a whimper. They were at their most influential as junior partners in the two Fianna Fáil-led governments between 1997 and 2007 where they wielded considerable influence on government policy and on Ahern himself.

In the immediate years after the re-election of the Fianna Fáil–PD coalition in 2002, Ireland was considered in some reputable, albeit conservatively oriented, rankings to have the most open economy in the world. The A. T. Kearney / Foreign Policy Globalization Index placed Ireland first in the world in 2002, 2003 and 2004 in its annual empirical measure of globalisation and its impact using a variety of macroeconomic indicators such as such as trade and investment flows, movement of people across borders, volumes of international telephone traffic, Internet usage, participation in international organisations, and data on trade and foreign direct investment inflows and outflows. Moreover the *2005 Index of Economic Freedom*, compiled jointly by the *Wall Street Journal* and the Heritage Foundation, found Ireland's was the world's fifth-freest economy, and the second most free in the EU (after Luxembourg). This *Index of Economic Freedom* measured 161 countries against a list of fifty indicators divided into ten broad factors of economic freedom: Trade policy, Fiscal burden of government, Government intervention in the economy, Monetary policy, Capital flows and foreign investment, Banking and finance, Wages and prices, Property rights, Regulation, Informal market activity. This index ultimately concluded that Ireland had one of the world's most probusiness environments, especially for foreign businesses and investments wherein 'Ireland's policy framework promoted an open and competitive business environment and where regulations were applied uniformly and were not particularly onerous' (Murphy, 2006b: 302).

But the PDs' brand of neoliberalism was in many ways uniquely Irish in character and scope and was best signified by the Fianna Fáil–PD government's approach to the taxi industry, when it decided in late 2000 to deregulate the licensing of the industry amidst huge protests from within the industry itself. Such deregulation within Irish public policy was symptomatic of moves to, as Taylor describes it, 'deliver a world-class economy while retaining some measure of commitment to the avoidance of social dislocation' (Taylor, 2002: 501–23). For Taylor, Ireland had in essence pursued a neo-corporatist approach to economic growth, which remained quite different from the neoliberal forms of economics practised in for instance New Zealand, the United Kingdom and the United States of America. This was something the OECD also espoused. In analysing Irish regulatory reform in 2001 it made the point that countries such as the United Kingdom and New Zealand pursued contentious ideological reform, unlike Ireland, which pursued a more pragmatic agenda in building consensus through processes of national partnership and was quite happy not to liberalise certain utilities such as transport, electricity, postal services and the issuing of licences in the drinks industry (Murphy, 2006b, 304). Ultimately the OECD deduced that privatisation in Ireland was based on a practical, non-ideological and case-by-case approach, under the Fianna Fáil–PD coalition whereby policies were developed in close consultation with trade unions and effected, in some cases, through 'strategic alliances' where union support was linked to immediate benefits. The PDs clearly picked their ideological battles while in government. There was no clamour for wholescale or ideological privatisation in Ireland. What the PDs were interested in was less an ideological commitment to privatisation but rather an ideological commitment to reducing what it considered to be overtly bureaucratic regulation. In this it was extremely successful, as the regulatory regime in Ireland in the decade from 1997 to 2007 was minuscule. The results of this were to be devastating.

By 2007, however, the electorate, always somewhat suspicious of the PDs, had finally wearied of them and decided that they could live without the party that had played a key role in Irish politics since its foundation in 1985. Its unique brand of neoliberal economics and devotion to the manna of deregulation would ultimately shake Irish politics and society to its core once the banking crisis hit the country with a vengeance in September 2008 just a few months after the Party had been wound up.

On the other end of the ideological spectrum the decade between 1997 and 2007 had been nothing short of a disaster for Ireland's oldest party, Labour. After a decade in the opposition doldrums the result of the 2007 general election brought yet another bout of soulful introspection for the party that had thought it had broken the mould with its spectacular breakthrough in 1992. But for the third general election in a row Labour remained rooted on just over 10 per cent of the vote and actually lost a seat. After ten years in opposition, such a result was utterly devastating for Labour. It led inevitably to yet another change in leadership.

Beaten by Pat Rabbitte for the Labour leadership in 2002, Eamon Gilmore eventually became Labour's tenth leader in September 2007 after Rabbitte announced his resignation the previous month. Gilmore was elected unopposed, having set out an ambitious plan to have Labour lead the next government and offer itself as an alternative option to the voters beyond Fianna Fáil and Fine Gael. This would ultimately manifest itself in the 'Gilmore for Taoiseach' posters that sprang up during the 2011 general election campaign. Given Labour's anaemic performance since 1992 and the fact that the merger with Democratic Left had actually seen the Party lose support, this seemed nothing but the normal hyperbole associated with desperate politicians talking up their party and themselves. But Gilmore and Labour did have Dick Spring's barnstorming opposition performances from 1989 to 1992 as a potential template to make gains from the grimness and grind of opposition. And from his election as leader Gilmore began aping the Spring tactic of attacking Fianna Fáil unmercifully and was very vocal in his positing of the view that under no circumstances would Labour enter into a coalition with Fianna Fáil after the following election. This was to counter the speculation which haunted Labour throughout the 2007 campaign that if the numbers had stacked up they might well have entered government with Fianna Fáil. It was clear in that context that the fateful decision by Dick Spring to bring Labour into government with Fianna Fáil after its great breakthrough in the 1992 general election still scarred the Labour Party. The strident approach of Gilmore was best expressed when in an emotive Dáil debate in March 2010 he took the unprecedented step of accusing the then Taoiseach, Brian Cowen, of 'economic treason' for signing off on the state guarantee of Anglo Irish Bank in September 2008, noting that the decision had been made 'not in the best economic interest of the nation but in the best personal interests of those vested interests who I believe the Government was trying to protect on that occasion' (Dáil Debates, vol. 706, col. 1, 31 March 2010). Even the normally combative Cowen was taken aback at this assault on his character, merely noting that it was beyond the pale and that he himself would never accuse another Irishman of any such thing. But all this was in the future when Fianna Fáil basked in the afterglow of its third general election victory in a row in May 2007 on the back of its reputation for economic competence.

So smug was Fianna Fáil with its affirmation from the electorate that Bertie Ahern, seemingly quite satisfied with the work he had achieved, declared that he would retire from public life by the time he was sixty in 2011, and before the ending of the thirtieth Dáil. He then announced that Brian Cowen would be his anointed successor. Deputy leader since 2002, Minister for Finance since 2004 and Tánaiste since 2007, Cowen was widely popular in the Party. Once popular support ebbed away from Bertie Ahern after his travails with the Mahon Tribunal, there was little doubt that Cowen would take the Fianna Fáil leadership after Ahern finally decided to exit as Taoiseach and leader of Fianna Fáil on 2 April 2008.

Two days after Ahern stepped down, Cowen was nominated by his fellow ministers Brian Lenihan and Mary Coughlan for the leadership, and the following day Fianna Fáil confirmed he was the sole nominee for the position. He was elected on 9 April 2008 and would succeed Ahern as Taoiseach in early May. Cowen immediately repaid the faith shown in him by his nominators by naming Coughlan Tánaiste and Minister for Enterprise, Trade and Employment, and even more crucially and surprisingly naming Lenihan as Minister for Finance. He thus overlooked the claims of more senior members of Bertie Ahern's cabinet for two of the most crucial positions in government. By the time Cowen resigned the leadership of Fianna Fáil and was replaced as Taoiseach just over two and a half years later, he had presided over the implosion of both the Irish economy and Fianna Fáil's standing in the polls. The party that had dominated Irish politics would see its reputation in ruins, its competency and integrity called into question and its very survival put at risk. But when Brian Cowen was greeted by jubilant crowds in his native Offaly in May 2008, singing a song from a makeshift stage while drinking a pint of Guinness, none of this appeared to be anywhere on the horizon.

In fact Cowen originally had to face a much more mundane task on becoming Taoiseach, and that was to get yet another one of Ireland's seemingly interminable European referendum treaties passed and out of the way. This seemed like a routine task but it would turn out to be anything but. The Lisbon Treaty referendum of 12 June 2008 proved to be the beginning of Cowen's never-ending difficulties in his short period as Taoiseach. The Lisbon Treaty was mainly concerned with procedural changes including moving from unanimous to qualified majority voting in a number of areas and strengthening the power of the European Parliament. It was intended for the most part to complete the process began by the Treaties of Amsterdam and Nice to enhance the efficiency and democratic legitimacy of the EU. As with all such treaties in Ireland, however, the debate was based around completely different issues.

Just a week after attaining the most powerful office in the land, Cowen had confirmed that he had not in fact even read the treaty and seemed unable to come to terms with the vigorous opposition to it from both the right, in terms of the newly formed Libertas group and a number of extreme antiabortion groups, and the more usual anti-European-treaty suspects from the left in the form of Sinn Féin, and the People Before Profit alliance. To make matters worse for the pro-Lisbon advocates, Ireland's European Commissioner, Charlie McCreevy, also declared that he had not read it either nor would he expect any sane sensible person to do so (Quinlan, 2009: 113). While this was probably an accurate summation of the treaty, it was clearly politically naive and played into the hands of the No campaigners. This rather blasé attitude to the voters also spoke of a mindset where Yes campaigners believed that European referendums could somehow be passed by faith alone (Murphy and Puirséil, 2010: 94). In that context nothing much had changed or indeed been learned from the failed Nice campaign of 2001. For their part the No campaigners were much more engaged with the issues and had been preparing for the campaign since the beginning of 2008. Moreover Cowen's robust partisan political nature came to the fore when, after an opinion poll showing that a majority of Fine Gael voters were intending to vote No, he stated that all parties would have to 'crank up their campaign'. This was widely seen across the political spectrum as an attack on Fine Gael, although Cowen later claimed that his remarks had been taken out of context (Quinlan, 2009: 113). Nevertheless, such normal party political jousting distracted attention from the real issues and from the Yes campaign's attempt to fend off the aggressive and sometimes misinformed views on what the treaty, if adopted, would mean for Ireland. These included the perpetual concerns in EU referendums of a further erosion of sovereignty, the spectre of military conscription for Irish citizens into an EU army, the threat to Irish neutrality and a permissive abortion policy being introduced into Ireland via some sort of morally lackadaisical back door. The Yes campaign never gained any traction, not least because those in favour of it never gave the electorate a good reason for which to vote for it. Moreover the Yes campaign had also been put on hold until after Bertie Ahern's valedictory farewell tour as Taoiseach, which contributed in no small manner to its defeat. The failure to convince the electorate that issues surrounding abortion, conscription and corporate taxation, were not part of the treaty played a significant part in the defeat of the referendum by 53.4 per cent to 46.6 per cent on a turnout of 53 per cent (Sinnott et al., 2009: 27, 39). This was a significant if not exactly fatal blow to Cowen, barely a month in office. A European referendum had been lost only seven years before without any serious political impact for the governing parties. It was, however, a very inauspicious start, and the campaign itself, marked initially by government laziness, then complacency, and in the final days a certain fatalism as to the result, would come to characterise the rest of the government's tenure in office.

Guaranteeing the banks: a peculiar form of private enterprise

Nevertheless, by the time of the state guarantee of the banks in September 2008 the government and Fianna Fáil in particular had retained their support with the public in the fifteen months since the election. A series of polls up to the beginning of September 2008 showed Fianna Fáil consistently achieving 40 per cent and comfortably Ireland's most popular party. However, once the guarantee was enacted and the consequences of that decision began to become apparent, support for Fianna Fáil plummeted to a degree never witnessed before. The first TNS MRBI poll after the guarantee had Fianna Fáil at 27 per cent, a gargantuan drop in Irish terms of 15 percentage points from which it would never recover, while the first Red C poll taken in late October 2008 had it at 26 per cent. Once it became clear throughout 2009 that the bailout of the banks and the establishment of the National Assets Management Agency (NAMA) to deal with the banks' distressed assets were not the panacea for the Irish economy that they had been portrayed by Fianna Fáil as being, then it simply became a matter of how low Fianna Fáil would go (Farrell et al., 2011: 36–7). The social categories it had created in its image right across the Irish state would begin to desert it once its reputation for economic competency was lost. This can be traced to the infamous government decision to, in essence, give the private banks a free pass on their debts by guaranteeing all their obligations without knowing what cost this would bring to the state. The reality was that the decision was taken not by the government in full but basically by its head, the Taoiseach, Brian Cowen. As told by the Governor of the Central Bank, Patrick Honohan, Lenihan argued strongly for 'the immediate nationalisation of both Anglo and INBS – but officials cautioned that there would be operational risks in taking such action mid-week, and the idea certainly would not have appealed to all of his political colleagues; he was overruled on the night' (Honohan, 2014: 69). There was only one man who could have overruled the Minister for Finance, and that was his boss, the Taoiseach. And thus Cowen signed off on probably the most important decision in the history of the Irish state. How did this happen?

On the night of Monday 29 September 2008, Brian Goggin, chief executive of Bank of Ireland, and Eugene Sheehy, chief executive of Allied Irish Banks, Ireland's two largest and most important banks, came together at 6.30 p.m. to ring Brian Cowen requesting an immediate and urgent meeting with him and his Minister for Finance, Brian Lenihan. Although the request was granted by the government, the dapper bankers who turned up at the Department of Finance at 9.30 p.m. were made to wait until 11.30 p.m. to have their case heard. In the meantime Cowen, Lenihan, the governor of the Central Bank, the secretaries general of both the Department of the Taoiseach, and of Finance, the chief executive of the Financial Services Regulatory Authority, the Attorney General and a whole raft of advisers were grappling with a crisis of unprecedented proportions within the history of the Irish state: the very survival of the Irish banking system. The bankers outlined their case, which was that they feared the immediate collapse of Anglo Irish Bank and perhaps one more financial institution, Irish Nationwide, and that if that was allowed to happen contagion in the banking system could well sweep away their institutions as well. Shares in Anglo Irish Bank had fallen by close to half that day alone and threatened to be much worse the following day, leading to what would be the inevitable failure of that bank and the very likelihood of a domino effect on all other Irish banks, the dreaded run which would literally take all the banks out. Goggin and Sheehy were joined by their respective chairmen, Richard Burrows and Dermot Gleeson, at the meeting and told the politicians in no uncertain terms that the government had to act or the entire Irish banking system could well fail and the Irish economy plunged into a nuclear winter of economic catastrophe. One of their suggestions was that the government could nationalise Anglo Irish Bank. In angry terms, the Taoiseach told them that the government would not be taking that course, using the immortal line: 'We're not fucking nationalising Anglo' (Leahy, 2009: 332).

That September night was, for the Irish government, the culmination of a six-month period of acute national and international turbulence on the stock market which had spawned a fiscal crisis that threatened to undermine the very solvency of the state. The Irish stock market lost €3.5 billion of its value on 17 March 2008 after the US investment bank Bear Sterns collapsed due to its exposure to the sub-prime property market. Shares in Anglo Irish Bank fell 15 per cent on the same day, leading Sean FitzPatrick, chairman of Anglo Irish Bank, to ring Cowen, then Minister for Finance, who was in Malaysia, over fears of a run on the bank's deposits. Cowen attempted to assuage market fears through issuing a statement saying that the situation was an international development rather than a national development (Lyons and Carey, 2011: 129–30). Nevertheless, it was the beginning of a prolonged period leading up to the guarantee where it would become clear that Anglo Irish Bank's overexposure to the property market would have a traumatic effect on both the Irish state and its economy. In the weeks leading up to the guarantee, the government began to put in place contingency measures for a worsening of the banking sector and prepared for the possible nationalisation of one or more of the state's financial institutions, considering even a merging of Allied Irish Bank and Bank of Ireland. Moreover according to evidence given by Kevin Cardiff – assistant secretary general of the Department of Finance during the crisis and present on the fateful night – at the Oireachtas banking inquiry in June 2015, a whole range of people had been lobbying the government in the months coming up to the guarantee to actually provide some form of overarching state guarantee of the banks. This included such luminaries as the former Minister for Finance, Charlie McCreevy, one of Ireland's richest entrepreneurs, Dermot Desmond, and a whole range of bankers including Sean FitzPatrick (*Irish Times*, 19 June 2015). Just two days before the fateful night of 29 September, the Department of Finance had commissioned an emergency report from the global financial giant Merrill Lynch, seeking an outline of the state's options in a rapidly worsening economic climate. The sixteen-page report was emailed to Kevin Cardiff that evening at 6.43 p.m., and outlined as one option, in just seven lines, a blanket guarantee of all deposits and obligations of the six Irish banks, but warned that the wider market 'will be aware that Ireland could not afford to cover the full amount if required'. It staggeringly estimated that this amount could be in excess of €500 billion (Lyons and Carey, 2011: 181–2).

The two politicians, Cowen and Lenihan, and their cabal of civil servants and advisers who met on that September night had taken the view that doing nothing was not an option. Leaving the markets to decide would inevitably lead to the loss of Anglo Irish Bank within days, almost certainly Irish Nationwide Building Society and perhaps others as well. The experience of the fall of Lehman Brothers, the enormous Wall Street investment bank, just two weeks earlier in the United States showed the huge risk with the approach of leaving the market to decide. In that context the group led by Cowen had concluded that some form of state underwriting of the banking system was necessary. When told by Sheehy and Goggin that Ireland's two largest banks were at risk, Cowen was initially suspicious. Allied Irish Banks in particular had some past history in relation to being aided by the state. In 1986, during a serious recession, it sought government help to the tune of £100 million after its purchase of the Insurance Corporation of Ireland went disastrously wrong. The scale of that particular rescue was seen as overly generous to the bank, and here it was again seeking government assistance. But Cowen and his team were clearly in a bind and had to do something. Not wanting an Irish bank to fail or be taken into public ownership, the decision was taken to guarantee the deposits, loans, obligations and liabilities of the six Irish banks, a total sum of €440 billion, more than twice the country's Gross National Product. Despite Honohan's view of a dispute between Lenihan and others on the night, most notably his boss, Cowen, Donovan and Murphy note that it seemed that 'the guarantee commanded widespread support from all those who were present' (Donovan and Murphy, 2013: 200). An incorporeal cabinet meeting took place to approve the measure, with ministers contacted by phone between 3 a.m. and 5 a.m. to gain their assent, although there was no substantive discussion about the decision during these phone calls. In perhaps a sign of the coming confusion and dissension that would tear the government asunder over two years later, the Minister for the Environment and Green Party leader, John Gormley, could not be contacted on the fateful night and had to be roused from his bed by the Gardai with a message to ring the Taoiseach's office. Ultimately, as Cooper pithily points out, 'the decision was approved because it was the one Cowen told the cabinet he wanted' (Cooper, 2009: 319). But it was the height of folly to approve deals that banks had made with their depositors and creditors without knowing what these arrangements were and how much they would cost. In that context the main fault to be laid at the door of Cowen and his government is not that they were forced on the infamous night to make such a momentous decision but that they made it in ignorance of how much it would cost, and, even more importantly, that they let such a situation develop in the first place. It was also the height of political folly, as in the minds of ordinary citizens it seemed that Fianna Fáil was more interested in the survival of bankers rather than in the well-being of ordinary citizens. For a party that had made its name as looking after the ordinary people of Ireland, and being indeed made in their image, this was a fatal mistake.

The trouble with the Irish banks was that they were massively reliant on borrowed money from international banks and regularly had to borrow new money to cover loans that were due for repayment. Moreover recourse to foreign funds began to quickly dry up from early 2007 when foreign investors started dumping Irish bank shares because of the banks' heavy exposure to a property sector that had 'all the hallmarks of a bubble' (Ross, 2009: 83). As the Irish property market began to crash spectacularly in the autumn of 2008, a concomitant collapse of the banks' liquidity ensued due to the enormous sums loaned by all the main banks, but particularly Anglo Irish Bank and Allied Irish Banks, to property developers. With the fear that the Irish banks would be unable to borrow if one or two of them went under, and the realisation that such an event could lead to the collapse of the entire Irish economy, the bank guarantee scheme was announced at 7 a.m. on Tuesday 30 September to an initial welcoming at home from both the media and the opposition political parties, with the exception of the Labour Party, but a much less friendly reception from abroad highlighted by downright hostility from the British government and a statement from the European Commission that the guarantee would be investigated. Meanwhile the government congratulated itself on a political masterstroke, encouraged everyone in the state, including their political opponents, to don the green jersey and bullishly declared through Lenihan that it would be the 'cheapest bailout in the world so far' (*Irish Times*, 24 October 2008). This was hubris on a grand scale. Nemesis was just around the corner.

This hubris first manifested itself with a government decision to bring forward the budget for 2009 from its normal date in early December to the middle of October. This seemed more to do with the idea of a government seeing to be getting things done rather than anything more substantive, and the budget when produced was nothing short of a public relations disaster. Ending his budget speech with a rhetorical flourish that it was a call to patriotic action, one of Lenihan's initiatives was to abolish the automatic entitlement to a medical card for people over seventy giving them free medical treatment no matter their ailment. Introduced for no particular reason except as a stroke of political opportunism by a previous Fianna Fáil Minister for Finance, Charlie McCreevy, just before the 2002 election, as the prince of all gimmicks, the entitlement to free medical care was likely to cost the state significant sums in a country with an increasingly elderly population. When Lenihan decided that the now near bankrupt state could not afford such a financial luxury, the elderly constituency revolted. The result was government vacillation and weakness. Numerous Fianna Fáil TDs threatened to vote against the government, and one backbencher, Joe Behan, resigned from the parliamentary party. The independent TD Finian McGrath then announced to no one in particular that he would no longer be supporting the government. In the ultimate show of political cowardice, Cowen once more overruled Lenihan and announced an about-turn on the medical card issue (Leahy, 2009: 335–6). It was a spectacular display of political ineptitude and a sign of how weak Cowen's leadership had become in just six months as Taoiseach.

Just four months after categorically stating that the government would not nationalise Anglo Irish Bank, Lenihan announced on 15 January 2009 that Anglo was to be immediately nationalised, thus negating in one fell stroke of the pen one of the main reasons for the introduction of the bank guarantee scheme. Revelations that its chairman, Sean FitzPatrick, had arranged for loans of well over €100 million for himself from the bank, and had then colluded with the help of the Irish Nationwide Building Society chief executive, Michael Fingleton, to conceal this from Anglo's own auditors and shareholders, were the final nail in the coffin of Anglo's reputation (Cooper, 2009: 211–17). Its demise was followed by the news that FitzPatrick was declared bankrupt. Politically the result was to be the slow strangulation of Fianna Fáil's hegemony in Irish politics.

As it became clear that the bank guarantee scheme was not a panacea to get out of the economic crisis, but rather a gigantic millstone around the necks of ordinary Irish people and of the Irish state itself, the government in January 2010 agreed to a framework of inquiry into the banking crisis and commissioned a number of reports for consideration by the Dáil. Findings by the former IMF officials Klaus Regling and Max Watson in their report of May 2010 clearly concluded that the banking meltdown was a result of 'home made' decisions rather than the global economic crisis. In their executive summary they came straight to the point, stating: 'Ireland's banking crisis bears the clear imprint of global influences, yet it was in crucial ways "home-made".' A parallel report by the new governor of the Central Bank, Patrick Honohan, concluded that in its budgetary and macroeconomic policy the government relied to an unsustainable extent on the construction sector and other transient sources for revenue, while principally focusing on failures of the regulatory agencies of the state. Ten months later in March 2011 a third report by the former IMF economist Peter Nyberg found that the main reason for the crisis was 'the unhindered expansion of Ireland's property bubble' and went on to criticise the herd-like mentality that saw all financial institutions copy the risky lending practices of Anglo Irish Bank (Regling and Watson, 2010; Honohan, 2010; Nyberg, 2011). Unfortunately for the citizens of the Irish state, the consequence of this behaviour was to saddle the country with a colossal debt. It also saddled Fianna Fáil with an unenviable reputation for economic incompetence on a grand scale and for that it would pay an enormous price at the polls. A fourth inquiry set up by the Oireachtas itself began in 2015 and is ongoing at the time of writing.

The Fianna Fáil meltdown

The first manifestation of the Fianna Fáil meltdown came on 5 June 2009 when the governing parties faced into European, local government and two by-elections that two years into their tenure would serve as an accurate barometer of its standing with the public. The results would be nothing short of catastrophic for both Fianna Fáil and the Greens. The rejection of the Lisbon Treaty had brought on to the political scene the Libertas group, which, rejoicing in its role in defeating the treaty announced that it was considering running candidates in the 2009 elections to the European Parliament and reckoned in another astonishing display of deluded hubris that it could win up to 70 seats across Europe (*Irish Times*, 16 July 2008). In December 2008, under the leadership of Declan Ganley, it reconstituted itself as a pan-European political party, declaring its intention to run candidates in all the states of the European Union, and in March 2009 Ganley announced he would spearhead this assault by running in the Ireland North-West constituency. In that context Ireland's election to the European Parliament in June 2009 would see a completely new dynamic at work, with a high-profile group putting candidates up for election to an institution which they basically accused of failing both the Irish and the European people. Once the campaign began, however, it was clear that Ganley and Libertas had vastly overreached themselves. While Ganley himself ran a high-profile campaign, his candidates both in Ireland and across Europe had minimal impact and suffered from a rather inchoate campaign structure and little voter recognition on the ground. Libertas eventually contested elections in fourteen European states, running over six hundred candidates, but performed spectacularly badly, winning only one seat in France. Ganley came close to winning a seat in the Ireland North-West constituency, but on coming up short subsequently declared that he was retiring from politics. He would return, however, to the Irish political scene just three months later to campaign, unsuccessfully this time, against the second Lisbon Treaty referendum (Murphy, 2012: 155). That referendum was passed in October 2009 with an overwhelming majority of 67 per cent in favour, a switch of over 20.5 per cent from the first Lisbon referendum, with forty-one of the country's forty-three constituencies voting Yes. It was the highest Yes vote in a referendum on Europe since the Maastricht Treaty in 1992, and the turnout of 58.5 per cent was the highest in a European referendum since the original vote on joining the EEC in 1972. In a phenomenon akin to the second referendum on the Nice Treaty there was an increased effort both by the main political parties of the state and by a variety of civil society groups to persuade the public that being part of the European project better protected Ireland's national interest. In that context the central appeal from the Yes side was that the national interest had to take precedence over simple partisan politics (McGraw, 2015: 139). The overriding rationale of the electorate seemed clearly to be that it was safer to be an integral part of the European Union in troubled economic times, with the 'vote yes for jobs' slogan of the Yes side being particular resonant. But it was a false hope. The Irish state would certainly need Europe in the near future but it was to bail out the country not to transplant it into a hive of economic honey as the Yes voters in Lisbon Two had rather plaintively hoped.

The 2009 European Parliament election results would set in train the relatively quick demise of the Fianna Fáil electoral machine. On a decent turnout of 58.6 per cent, Fianna Fáil garnered just 24.1 per cent of the national vote, down 5.4 percentage points on the 2004 result, and lost its seat in Dublin. This marked the first time since it first entered politics in the 1927 general election that Fianna Fáil had failed to win the most votes in a national election. It did retain its seat in North-West where the veteran Donegal sitting TD Pat 'the Cope' Gallagher was victorious. The delay in holding a by-election to fill his vacated Dáil seat would, however, come back to haunt the government as over a year later in July 2010 the High Court granted Sinn Féin's Pearse Doherty a judicial review into why the by-election had not been held in the intervening twelve months. The court ultimately ruled that the delay offended the terms and spirit of the Constitution and the government announced it would hold the by-election on 25 November 2010, which Doherty comfortably won, gaining 39.8 per cent of the first preference vote. The failure to hold a by-election was symptomatic of the government's fear in facing the electorate at all. That by-election win was also crucial for Sinn Féin after disappointing local and European election results. Its rising star Mary Lou McDonald lost her Dublin seat in the European election to the maverick socialist Joe Higgins, just two years after the voters of Dublin West had turfed Higgins out of the Dáil (Quinlan, 2010: 289–301). Moreover Sinn Féin also had a poor local election in that it saw its share of the vote slightly decrease to 7.4 per cent while returning the exact same number of seats at 54. The stagnation in the Sinn Féin vote, in a second-order election where the government of the day was deeply unpopular, on top of its disappointing 2007 general election result left many in the party wondering whether the Irish electorate would ever be receptive to Sinn Féin's charms.

After their historic decision to go into government, these elections were the first electoral test for the Greens, and proved nothing short of calamitous, with their two European election candidates, Deirdre de Burca and Dan Boyle, failing to get even enough votes to redeem their expenses. Fine Gael, although it lost a European seat, saw its share of the national vote increase and it also overtook Fianna Fáil in first preferences in a national election for the first time in its history, taking 29.1 per cent of the first preference vote. There was jubilation in Labour as the Party gained two seats at the expense of Fine Gael in the East constituency and the independent Kathy Sinnott in the South constituency. The independent MEP Marian Harkin held off the challenge of Ganley in North-West.

The local government election results mirrored those of the European elections, with Fine Gael again emerging as the largest party in terms of votes and seats. The election campaign was dominated by the state of the economy, with one candidate declaring the election to be 'the most national election I have been involved in as a local councillor' (Quinlivan and Weeks, 2010: 317). Coming just after an emergency budget in April that increased taxation and cut public expenditure yet again, these elections promised more grim news for the governing parties. Fianna Fáil in particular suffered a crushing reverse, losing 84 seats from what was seen as a terrible result in 2004, finishing with 218, and seeing its share of the vote fall nearly 8 percentage points to 24.4 per cent. The results were even worse for the Green Party, which lost 15 of its 18 seats and received a negligible 2.3 per cent of the vote. For a party that had prided itself on devolving government to as local a level as possible, this was a terrible blow to sustain. Only one-third of voters who supported the Greens in the 2007 general election stuck with them at this election (Quinlivan and Weeks, 2010: 320). While the coalition parties stuck to the line that this was a typical mid-term second-order election, there could be little doubt that as the recession continued to hit home these results did nothing but presage electoral carnage come a general election. Fine Gael won 32.3 per cent of the national vote to open up a significant gap between it and Fianna Fáil in the quest for public support. For its part Labour increased its number of seats and, although it continued to poll remarkably poorly in the west of Ireland, winning only 5 of 208 seats in Connaught–Ulster, crucially for the future general election it did very well in Dublin and gained the largest number of seats in three of the four city and county councils. This was certainly a good harbinger for the Party as its performance in Dublin would be central to its general election prospects.

Overshadowing the European and local government elections, however, were the two by-elections held on the same day in Dublin Central and Dublin South. Fine Gael, in a major coup managed to persuade the well-known RTÉ broadcaster George Lee to be the Party's standard bearer in the Dublin South by-election caused by the death of the long-standing Fianna Fáil minister Seamus Brennan. Lee had previously entertained, but decided against, the idea of standing for the Party in the 2002 general election in the Dun Laoghaire constituency. In 2009 he succumbed to the approach made by the Fine Gael apparatchiks Frank Flannery and Tom Curran. His candidacy immediately gave Fine Gael an immense credibility boost, as a man generally trusted by the public as an economics expert in a time of unprecedented financial turmoil had made a significant political investment (Rafter, 2009: 231–2). Lee romped home gaining over 27,000 first preference votes and winning over 53 per cent of the vote. His time in Fine Gael was, however, to be both short-lived and underwhelming. He failed to adapt at all to life in Leinster House, was somewhat irate that Fine Gael neither immediately put him on the front bench nor made much use of his talents, claiming to 'have had virtually no influence or input into shaping Fine Gael's economic policies at this crucial time', and eventually he resigned as a TD after only eight months (Rafter, 2011b: 267). In Dublin Central the vacancy was caused by the death of the long-serving independent TD Tony Gregory, and Fianna Fáil, in yet another astonishing show of hubris combined with a nod to the Bertie Ahern political machine, decided to run the former Taoiseach's brother Maurice Ahern, who was then seventy years old and could hardly be described as the new face of Fianna Fáil, rather than the former Dáil candidate Mary Fitzpatrick, who was known to be outside the Ahern tent. The voters of Dublin Central delivered a brutal rebuke to the Ahern name when Maurice Ahern won just 12 per cent of the first preference vote and polled in a humiliating fifth place, making this Fianna Fáil's worst result in any election it had ever fought. To make matters worse he also lost his council seat on the same day, while Mary Fitzpatrick comfortably won a seat in the same ward. It was an eloquent verdict on the Ahern years, with the political journalist Pat Leahy astutely commenting that 'showtime politics was buried in a Dublin Central grave' (Leahy, 2009: 341).

Notwithstanding Fine Gael's successes in the June 2009 elections doubts about Enda Kenny's leadership and his ability to win the next general election continued to cause much anxiety within the Fine Gael parliamentary party in particular. The exit of George Lee from the political stage certainly spooked many, as did the real fear that the Fianna Fáil bogeyman in the guise of Brian Cowen might make some sort of miraculous comeback. Static opinion polls, and a generally received wisdom that Kenny had a poor public persona and had not connected with the electorate sufficiently enough to win the next election, ultimately compelled those opposed to Kenny to act.

Richard Bruton, deputy party leader and spokesman on finance, who rather ironically was seen as preventing Lee from having any major input into Fine Gael economic policy, launched a leadership heave against Enda Kenny in June 2010 when he refused to back his leader publicly. The backdrop to the heave was the publication of an Ipsos/MRBI opinion poll on 11 June 2010 which showed Fine Gael falling below 30 per cent for the first time since September 2008, at 28 per cent, and putting it in second place behind the

Labour Party. Given that Fine Gael was only a single percentage point higher than its 2007 general election performance, despite being in opposition to the most unpopular government in the history of the state, it was too much for Bruton, and he attempted to oust Kenny as leader. However, Bruton's strategy was botched from the beginning, as many of his followers had no idea that he was in the process of launching a heave at all. Moreover his campaign, if it could even be called that, had assumed that, once Kenny was faced with the challenge from the well-heeled blue-blood Bruton, he would voluntarily resign and there would be a 'seamless transfer of power' (Rafter, 2011b: 291). This was to underestimate Kenny seriously. The idea that Kenny, having led Fine Gael out of the doldrums of the 2002 election, would then quietly step aside with his party on the brink of power, notwithstanding static opinion polls, without putting up any sort of fight, clearly never dawned on Bruton or any of his supporters. The Bruton leadership campaign also clearly had a touch of self-entitlement about it. In that context he and his supporters seemed somewhat surprised that Kenny did not simply resign in the face of such open revolt in his parliamentary party. Spurred on principally by his trusted aide, the Carlow Kilkenny TD Phil Hogan, who, one Kenny loyalist Frank Feighan noted, was 'instrumental in Kenny remaining leader' (O'Connell, 2015), the Fine Gael leader showed his political mettle by sacking Bruton from his front bench, much to the deputy leader's surprise and dismay: 'Kenny has just sacked me', he disbelievingly told one of his chief supporters, Brian Hayes, 'and started giggling' (Leahy, 2013: 7). Kenny then, in another dramatic move, dissolved his entire front bench, the majority of whom were against him, at a subsequent meeting, leaving no one in the party or in the wider electorate in any doubt that he intended to fight to hold on to his position as leader and, as he saw it, Taoiseach in waiting. Kenny ultimately prevailed in the leadership battle, due to the support of a number of rural backbenchers, senators and MEPs, and won a confidence motion on 17 June 2010. Still, with a divided party, a resurgent Labour and the constant suspicion that Fianna Fáil might actually rise from its political slumbers there was no guar-antee that Kenny would be able to lead Fine Gael into office at the next election. That view was, however, to change dramatically over the next six months. And the reason continued to be the ever worsening recession and the dawning on the electorate and indeed the political elites that the government, and Fianna Fáil in particular, had no panacea for the economic travails visited upon the country.

Over a year earlier, in April 2009, the government had announced its inten-tion to deal with the problem of impaired assets in the banking system by setting up the National Asset Management Agency. The Minister for Finance, Brian Lenihan, confidently predicted that NAMA would stabilise the banking sector and was an essential component of the state's economic recovery.

Eventually established in September 2009, NAMA's principal function was to acquire the distressed-property-related loans of the Irish banks, estimated at that stage at some €80 billion, in return for government bonds with the aim of allowing the banks to begin lending to viable businesses and increase credit generally within the Irish economy. However, as the Irish economy continued to plummet, with concomitant increases in both emigration and unemployment, and the government was faced with rapidly and seemingly never-ending rises in interest rates for borrowing money on the international bond markets, NAMA soon became associated in the public consciousness as the agency through which the government put the interests of the banks ahead of the interests of its people. Public spending on education, health and social welfare was slashed and a pay cut in public sector pay was introduced. Unemployment and emigration continued to rise, and the banks needed yet more injections of government capital – capital which the government simply did not have but had to find due to the bank guarantee decision.

If the solvency of the Irish state was being threatened by the banking crisis, then the competency of the Irish government was also brought into question by a series of scandals from the autumn of 2009. This began with the resignation as Ceann Comhairle of John O'Donoghue in October 2009 after a lengthy succession of newspaper reports over lavish expenses he incurred during overseas trips (Foxe, 2010). It continued with the resignation of Willie O'Dea as Minister for Defence in February 2010. O'Dea had got himself into some significant difficulty when it transpired that he had made a sworn statement in the summer of 2009 in connection with a High Court case taken by the Limerick Sinn Féin local election candidate Maurice Quinlivan. While O'Dea initially accepted making comments about Quinlivan which were published in a local paper, he denied making other unpublished comments which figured in the court case. It later transpired that O'Dea had in fact made the comments. Amidst allegations from Fine Gael in particular that O'Dea had committed perjury, the government initially won a vote of confidence in the minister, but he resigned the following day, stating that his continuance in office would distract from the vital work of the government, though it was widely believed in political circles that he could not remain in office. Less than a week later, the former Green Party leader, Trevor Sargent, resigned as minister of state in the Department of Agriculture after accepting that he had 'made an error of judgement' in contacting the Gardai about a case involving a constituent, although he defended his motivation in taking the action, making yet another tortuous point, which few could understand, about doing the right thing (Minihan, 2011: 123).

And although no one resigned over it, the nadir of these scandals was reached when the Taoiseach, Brian Cowen, at the annual Fianna Fáil pre-Dáil session think-in, gave what would turn out to be one of the most extraordinary interviews ever broadcast in Irish politics on 14 September 2010. Sounding uninvolved and hung over or like someone who, as Leahy perceptively put it, 'has given up trying to talk to people, who has actually given up on politics', Cowen mumbled his way through what should have been an instantly forgettable interview (Leahy, 2013: 39). But when the Fine Gael grandee Simon Coveney tweeted that Cowen was half-way between drunk and hung over, a narrative storm unlike any other in Irish politics about the drinking habits of the leader of the government was unleashed. Rumours of the Taoiseach's drinking had long swarmed around the confines of Leinster House but had never really reached the public, largely because of the media's queasiness about discussing the issue. All that instantly faded away once Coveney's tweet went viral. The result was an unedifying sight as Cowen was bombarded by the national media as to whether he was in fact hung over during the infamous interview and suffered the humiliation of having his drinking habits assessed and lampooned worldwide. But still his Fianna Fáil cabinet colleagues, like lemmings hopelessly running to jump off the cliff, were paraded out one after the other to defend their leader with suggestions as to why he had performed so spectacularly badly. These ranged from him having a bad cough to too much background noise interfering with the interview and the Taoiseach's concentration. In these excuses Fianna Fáil had committed the cardinal error of taking the citizens of the country for fools. The electorate's revenge would not be long in coming.

Nemesis: the arrival of the Troika

Cast adrift in a hopeless sea of incompetence, the government ambled aimlessly towards political and economic Armageddon, which duly arrived in November 2010. As the interest rate for government borrowing became more punitive by the week, rumours abounded both nationally and globally that Ireland would have to seek a bailout of its own from the EU or IMF or both. Government ministers had no idea of what was going on. In the second week of November the Minister for Communications, Energy and Natural Resources, Eamon Ryan, received a phone call from the media agency Bloomberg asking whether he knew that Ireland would be entering a programme with the Troika of the European Commission, the European Central Bank and the International Monetary Fund. The question was put in the form of a statement. It was not an inquiry whether Ireland would be entering a programme; it was a statement that Ireland would be entering a programme and did Ryan know anything about it. He did not, stating later that after the journalist's call he 'rang Brian Lenihan, who said he had heard the rumours but downplayed the issue saying there were only exploratory discussions without real substance' (Ryan, 2014: 235). A few days later on Sunday 14

November the Minister for Justice, Dermot Ahern, haplessly told RTÉ that speculation that the government was going to seek aid from the EU and the IMF was 'a fiction'. The following day the Taoiseach, Brian Cowen, insisted that his government was not making an application to the EU or IMF for funding as the state was fully funded until at least the middle of the following year. This line was reiterated by other senior ministers and by the Department of Finance throughout the week. On 18 November, however, Honohan, the governor of the Central Bank, went on Ireland's leading and most-listened-to radio programme, *Morning Ireland*, to state that the Irish government would indeed be entering a Troika programme to receive substantial financial assistance from the IMF in the region of tens of billions of euros. Honohan has since defended his public action by stating that things 'had got to the point where, had it remained silent on the state of play, the Central Bank would have not only failed in its responsibility to use timely communication to steady confidence, but would also have dashed a legitimate public expectation in Ireland that it could be trusted not to deceive through omission' (Honohan, 2014: 80). What the half a million people who listened to *Morning Ireland* that day thought of this can only be imagined, when for weeks they had been told by their sovereign government that no such thing was even being considered. The following day the government plaintively declared that it had indeed officially opened up talks with the EU and the IMF. But of course Brian Lenihan had been talking all along to the Troika, who were insisting that there had to be a formal application and that there was no question of a purely precautionary programme, with the ECB feeling it necessary to write to Lenihan that continued emergency lending by the Central Bank to the Irish banks could not be assured unless there was such an application (Honohan, 2014: 80). Lenihan, apoplectic with rage over what he considered a stab in the back by Honohan, wanted to sack him immediately but Irish economic sovereignty, which he was presiding over, had to all and purposes ceased to exist. The Irish state was being told by a financial institution what it had to do. And it had no option but to do it. The sacking of the governor of the Central Bank was not going to make any difference to that. And of course Lenihan really should have been the last one to complain of such behaviour, given the opprobrium brought on those like Dermot Ahern and Noel Dempsey who were insisting publicly that Ireland was not in negotiations for a bailout when Lenihan himself clearly knew that the opposite was the truth. The narrative that Ireland was bounced into the bailout has been mentioned ever since, and, though there is certainly some truth in it, the inescapable fact remains that the Fianna Fáil–Green–PD coalition government led by Brian Cowen had lost control of the country's economic sovereignty and no amount of complaints about being forced into a bailout by nameless bureaucrats in Europe can alter that fact.

On Sunday 28 November 2010 the government finally accepted access to an €85 billion rescue package for the Irish state. The loan ultimately comprised €22.5 billion from the IMF and further contributions of €22.5 billion from the European Financial Stability Mechanism, €17.5 billion from the European Financial Stability Fund, €12.5 billion from the Irish National Pension Reserve Fund, a further €5 billion in Ireland's cash reserves and finally €5 billion in bilateral loans from the United Kingdom, Denmark and Sweden (Breen, 2013: 118). It was the ultimate surrender of Irish economic sovereignty. A week earlier on 22 November the Green Party announced that it would stay in government to pass the December budget but that it then wanted an election to take place in the second half of January 2011. Of course having an election in January was not something within the Greens' gift. Helpless in government, ignored for the most part by their Fianna Fáil partners, and increasingly viewed with opprobrium by the public, the Greens had been nervous about their continued participation in the coalition for some time. Once Honohan uttered his famous words, the Green leader, John Gormley, wanted to lead his party out of coalition there and then 'rather than going through with the worst budget in the history of the state. The combination of the IMF coming in here and the budget could only result in electoral meltdown' (Minihan, 2011: 196). True words indeed. But the Greens decided to stay on to help pass the budget and then leave the people to decide on Ireland's political fate. It was yet another odd decision. The Greens could have pulled out and supported the budget from the opposition benches. They were having no input into the makeup of the budget in any event. But they took the tortuous route of staying in government. They were 'leaving but staying', a concept that Gormley rather pompously stated afterwards was too complex for most observers to understand (Minihan, 2011: 219). The trouble was that the Greens continued to cling to office after the December budget was passed, insisting that bills on climate change, corporate donations and directly elected mayors be passed. This was to fatally underestimate the electorate's indifference to such issues in the continued light of the country's bailout programme. In any event the Greens' electoral fate was not long in coming.

The same was true of Fianna Fáil. By the end of 2010 the party that had dominated Irish politics since 1932 was polling at 17 per cent in opinion polls. It had overseen the demise of Irish sovereignty. But while the Troika deal was keeping the state on economic life support, political sovereignty was something that could still be expressed by the people at the ballot box. The decision by the Greens to seek an early election, notwithstanding their tardiness in actually pulling the government down, had massive implications for Fianna Fáil. The first poll of 2011 by Red C showed Fianna Fáil on 14 per cent, prompting more and more disquiet within the parliamentary ranks of the party and persuading the Minister for Foreign Affairs, Micheál Martin, to act. On 18 January 2011, with speculation that Martin was about to launch a no confidence motion in Cowen, the Taoiseach, in an attempt to take the initiative, declared a motion of confidence in his leadership of Fianna Fáil. Martin retorted that he would be opposing the motion, declaring to RTÉ that the 'presentation of the IMF coming into the country that to me was a watershed moment' (*Irish Times*, 19 January 2011). Yet only a month earlier on the RTÉ *Frontline* television programme of 13 December 2010, weeks after the Troika had arrived in Dublin, in which this author was a guest alongside Martin, he offered unequivocal support to his leader, and stated that while he did have leadership ambitions he would act on them only once a vacancy had arisen. Things had obviously changed. No other cabinet member joined this purported leadership coup, with the Minister for Finance, Brian Lenihan, denying that he had called on dissident Fianna Fáil TDs to seek a no confidence motion in Cowen, although this was about as credible as his denials that the Troika was about to bail out the country. This was shown to be the case when the Fianna Fáil TD John McGuinness went on RTÉ to state categorically that Lenihan had been encouraging him and others to mount a campaign against Cowen (Leahy, 2013: 59). Thus Martin went alone and failed dismally, with Cowen winning a confidence motion by what was considered to be a comfortable margin on 18 January 2011. Martin then resigned as Minister for Foreign Affairs and considered his future. Leahy argues that Fianna Fáil had given up on Cowen back in September on the back of his infamous hung over interview (Leahy, 2013: 40) but when it had the chance to get rid of him just four months later the same party baulked and stood by him.

This was to prove a terrible mistake. Shortly after midnight on the following night, Wednesday 19 January 2011, Cowen rang the Minister of State for Children, Barry Andrews, at his home to offer him the post of Minister for Justice as part of a purported cabinet reshuffle that Cowen was intending to announce to the Dáil the following day. Andrews refused the offer, claiming that while he was flattered he had to decline on the basis that he was anxious to press ahead on the referendum for children's rights that he had long been piloting. This was a rather bizarre answer in itself, as by refusing Andrews must have known that he was in fact hastening the demise of the coalition government he was being asked to serve in. The offer of a senior ministry to Andrews was the sequel to a carefully choreographed but ultimately futile series of ministerial resignations, whereby Mary Harney, Dermot Ahern, Noel Dempsey and Tony Killeen gave their letters of resignation to the Taoiseach earlier that night. These were then disclosed to an astonished national media. They were later joined by the Cowen loyalist Batt O'Keeffe just before midnight, although that resignation was not announced. With the resignation of

Micheál Martin the previous day, the Taoiseach had expected to announce six new ministers to the Dáil in a last-ditch desperate attempt by Cowen to refresh the Fianna Fáil faces in his government for the coming election; an election that Fianna Fáil supporters hoped to delay into the spring and perhaps summer of 2011 when they thought they would be able to campaign with the sun at their backs. But Cowen's cabinet reshuffle, with its rationale of presenting a revitalised and unified party to a jaded electorate, was to backfire spectacularly once his coalition partners the Greens interpreted it as a cynical return to stroke politics, which of course it was, and refused to agree to it. It is hard to imagine this botched reshuffle as anything else but a return to the stroke culture and cute hoorism with which Fianna Fáil had long been associated, not that it ever did it much harm at the ballot box. And it is also difficult to discern what Brian Cowen was actually up to with this frankly idiotic plan.

Thursday 20 January 2011 would prove to be one of the most amazing days in the history of Irish politics. The Minister for the Environment and leader of the Greens, John Gormley, had become aware of the ministerial resignations and impending reshuffle only on the early morning news bulletins. At an emergency meeting of the Greens at 9.30 a.m. they decided they would not immediately pull out of government but would first tell Cowen that they would not support any new appointments. With the government dependent on their support, Cowen was in a bind but he initially refused to back down from his reshuffle plan. At this stage it was not even clear that he had six replacements lined up, but he told the Greens he was preparing to push ahead with a new cabinet as was his prerogative as Taoiseach. The Greens told him they could not be a part of it, prepared a statement, and readied themselves for an appearance on the famous plinth of Leinster House to announce they were withdrawing from government. Cowen blinked first and, after a third meeting with Gormley that morning, stated that he would be reassigning his existing ministers to new portfolios.

He announced this to a stunned Dáil at 1.30 p.m., and named 11 March 2011 as election day; the Greens declared that they were staying in government. Then the recriminations began. Both Cowen and Gormley went on RTÉ's Six One news to give their side of a meeting that representatives of Fianna Fáil and the Greens had had the previous day where the issue of the reshuffle was brought up by Cowen. An angry Taoiseach maintained that, while the Greens had reservations, they understood that it was his prerogative to change the Fianna Fáil ministers and that by refusing to recognise this they had altered a long-standing tradition relating to a Taoiseach's right to change his cabinet. For their part Gormley stated that the Greens could not have been any clearer in telling Fianna Fáil that a reshuffle was the wrong signal to send out to the Irish people, currently going through the worst recession in living memory, and that they could not and would not support it. Clearly Cowen knew that the Greens were hostilely opposed to his plan, but he simply did not care and went ahead with it anyway (Murphy, 2011: 1–2).

Just two days after receiving a newly endorsed mandate from his party, Brian Cowen, with his botched reshuffle, had made one of the greatest errors in modern Irish political history. While the government was clearly in its last days, Cowen was desperate to lead his party into the general election in the hope of revisiting his barnstorming performance in the 2007 election where he was widely seen as the man who had turned around that particularly campaign for Fianna Fáil. He thus risked all on appointing a new ministerial team that he could bring to the electorate as the renewed face of Fianna Fáil. In fact to all but the most partisan Fianna Fáil activist it seemed an act of utter folly and a statement of Neroesque hubris from a Taoiseach who had lost all grip on reality.

Once the Greens refused to agree, Cowen had literally nowhere to go. Two days later he paid the ultimate price when he announced on Saturday 22 January 2011 that he was stepping down as leader of Fianna Fáil but would stay as Taoiseach until a new government had been formed, a position he had only days earlier described as nonsensical. The following day the Greens finally pulled out of government, leaving Cowen leading a cabinet with just seven members out of the maximum of fifteen. The date of the general election was then moved from March back to February once the Greens, from the opposition benches, agreed to support the passing of the finance bill, which was deemed necessary under the conditions of the Troika rescue package. The annual finance bill was hurriedly rushed through both houses of the Oireachtas and passed by the Seanad on Saturday 29 January 2011. This paved the way for the Dáil to be dissolved on 1 February and Brian Cowen called the election for 25 February.

The thirtieth Dáil had truly seen a series of extraordinary events. From Bertie Ahern's third election victory in a row to the time Cowen resigned as leader of Fianna Fáil and called the election, Irish politics had witnessed the following: Ahern resign from office as Taoiseach over his own extraordinary finances; the PDs, who had such an influence on the state and its people, wind themselves up; the state bail out the banks by guaranteeing all their deposits and obligations in the most momentous political decision taken by any government in the history of the Irish state; the country enter a severe and prolonged recession; and finally the state lose its economic sovereignty when the Troika come to the rescue of the Irish economy in the form of a multi-billion-euro contingency fund to ensure that the country remained solvent.

Perhaps most astonishingly of all, on the eve of the election Fianna Fáil, which had received 41.6 per cent of the vote at the 2007 election, stood at between 12 and 16 per cent in the opinion polls. The proposed saviour for the party was, astonishingly enough, Micheál Martin – the only member of the cabinet to have opposed Cowen's leadership the previous week. The Fianna Fáil leadership field summed up the intellectual bankruptcy which had inflicted the Party. Martin was the obvious candidate but he had served in cabinet with Cowen since 1997. Brian Lenihan, although he knew he had terminal cancer, having first been diagnosed with the illness in late 2009, and was the face of the bailout, put himself forward. So did Éamon Ó Cuív, grandson of the founder of the Party, Eamon de Valera. Ó Cuív's main contribution to the debate was that Fianna Fáil needed to get back to the ideals of de Valera, whatever they meant in Troika Ireland. The fourth candidate was Mary Hanafin, who in a rather odd way of campaigning asked none of her supporters to declare publicly for her. This, however, had more to do with the fact that those supporters could be counted in single figures. Why Lenihan felt the obligation to run remains a mystery as, 'damaged by the bailout and limited by his diagnosis', he had little to offer Fianna Fáil as leader, 'except to front a containment mission in the forthcoming election' (Whelan, 2014: 10). But his decision to run was a poor one detached from reality.

Micheál Martin was elected leader of Fianna Fáil on 26 January 2011, the third leader in just over two and a half years, and barely a week in the job he had to fight a general election where the most likely result was the decimation of his party. And where were the Irish people looking for their own political saviours come the general election? Where else but Fine Gael and Labour. Fine Gael and Labour, who had been rejected with such force at the 1987 general election, the last time Ireland had experienced such a severe recession, and who, notwithstanding one brief period in power from 1994 to 1997, had been in the doldrums ever since, were viewed by the public as the saviours of the Irish economy and indeed Irish society in 2011. Irish politics had come full circle since 1987.

Conclusion:
The politics of Troika Ireland

Never was any such event, stemming from factors so far back in the past, so inevitable and yet so completely unforeseen.
                    Alexander de Tocqueville on the French Revolution, 1856

We can sum up the 2011 general election as the 'Ireland has failed' election. A sorry trail of self-destruction, produced in part by a sad record of misman-agement and corruption, led to a paralysis of leadership whereby by the beginning of 2011 the democratically elected government of the state was barely functioning. That government eventually collapsed in what would have been laughable circumstances if the context had not been so serious. In the Ireland of clientelism it is worth noting that Ireland's earthquake election of 2011 saw national priorities come to the fore, with a plurality of voters viewing national issues as the most important criterion in deciding how they would vote (Mair, 2011: 291; Marsh and Cunningham, 2011: 185). Fianna Fáil had clearly hoped that the relationships it had built with the people in its long tenure as Ireland's natural party of government would save it a signifi-cant number of seats. But the polls did not lie. It was also easy for the elec-torate to blame a small coterie of individuals within Fianna Fáil and the PDs in whom power had been concentrated since the parties first came to power in 1997. As Ó Riain perceptively points out, the crucial positions in Irish politics were held by an inner core of four people within the cabinet for the vast majority of the years between 1997 and 2011, namely Bertie Ahern, Brian Cowen, Mary Harney and Micheál Martin. These four were supplemented by an outer core of individuals, namely Dermot Ahern, Mary Coughlan, Noel Dempsey, John O'Donoghue, Charlie McCreevy and Michael McDowell, who combined to 'produce an oligarchy within Irish democracy from 1997 to 2011' (Ó Riain, 2014: 230). In that context it was relatively easy for the electorate to punish Fianna Fáil at the 2011 election.

Prior to the economic meltdown, political parties freed from strong ideo-logical class-based identities had demonstrated 'the flexibility to adjust readily to changing circumstances without risking loss of support' (McGraw,

2008: 630). In that context the catch-all nature of Irish politics made it extremely difficult for new groups or parties seeking electoral support. Once such a grouping began to show signs of gaining support around an issue, larger parties had simply moved their policies to accommodate them. This, in essence, is what happened to the PDs, as once Fianna Fáil adopted their low taxation mantra, they found themselves without political support as there was not really much point for the electorate to vote for them. This then left the Irish electorate with a traditional choice. If the electorate was not going to go back to Fianna Fáil, then it could only look to the conservative revolutionaries of Fine Gael and Labour. Sinn Féin was a different type of political animal; anti-austerity certainly and also against the bailout (but then again who wasn't?), it still struggled in Irish general elections, in no small part because of its birth in violence in Northern Ireland. Yet Sinn Féin's 2011 result, winning 14 seats on just shy of 10 per cent of the vote, was, if not quite remarkable, then certainly noteworthy considering its poor local and European result just over eighteen months earlier. Its big problem in moving from a party of perpetual opposition to a party of government, though, was that none of the major parties was willing to coalesce with it. This somewhat paradoxically suited Sinn Féin just fine as it would set out its stall after the general election to build up its electoral strength by focusing on offering a left-wing anti-austerity message while to all intents and purposes ignoring its traditional rhetoric of a thirty-two-county socialist republic: a rhetoric which left the vast majority of Irish voters considerably cold.

And those voters, disenchanted with the party system, have begun to consider the attraction of independent candidates carefully. The decline in the independent vote in the 2007 general election from 13 to 5 seats seemed to suggest that Irish voters had made up their minds that in a tight election it was better to plump for a party that might actually be in power and be able to do something (Gallagher, 2008: 91–2). But minority governments, or governments with very small majorities, have in the past had to rely on independents who have used their position to gain significant investment in their constituencies. Hence Bertie Ahern's deal making with three of these independents to shore up his 2007 government. But the collapse in the Fianna Fáil and Green vote in 2011 presaged an unparalleled rise in votes for independents, with their vote reaching an eighty-year-high with fourteen independents elected. Another five members of the United Left Alliance, featuring two Socialist Party candidates, two People before Profit candidates and one other independent, were also elected. The combined vote for independents of over 12 per cent was the highest since June 1927 (Gallagher, 2011a: 151), when ironically enough the stability of the nascent state was also threatened, albeit for different reasons than in 2011. This dramatic increase gives sustenance to the Mair and Weeks (2005) view of voters relying more heavily on competing personal appeals, particularly in times of economic uncertainty. This then led to increased voter volatility, which by 2002 was three times the level recorded in the early 1980s and had moved even further by 2011. Yet despite this volatility no radical parties have emerged. While the radical left had some minor success in by-elections in 2014, no radical right-wing party has emerged despite relatively conducive social and political conditions (O'Malley, 2008b: 974).

While the three main parties of Fianna Fáil, Fine Gael and Labour collectively are weakening, they still claimed an average of 78 per cent of the votes at the elections between 1987 and 2011 compared to an average of 87 per cent of the votes at the elections from 1923 to 1982 (Gallagher, 2011b: 538). Part of the explanation for this lies in the fact that, beyond tending to the constituency, political parties in Ireland, and indeed independents, now compete on an increasingly narrow base. The ingrained nature of social partnership removed much of the economic debate from the political sphere, and what was left was a sterile debate as to who could best manage the economy. In essence over twenty years of social partnership ultimately led to a scenario whereby no one in either the bureaucratic or political elite had any idea at all of how to get the state out of the economic quagmire it found itself in as a result of ineffective regulation, greed, corruption and downright incompetence. This paucity of intellectual rigour in political thinking essentially led to the infamous bank guarantee scheme of September 2008 where the easiest decision to let the state take responsibility was the one ultimately plumped for by the Taoiseach of the day, Brian Cowen. It had all the hallmarks of a let's-hope-for-the-best mentality that had riddled public policy-making and indeed decision-making by politicians in Ireland since its independence. As this book has attempted to show, the political agency of Irish politicians from all the parties who had been in government since the foundation of the state was that when big business found itself in difficulty the state would come to its aid. It was this mentality that led the state to bail out the Insurance Corporation of Ireland in 1986 and to provide export credit insurance to a number of beef companies, most notably those associated with Larry Goodman, in 1987. The reductionism in economic policy-making in modern Ireland then dwindled even further as the parameters of independent government action were deeply constrained by Ireland's paymasters in the Troika.

The collapse in the Fianna Fáil vote in 2011 saw direct gains for the established political alternatives of Fine Gael and Labour but also Sinn Féin, a number of hard-left groups and various classes of independents. But what did not happen was the emergence of a new political party which could attract enough votes to make a difference. A number of new political groupings did put themselves forward as having the magic elixir to the woes of the Irish state by articulating opposition to the bailout and running on the general notion of restructuring bank debt and ending Irish cronyism. All, however, substantially underestimated the hurdles to be overcome in facing the electorate in a general election, and disappeared as they simply could not organise a national campaign with candidates in every constituency (Reidy, 2011: 47). Fís Nua, an offshoot of disaffected Green Party members, and New Vision, a hotchpotch of independents led by Eamonn Blaney, a son of the former Fianna Fáil minister and later independent Fianna Fáil MEP Neil Blaney, put forward a small number of candidates under their respective banners to no effect with the electorate. Luke Ming Flanagan, successfully elected in Roscommon–South Leitrim, aligned himself with New Vision but had a long history as an independent activist. There was some excitement, in media circles at least, when a group known as Democracy Now and which included several high-profile media commentators including Eamon Dunphy, David McWilliams and Fintan O'Toole, emerged on the scene and floated the idea in private, and eventually in public, of running as a specific group; but in the end, claiming lack of time and a skewed electoral playing field in favour of the established political elites, they opted off the electoral pitch (Reidy, 2011: 47; Leahy, 2011: 77). The Irish people, cautious in the use of their votes, ignored these groups as there were established political alternatives on offer.

Notwithstanding that these traditional alternatives had failed in the past, the electorate in 2011 was simply not willing to countenance supporting a new party. While these established political parties may not be able to respond to the demands of their voters or meet their specific interests, an alternative to tap into the discontent of voters has failed to appear (Mair, 2011: 296). This can be put down to the difficulties in attracting both candidates and canvassers, in financing and running campaigns, and perhaps most fundamentally to a general apathy towards politics and elections as a plague on your houses. The story of Irish political competition from 1987 to 2011 can still be interpreted as one of a continuing trust by major proportions of the electorate in traditional political alternatives, despite the chronic mismanagement of the state by these self-same political elites. In that context there remains a strong tendency towards political continuity in the Irish state.

But despite this continuity there is clearly significant disquiet in and about Irish politics. The Fine Gael–Labour coalition was a government born in crisis and was unable to offer any quick fixes to the woes of the Irish economy. This was wryly summed up by the Minister for Education, Ruairi Quinn, writing in his diary in early January 2012: 'The Troika return today. Our debt mountain rises and I continue to worry about our future and money in this little country of ours. Keep to the knitting!' (Walshe, 2014: 86). The political consequence of this state of affairs was an electorate impatient with the pace of the economic recovery. In that context political competition in Troika Ireland became more congested. And while the Troika ultimately exited Irish shores in December 2013, they left significant political uncertainty behind them. One manifestation of this came in January 2015 when the former Fine Gael Minister of State for European Affairs, Lucinda Creighton, announced she was forming a new political party. Two months later Renua Ireland was born, proclaiming a generally centre-right view on economic issues and a free vote for its members on social issues such as abortion. Declaring that it did not believe that party politics in Ireland had a place for issues of conscience, Renua revealed a twenty-first-century updating of the PD policy of rolling back the state by advocating that the state should as far as possible stay out of the lives of citizens. Renua also argued that Ireland needed to build an economy for entrepreneurs across the social, private and public sectors. Moreover, without really explaining what it meant, Renua also declared that it wanted to make the public sector public and give politics back to the people. The latter sounded eerily like the Fianna Fáil manifesto of 1997, 'People Before Politics', or the Fine Gael–Labour coalition's local government policy document of 2012, 'Putting People First'.

Four months later, in July 2015, another new political party came into being with the formation of the Social Democrats by the independent TDs Stephen Donnelly, Catherine Murphy and Róisín Shortall. This new party, offering a generally centre-left view of politics, was also keen on ensuring that Irish democracy would empower people, ensuring that Irish citizens could play full roles in civic and political life. Something similar was promised by a variety of left-wing groups, loosely termed the Anti Austerity Alliance, which not only had found their political voice in opposing austerity but also drew support for their opposition to the government's decision to introduce water charges to be implemented by a new quango, namely Irish Water. The first major manifestation of this discontent with continuing austerity was the by-election victory in Dublin South-West of the Socialist Party activist Paul Murphy in October 2014. Running basically on a single issue of refusing to pay water charges, Murphy won a seat widely expected to go to Sinn Féin and promptly hailed his victory as one for the people.

This all goes to show that Irish politicians are generally enthusiastic if rather confused about the link between politics and people. Creighton and two other TDs, Billy Timmins and Terence Flanagan, were expelled from the Fine Gael parliamentary party in July 2013 for voting against the government's Protection of Life During Pregnancy act. Both Creighton and Timmins had been strongly behind the attempted heave by Richard Bruton to get rid of Enda Kenny as Fine Gael leader in 2010, and both ultimately decided that Fine Gael under Kenny was no place for them. Thus they established a new party in an attempt to win enough seats at the next general election to be in contention to be part of a possible coalition government. To that end Renua is like any other party in Irish politics. Its short- and long-term future will ultimately depend on the Irish voter, who has shown very little enthusiasm about new parties. The same goes for the Social Democrats and the variety of left-wing offerings on display to the electorate. The fact that Renua has declared no position on abortion suggests that at last politicians in Ireland have finally realised that when it comes to general elections voters are not remotely inclined to be influenced by social matters. While Creighton and Timmins left Fine Gael over the Protection of Life During Pregnancy Act, the government's solution to the ongoing and inordinately tangled problem of abortion in Ireland, all the evidence suggests that abortion and indeed pretty much all social issues are marginal at best when it comes to voters casting their ballots. The original 1983 right-to-life constitutional referendum ultimately spawned a controversial Supreme Court decision and four other referendums before the 2013 act was finally passed. And while voices on both the liberal and conservative ends of the spectrum have constantly complained about that act, the reality remains that both Irish politicians and indeed Irish voters are relatively happy to see it as a non-mainstream electoral issue.

The political system itself, however, has become an issue of crucial importance for the state and its citizens. A key aspect of the 2011 general election was the focus placed on political reform as a solution to the economic woes of the state. As the economy failed, the state's political structures were not robust enough to protect a loss of economic sovereignty. In that context how to reform the political system to ensure that a similar economic collapse could not happen again became a question that exercised both political parties and citizens alike in the lead up to the general election. In March 2010 Fine Gael published a comprehensive political reform plan entitled 'New Politics'. This document called for substantial political and constitutional reform, with Fine Gael itself proclaiming that it was the most ambitious programme for political reform since the 1930s. Moreover it advocated the view that political reform was central to the economic recovery of the state. The main headline act of the Fine Gael plan was the proposal to abolish the Seanad. This had been announced by Enda Kenny in October 2009 without any consultation with his party's own TDs and Senators. Despite reported heated opposition within the party to the proposal, abolishing the Seanad became official Fine Gael policy with the publication of 'New Politics' (MacCarthaigh and Martin, 2015: 122). Fine Gael also pledged to reduce the numbers of TDs in the Dáil by twenty, to strengthen the Dáil committee system, to give a vote in presidential elections to Irish citizens living abroad and to introduce an Open Government Bill which would significantly strengthen Freedom of Information, register all lobbyists and protect whistleblowers. The Seanad referendum was run in October 2013, with the government suffering a rather shock defeat. Its generally simplistic campaign, based around reducing the number of politicians in the country while claiming that the Seanad was unreformable, was countered by, amongst others, the group specifically set up to defeat the amendment, Democracy Matters, of which the current author was a member.

For its part the Labour Party in November 2010 published proposals setting out an equally wide range of reform measures, including a promise to enact legislation on Dáil reform, cabinet confidentiality, freedom of information, registration of lobbyists, whistleblowers' legislation, political contributions and electoral spending limits. By the time of the election campaign, Fianna Fáil had decided that it too needed to present a comprehensive reform agenda to the people, with its new leader, Micheál Martin, going as far as appointing a spokesperson on political reform, the candidate for Dublin North-East, Averil Power. The Fianna Fáil manifesto significantly pointed to the electoral system as being the chief culprit in encouraging an almost perpetual campaign in Irish politics, thus moving representatives away from their most important roles of passing legislation and overseeing the work of government. It advocated instead a mixed system of single-seat constituencies elected through the single transferable vote and a top-up national list which was to ensure proportional representation. Why of course it did not decide to do anything about this during its long tenure in power was not lost on the electorate. The three main political parties of the state also saw political reform as being central to budgetary reform, with all suggesting that some form of independent advisory council be established to provide independent commentary on the government's budgetary strategy. Labour for its part stated that its fiscal advisory council would report to the Dáil and the general public, while Fine Gael went even further saying that it would allow both the opposition and the wider public to examine in detail the key underlying financial assumptions on which it was basing its actions in government before the budget was published. Yet looming over the negotiations between Fine Gael and Labour around the formation of the new government was the fact that any discussions around budgets, and the budgetary process, were to a certain extent redundant in that the final deal had to come within parameters set by the Troika (O'Malley, 2011b: 272).

There was a sense of inevitability about the eventual Fine Gael and Labour government which took power in March 2011, offering all these radical solutions to the woes of the Irish state and its people after Ireland's earthquake election of 2011. But what really changed? Yes, Fianna Fáil had been routed, but in the midst of the worst recession to hit the Irish state since the 1950s it still persuaded over 387,000 people to give it their first preference vote. In a country where economic sovereignty had been lost, and where the new government had to report on its spending and taxation policies to the Troika, the fact that Fianna Fáil had not been completely obliterated showed that the

ties that bound citizens to established political parties had not been completely eradicated. In fact Fianna Fáil would resurrect itself within two years
by winning the most seats in the 2014 local elections and receiving the largest
number of votes cast, with some quarter of the voting public, over 430,000
people, casting their ballots for the party that had presided over the greatest
calamity to hit the Irish state since it won its independence. Yes, it was a
second-order election and it was still the second worst election result that
Fianna Fáil had endured in its long history, but it showed that Fianna Fáil
remained relevant in Irish politics. But it was now just one of many parties
in the marketplace rather than the dominant behemoth that had bestridden
Irish politics colossus like and treated other parties as somehow not worthy.
Fianna Fáil ultimately remained relevant not only because it was able to
persuade people that it was worth voting for but because the alternatives in
the guise of Fine Gael, Labour and even Sinn Féin were so similar to it. They
all relied on the Troika to fund the state, and, even when the Troika left, the
spending and taxing parameters in which to direct macroeconomic policy
would remain extraordinarily narrow. Although social partnership was over,
they all still relied on the social partners to maintain industrial and economic
harmony. They all relied on a troubled civil service bureaucracy which in
itself had failed the state. In that context the years from 1987 are best characterised not as the politics of change but perhaps more as the politics of
continuity where the policy choices of Ireland's main political parties resulted
in a bankrupt state leading to misery and despair for much of the state's
population. But when that population had the option politically of doing
something to alleviate the crisis, it decided instead to seek remedies from the
traditional alternatives it was comfortable with. The hubris of Ireland's political elite had cost the state its economic sovereignty. But in keeping with those
political elites the Irish electorate had contributed in no small way to that
situation. Nemesis began with the Irish voter. By late 2015 that voter had
more options than ever before on the eve of a general election that would
inevitably lead to Ireland's most politically fragmented Dáil, given the general
dissatisfaction of the electorate with the governing parties of Fine Gael and
Labour, the rejuvenation of Fianna Fáil, the increasing popularity of Sinn
Féin and the plethora of new political parties and groupings promising an
end to austerity. In that context the continuity long associated with Ireland's
party system was destined to change for ever. It was up to the voter to decide
how Ireland's new political landscape would look. Whether that politics
would lead to triumph or despair was a question which remained very much
in doubt.

Bibliography

Adshead, Maura (2011). 'The Exercise and Impact of Social Partnership', in O'Malley, Eoin and Muris MacCarthaigh (eds), *Governing Ireland: From Cabinet Government to Delegated Governance*. Dublin: Institute for Public Administration, 173–89.

Adshead, Maura, Peadar Kirby and Michelle Millar (eds) (2008). *Contesting the State: Lessons from the Irish Case*. Manchester: Manchester University Press.

Adshead, Maura and Jonathan Tonge (2009). *Politics in Ireland: Convergence and Divergence in a Two-Polity Island*. Basingstoke: Palgrave.

Ahern, Bertie (2010). *Bertie Ahern: The Autobiography*. London: Hutchinson.

Allen, Kieran (1997). *Fianna Fáil and Irish Labour: 1926 to the Present Day*. London: Pluto Press.

Allen, Kieran (2000). *The Celtic Tiger: The Myth of Social Partnership in Ireland*. Manchester: Manchester University Press.

Arnold, Bruce (2001). *Jack Lynch: Hero in Crisis*. Dublin: Merlin.

Barrington, Ruth (1987). *Health, Medicine and Politics in Ireland 1900–1970*. Dublin: Institute for Public Administration.

Barry, Frank (ed.) (1999). *Understanding Ireland's Economic Growth*. Houndsmill: Palgrave.

Benoit, Kenneth and Michael Laver (2003). 'Estimating Irish Party Policy Positions Using Wordscoring: The 2002 Election – A research note', *Irish Political Studies*, 18:1, 97–107.

Benoit, Kenneth and Michael Laver (2005). 'Mapping the Irish Policy Space: Voter and Party Spaces in Preferential Elections', *The Economic and Social Review*, 36:2, 83–108.

Bew, Paul (2007). *Ireland: The Politics of Enmity, 1789–2006*. Oxford: Oxford University Press.

Bolleyer, Nicole (2010). 'The Irish Green Party: From Protest to Mainstream Party?', *Irish Political Studies*, 25:4, 603–24.

Bolleyer, Nicole and Liam Weeks (2009). 'The Puzzle of Non-Party Actors in Party Democracy: Independents in Ireland', *Comparative European Politics*, 7:3, 299–324.

Boyle, Dan (2012). *Without Power or Glory: The Greens in Government*. Dublin: New Island.

Bradley, John (2000). 'The Irish Economy in Comparative Perspective', in Nolan, Brian, Philip J. O'Connell and Christopher T. Whelan (eds), *Bust to Boom? The Irish Experience of Growth and Inequality*. Dublin: Institute of Public Administration, 4–26.

Breen, Michael (2013). *The Politics of IMF Lending*. Basingstoke: Palgrave.

Byrne, Elaine (2012). *Political Corruption in Ireland 1922–2010: A Crooked Harp?* Manchester: Manchester University Press.

Carty, R. K. (1981). *Party and Parish Pump: Electoral Politics in Ireland*. Ontario: Wilfrid Laurier University Press.

Chari, Raj and Hilary McMahon (2003). 'Reconsidering the Patterns of Organised Interests in Irish Policy Making', *Irish Political Studies*, 18:1, 37–50.

Clark, Christopher (2012). *The Sleepwalkers: How Europe Went to War in 1914*. London: Penguin.

Clifford, Michael and Shane Coleman (2009). *Bertie Ahern and the Drumcondra Mafia*. Dublin: Hachette Books.

Coakley, John (1990). 'Minor Parties in Irish Political Life, 1922–1989', *The Economic and Social Review*, 21:3, 269–97.

Coakley, John (2003). 'The Election and the Party System', in Gallagher, Michael, Michael Marsh and Paul Mitchell (eds), *How Ireland Voted 2002*. Basingstoke: Palgrave, 230–46.

Coakley, John (2010). 'The Rise and Fall of Minor Parties in Ireland', *Irish Political Studies*, 25:4, 503–53.

Coakley, John (2013). *Reforming Political Institutions: Ireland in Comparative Perspective*. Dublin: Institute for Public Administration.

Coakley, John and Michael Gallagher (eds) (2005). *Politics in the Republic of Ireland*, 4th edn. Abingdon: Routledge and PSAI Press.

Coakley, John and Michael Gallagher (eds) (2010). *Politics in the Republic of Ireland*, 5th edn. Abingdon: Routledge and PSAI Press.

Coakley, John and Kevin Rafter (eds) (2014). *The Irish Presidency: Power, Ceremony and Politics*. Dublin: Irish Academic Press.

Collins, Neil and Mary O'Shea (2000). *Understanding Political Corruption in Ireland*. Cork: Cork University Press.

Collins, Neil and Mary O'Shea (2003). 'Political Corruption in Ireland', in Bull, Martin J. and James L. Newell (eds), *Corruption in Contemporary Politics*. Basingstoke: Palgrave Macmillan, 164–77.

Collins, Neil and Aodh Quinlivan (2010). 'Multi-Level Governance', in Coakley, John and Michael Gallagher (eds), *Politics in the Republic of Ireland*, 5th edn. Abingdon: Routledge and PSAI Press, 359–80.

Collins, Stephen (1992). *The Haughey File: The Unprecedented Career and Last Years of the Boss*. Dublin: O'Brien Press.

Collins, Stephen (1993). *Spring and the Labour Story*. Dublin: O'Brien Press.

Collins, Stephen (2001). *The Power Game: Ireland under Fianna Fáil*. Dublin: O'Brien Press.

Collins, Stephen (2003). 'Campaign Strategies', in Gallagher, Michael, Michael Marsh and Paul Mitchell (eds), *How Ireland Voted 2002*. Basingstoke: Palgrave, 21–36.

Collins, Stephen (2005). *Breaking the Mould: How the PDs Changed Irish Politics.* Dublin: Gill and Macmillan.

Connolly, Frank (2014). *Tom Gilmartin: The Man Who Brought Down a Taoiseach and Exposed the Greed and Corruption at the Heart of Irish Politics.* Dublin: Gill and Macmillan.

Cooper, Matt (2009). *Who Really Runs Ireland: The Story of the Elite who Led Ireland from Bust to Boom and Back Again.* Dublin: Penguin.

Cooper, Matt (2011). *How Ireland Really Went Bust.* Dublin: Penguin.

Corcoran, Mary P. and Alex White (2000), 'Irish Democracy and the Tribunals of Inquiry', in Slater, Eamonn and Michel Peillon (eds), *Memories of the Present: A Sociological Chronicle of Ireland, 1997–1998.* Dublin: Institute of Public Administration, 185–96.

Corless, Damian (2007). *Party Nation: Ireland's General Elections, the Strokes, Jokes, Spinners and Winners.* Dublin: Merlin Press.

Cullen, Paul (2002). *With a Little Help from My Friends: Planning Corruption in Ireland.* Dublin: Gill and Macmillan.

De Tocqueville, Alexis (1856/1955). *The Old Regime and the French Revolution,* translated from the French by Stuart Gilbert. New York: Anchor Books.

Di Lampedusa, Giuseppe (1958/1961). *The Leopard,* translated from the Italian by Archibald Colquhoun. London: William Collins.

Donovan, Donal and Antoin E. Murphy (2013). *The Fall of the Celtic Tiger: Ireland and the Euro Debt Crisis.* Oxford: Oxford University Press.

Duignan, Seán (1995). *One Spin on the Merry-Go-Round.* Dublin: Blackwater Press.

Dunlop, Frank (2004). *Yes, Taoiseach: Irish Politics from Behind Closed Doors.* Dublin: Penguin.

Dunphy, Richard (1998). 'A Group of Individuals Trying to Do Their Best: The Dilemmas of Democratic Left', *Irish Political Studies,* 13, 50–75.

Elgie, Robert and Peter Fitzgerald (2005). 'The President and the Taoiseach', in Coakley, John and Michael Gallagher (eds), *Politics in the Republic of Ireland,* 4th edn. Abingdon: Routledge and PSAI Press, 305–27.

Fallon, Johnny (2009). *Brian Cowen: In His Own Words.* Cork: Mercier Press.

Fallon, Johnny (2011). *Dynasties: Irish Political Families.* Dublin: New Island.

Fanning, Bryan (2008). *The Quest for Modern Ireland: The Battle of Ideas 1912–1986.* Dublin: Irish Academic Press.

Farrell, Brian (1990). 'Forming the Government', in Gallagher, Michael and Richard Sinnott (eds), *How Ireland Voted 1989.* Galway: PSAI Press, 179–91.

Farrell, Brian (1993). 'The Formation of the Partnership Government', in Gallagher, Michael and Michael Laver (eds), *How Ireland Voted 1992.* Dublin: PSAI Press, 146–61.

Farrell, Sean, Ciara Meehan, Gary Murphy and Kevin Rafter (2011). 'Assessing the Irish General Election of 2011: A Roundtable', *New Hibernia Review,* 15:3, 36–53.

Faulkner, Pádraig (2005). *As I Saw It: Reviewing over 30 Years of Fianna Fáil and Irish Politics.* Dublin: Wolfhound.

Ferriter, Diarmaid (2005). *The Transformation of Ireland.* London: Profile Books.

Ferriter, Diarmaid (2009). *Occasions of Sin: Sex and Society in Modern Ireland.* London: Profile Books.

Fianna Fáil and Labour (1993). 'Fianna Fáil and Labour Programme for a Partnership Government 1993–1997', available at http://michaelpidgeon.com/manifestos/docs/pfgs/PfG%201993%20-%201994%20-%20FF-Lab.pdf.

Fianna Fáil (1977). *Manifesto: An Action Plan for National Reconstruction*: Dublin: Fianna Fáil.

Finlay, Fergus (1998). *Snakes and Ladders*. Dublin: New Island.

FitzGerald, Garret (1991). *All in a Life: An Autobiography*. Dublin: Gill and Macmillan.

FitzGerald, Garret (2005). *Reflections on the Irish State*. Dublin: Irish Academic Press.

FitzGerald, Garret (2010). *Just Garret: Tales from the Political Frontline*. Dublin: Liberties Press.

FitzGerald, John (2000). 'The Story of Ireland's Failure – and Belated Success', in Nolan, Brian, Philip J. O'Connell and Christopher T. Whelan (eds), *Bust to Boom? The Irish Experience of Growth and Inequality*. Dublin: Institute of Public Administration, 27–57.

Fitzgerald, Peter, Fiachra Kennedy and Pat Lyons (2004). 'The Irish Labour Party Leadership Election, 2002: A Survey of Party Members', *Journal of Elections, Public Opinion & Parties*, 14:1, 230–44.

Flood, Mr Justice Feargus (2002). *The Second Interim Report of the Tribunal of Inquiry into Certain Planning Matters and Payments*. Dublin: Stationery Office.

Foster, Roy (2007). *Luck and the Irish: A Brief History of Change, 1970–2000*. London: Allen Lane.

Foxe, Ken (2010). *Snouts in the Trough: Irish Politicians and their Expenses*. Dublin: Gill and Macmillan.

Gallagher, Michael (2003). 'Ireland: Party Loyalists with a Permanent Base', in Borchert, Jens and Jürgen Zeiss (eds), *The Political Class in Advanced Democracies*. Oxford: Oxford University Press, 187–202.

Gallagher, Michael (2005). 'Ireland: The Discreet Charm of PR – STV', in Gallagher, Michael and Paul Mitchell (eds), *The Politics of Electoral Systems*. Oxford: Oxford University Press, 511–32.

Gallagher, Michael (2008). 'The Earthquake that Never Happened: Analysis of the Results', in Gallagher, Michael and Michael Marsh (eds), *How Ireland Voted 2007: The Full Story of Ireland's General Election*. Basingstoke: Palgrave, 78–104.

Gallagher, Michael (2010). 'The Changing Constitution', in Coakley, John and Michael Gallagher, *Politics in the Republic of Ireland*, 5th edn. Abingdon: Routledge and PSAI Press, 72–108.

Gallagher, Michael (2011a). 'Ireland's Earthquake Election: Analysis of the Results', in Gallagher, Michael and Michael Marsh (eds), *How Ireland Voted 2011: The Full Story of Ireland's Earthquake Election*. Basingstoke: Palgrave, 139–71.

Gallagher, Michael (2011b). 'Parties and Referendums in Ireland 1937–2011', *Irish Political Studies*, 26:4, 535–54.

Gallagher, Michael (2014). 'The Political Role of the President', in Coakley, John and Kevin Rafter (eds), *The Irish Presidency: Power Ceremony and Politics*. Dublin: Irish Academic Press, 40–59.

Gallagher, Michael and Michael Laver (eds) (1993). *How Ireland Voted 1992*. Dublin: PSAI Press.

Gallagher, Michael, Michael Laver and Peter Mair (2006). *Representative Government in Modern Europe: Institutions, Parties and Governments*, 4th edn. New York: McGraw-Hill.

Gallagher, Michael and Michael Marsh (1992). 'The Presidential Election of 1990', in Hill, Ronald J. and Michael Marsh (eds), *Modern Irish Democracy: Essays in Honour of Basil Chubb*. Dublin: Irish Academic Press, 62–81.

Gallagher, Michael and Michael Marsh (2002). *Days of Blue Loyalty: The Politics of Membership of the Fine Gael Party*. Dublin: PSAI Press.

Gallagher, Michael and Michael Marsh (eds) (2008). *How Ireland Voted 2007: The Full Story of Ireland's General Election*. Basingstoke: Palgrave.

Gallagher, Michael and Michael Marsh (eds) (2011). *How Ireland Voted 2011: The Full Story of Ireland's Earthquake Election*. Basingstoke: Palgrave.

Gallagher, Michael, Michael Marsh and Paul Mitchell (eds) (2003). *How Ireland Voted, 2002*. Basingstoke: Palgrave Macmillan.

Gallagher, Michael and Richard Sinnott (eds) (1990). *How Ireland Voted 1989*. Galway: PSAI Press.

Galligan, Yvonne (1998). *Women and Politics in Contemporary Ireland: From the Margins to the Mainstream*. London: Pinter.

Galligan, Yvonne (2014). 'Activist Presidents and Gender Politics', in Coakley, John and Kevin Rafter (eds), *The Irish Presidency: Power Ceremony and Politics*. Dublin: Irish Academic Press, 126–47.

Garry, John (1995). 'The Demise of the Fianna Fáil / Labour "Partnership" Government and the Rise of the "Rainbow" Coalition', *Irish Political Studies*, 10, 192–9.

Garry, John, Niamh Hardiman and Diane Payne (eds) (2006). *Irish Social and Political Attitudes*. Liverpool: Liverpool University Press.

Garry John, Michael Marsh and Richard Sinnott (2005). '"Second Order" Versus "Issue Voting" Effects in EU Referendums: Evidence from the Irish Nice Treaty Referendums', *European Union Politics*, 6:2, 201–21.

Garry, John and James R. Tilly (2003). 'Fianna Fáil Activists: Coalition Preferences and Policy Priorities', *Irish Political Studies*, 18:2, 82–8.

Garvin, Tom (1981/2005). *The Evolution of Irish Nationalist Politics*. Dublin: Gill and Macmillan.

Garvin, Tom (2004). *Preventing the Future: Why Was Ireland So Poor for So Long?* Dublin: Gill and Macmillan.

Gilland, Karin (2000). 'The 1999 European Parliament Election in the Republic of Ireland', *Irish Political Studies*, 15, 127–33.

Gilland Lutz, Karin (2003). 'Irish Party Competition in the New Millennium: Change, or Plus Ca Change?', *Irish Political Studies*, 18:2, 40–59.

Girvin, Brian (1986). 'Social Change and Moral Politics: The Irish Constitutional Referendum 1983', *Political Studies*, 34:1, 61–81.

Girvin, Brian (1987a). 'The Campaign', in Laver, Michael, Peter Mair and Richard Sinnott (eds), *How Ireland Voted: The Irish General Election 1987*. Swords: Poolbeg, 9–29.

Girvin, Brian (1987b). 'The Divorce Referendum in the Republic, June 1986', *Irish Political Studies*, 2, 93–8.

Girvin, Brian (1990). 'The Campaign', in Gallagher, Michael and Richard Sinnott (eds), *How Ireland Voted 1989*. Galway: PSAI Press, 5–22.

Girvin, Brian (1993). 'The Road to the Election', in Gallagher, Michael and Michael Laver (eds), *How Ireland Voted 1992*. Dublin: PSAI Press, 1–20.

Girvin, Brian (1996). 'The Irish Divorce Referendum, November 1995, *Irish Political Studies*, 11, 174–81.

Girvin, Brian (1999). 'Political Competition 1992–1997', in Marsh, Michael and Paul Mitchell (eds), *How Ireland Voted 1997*. Boulder: Westview and PSAI Press, 3–28.

Girvin, Brian (2002). *From Union to Union: Nationalism, Religion and Democracy from the Act of Union to the European Union*. Dublin: Gill and Macmillan.

Girvin, Brian (2010). 'Continuity, Change and Crisis in Ireland: An Introduction and Discussion', in Girvin, Brian and Gary Murphy (eds), *Continuity, Change and Crisis in Contemporary Ireland*. Abingdon: Routledge, 1–18.

Girvin, Brian and Gary Murphy (eds) (2010). *Continuity, Change and Crisis in Contemporary Ireland*. Abingdon: Routledge.

Government of Ireland (2006). 'Towards 2016: Ten-Year Framework Social Partnership Agreement 2006–2015', available at www.taoiseach.gov.ie/attached_files/Pdf%20files/Towards2016PartnershipAgreement.pdf.

Gwynn Morgan, David. (2001). *A Judgement Too Far? Judicial Activism and the Constitution*. Cork: Cork University Press.

Hamilton, Mr Justice Liam (1994). *Report of the Tribunal of Inquiry into the Beef Processing Industry*. Dublin: Stationery Office.

Hardiman, Niamh (1988). *Pay, Politics and Economic Performance in Ireland, 1970–1987*. Oxford: Clarendon.

Hardiman, Niamh (2000). 'Social Partnership, Wage Bargaining and Growth', in Nolan, Brian, Philip J. O'Connell and Christopher T. Whelan (eds), *Bust to Boom? The Irish Experience of Growth and Inequality*. Dublin: Institute of Public Administration, 286–309.

Hardiman, Niamh (2002). 'From Conflict to Co-ordination: Economic Governance and Political Innovation in Ireland', *West European Politics*, 25:4, 1–24.

Hardiman, Niamh (ed.) (2012). *Irish Governance in Crisis*. Manchester: Manchester University Press.

Haughey, Charles, J. (2011) 'Social Partnership: Its Origins and Achievements', available at http://charlesjhaughey.ie.

Hayward, Katy (2003). 'If at first you don't succeed … The Second Referendum on the Treaty of Nice', *Irish Political Studies*, 18:1, 120–32.

Hayward, Katy (2009). *Irish Nationalism and European Integration: The Official Redefinition of the Island of Ireland*. Manchester, Manchester University Press.

Hesketh, Tom (1990). *The Second Partitioning of Ireland: The Abortion Referendum of 1983*. Dublin: Brandsma Books.

Honohan, Patrick (2010). *The Irish Banking Crisis: Regulatory and Financial Stability Policy 2003–2008*, available at www.bankinginquiry.gov.ie.

Honohan, Patrick (2014). 'Brian Lenihan and the Nation's Finances', in Murphy, Brian, Mary O'Rourke and Noel Whelan (eds), *Brian Lenihan: In Calm and Crisis*. Dublin: Merrion Press, 64–82.

Horgan, John (1997). *Seán Lemass: The Enigmatic Patriot*. Dublin: Gill and Macmillan.

Hogan, John, Paul F. Donnelly and Brendan O'Rourke (eds) (2010). *Irish Business and Society: Governing, Participating and Transforming in the Twenty–First Century*. Dublin: Gill and Macmillan.

Hughes, Ian, Paula Clancy, Clodagh Harris and David Beetham (2007). *Power to the People? Assessing Democracy in Ireland*. Dublin: Tasc.

Hussey, Gemma (1990). *At The Cutting Edge: Cabinet Diaries*. Dublin: Gill and Macmillan.

Jacobsen, John Kurt (1994). *Chasing Progress in the Irish Republic: Ideology, Democracy and Dependent Development*. Cambridge: Cambridge University Press.

Jones, Jack (2001). *In Your Opinion: Political and Social Trends in Ireland through the Eyes of the Electorate*. Dublin: Townhouse and Countryhouse.

Joyce, Joe and Peter Murtagh (1983). *The Boss: Charles J Haughey in Government*. Dublin: Poolbeg.

Kavanagh, Adrian (2004). 'The 2004 Local Elections in the Republic of Ireland', *Irish Political Studies*, 19:2, 64–84.

Keena, Colm (2001). *Haughey's Millions: Charlie's Money Trail*. Dublin: Gill and Macmillan.

Keena, Colm (2003). *The Ansbacher Conspiracy*. Dublin: Gill and Macmillan.

Kennedy, Fiachra (2002). 'The 2002 General Election in Ireland', *Irish Political Studies*, 17:2, 95–106.

Keogh, Dermot with Andrew McCarthy (2005). *Twentieth Century Ireland: Revolution and State Building*. Dublin: Gill and Macmillan.

Kirby, Peadar (2002). *The Celtic Tiger in Distress: Growth with Inequality in Ireland*. Basingstoke: Palgrave.

Kissane, Bill (2002). *Explaining Irish Democracy*. Dublin: University College Dublin Press.

Laffan, Brigid and Jane O'Mahony (2008). *Ireland and the European Union*. Basingstoke: Palgrave.

Laver, Michael (1998). 'Party Policy in Ireland: Results from an Expert Survey', *Irish Political Studies*, 13, 159–71.

Laver, Michael (1999). 'The Irish Party System Approaching the Millennium', in Marsh, Michael and Paul Mitchell, *How Ireland Voted 1997*. Boulder: Westview and PSAI Press, 264–76.

Laver, Michael and Audrey Arkins (1990). 'Coalition and Fianna Fáil', in Gallagher, Michael and Richard Sinnott, *How Ireland Voted 1989*. Galway: PSAI Press, 192–207.

Laver, Michael, Peter Mair and Richard Sinnott (1987). *How Ireland Voted 1987*. Swords: Poolbeg.

Leahy, Pat (2009). *Showtime: The Inside Story of Fianna Fáil in power*. Dublin: Penguin.

Leahy, Pat (2011). 'Campaign Strategies and Political Marketing', in Gallagher, Michael and Michael Marsh (eds), *How Ireland Voted 2011: The Full Story of Ireland's Earthquake Election*. Basingstoke: Palgrave, 68–88.

Leahy, Pat (2013). *The Price of Power: Inside Ireland's Crisis Coalition*. Dublin: Penguin.

Lee, J. J. (1989). *Ireland, 1912–1985: Politics and Society*. Cambridge: Cambridge University Press.

Lenihan, Brian (1991). *For the Record*. Dublin: Blackwater Press.

Lenihan, Brian (2008). 'Financial Statement of the Minister for Finance', available at http://budget.gov.ie/budgets/2009/FinancialStatement.aspx.

Lyons, Tom and Brian Carey (2011). *The Fitzpatrick Tapes: The Rise and Fall of One Man, One Bank and One Country*. Dublin: Penguin.

MacCarthaigh, Muiris (2005). *Accountability in Irish Parliamentary Politics*. Dublin: Institute of Public Administration.

MacCarthaigh, Muiris and Shane Martin (2015). 'Bicameralism in the Republic of Ireland: The Seanad Abolition Referendum', *Irish Political Studies*, 30:1, 121–31.

MacSharry, Ray (2014). 'The Poisoned Chalice', in Murphy, Brian, Mary O'Rourke and Noel Whelan (eds), *Brian Lenihan: In Calm and Crisis*. Dublin: Merrion Press, 102–14.

MacSharry Ray and Padraic White (2000). *The Making of the Celtic Tiger: The Inside Story of Ireland's Boom Economy*. Cork: Mercier Press.

Mahon, Mr Justice Alan (2012). *The Final Report of the Tribunal of Inquiry into Certain Planning Matters and Payments*, available at www.planningtribunal.ie/images/finalReport.pdf.

Mair, Peter (1987a). *The Changing Irish Party System: Organisation, Ideology and Electoral Competition*. London: Pinter.

Mair, Peter (1987b). 'Policy Competition', in Laver, Michael, Peter Mair and Richard Sinnott, *How Ireland Voted 1987*. Swords: Poolbeg, 30–47.

Mair, Peter (2011). 'The Election in Context', in Gallagher, Michael and Michael Marsh (eds), *How Ireland Voted 2011: The Full Story of Ireland's Earthquake Election*. Basingstoke: Palgrave, 283–97.

Mair, Peter and Liam Weeks (2005). 'The Party System', in Coakley, John and Michael Gallagher (eds), *Politics in the Republic of Ireland*, 4th edn. Abingdon: Routledge and PSAI Press, 135–59.

Mansergh, Lucy (1999). 'Two Referendums and the Referendum Commission: The 1998 Experience', *Irish Political Studies*, 14, 123–31.

Mansergh, Martin (ed.) (1986). *The Spirit of the Nation: The Speeches and Statements of Charles J. Haughey (1957–1986)*. Cork: Mercier Press.

Marsh, Michael (1999). 'The Making of the Eighth President', in Marsh, Michael and Paul Mitchell (eds), *How Ireland Voted 1997*. Boulder: Westview and PSAI Press, 215–42.

Marsh, Michael (2000). 'Candidate Centred but Party Wrapped: Campaigning in Ireland under STV', in Bowler, Shaun and Bernard Grofman (eds), *Elections in Australia, Ireland and Malta under the Single Transferable Vote*. Ann Arbor: Michigan University Press, 114–30.

Marsh, Michael (2005). 'Parties and Society', in Coakley, John and Michael Gallagher (eds), *Politics in the Republic of Ireland*, 4th edn. Abingdon: Routledge and PSAI Press, 160–82.

Marsh, Michael (2006). 'Party Identification in Ireland: An Insecure Anchor for a Floating Party System', *Electoral Studies*, 25:3, 489–508.

Marsh, Michael (2007). 'Candidates or Parties: Objects of Electoral Choice in Ireland', *Party Politics*, 13:4, 500–27.

Marsh, Michael (2008). 'Explanations for Party Choice', in Gallagher, Michael and Michael Marsh (eds), *How Ireland Voted 2007: The Full Story of Ireland's General Election*. Basingstoke: Palgrave, 105–31.

Marsh, Michael and Kevin Cunningham (2011). 'A Positive Choice, or Anyone but Fianna Fáil?', in Gallagher, Michael and Michael Marsh (eds), *How Ireland Voted 2011: The Full Story of Ireland's Earthquake Election*. Basingstoke: Palgrave, 172–204.

Marsh, Michael and Paul Mitchell (1999). *How Ireland Voted 1997*. Boulder: Westview and PSAI Press.

Marsh, Michael, Richard Sinnott, John Garry and Fiachra Kennedy (2008). *The Irish Voter: The Nature of Electoral Competition in the Republic of Ireland*. Manchester: Manchester University Press.

Martin, Micheál (2012). 'Response of Uachtarán Fhianna Fáil Micheál Martin TD to Report of Mahon Tribunal', available at www.fiannafail.ie/response-of-uachtaran-fhianna-fail-micheal-martin-td-to-report-of-mahon-tribunal/.

Martin, Shane (2010). 'Electoral Rewards for Personal Vote Cultivation under PR-STV', *West European Politics*, 33:2, 369–80.

Martin, Shane (2014). 'Why Electoral Systems Don't Always Matter: The Impact of "Mega-Seats" on Legislative Behaviour in Ireland', *Party Politics*, 20:3, 467–79.

McCracken, Mr Justice Brian (1997). *Report of the Tribunal of Inquiry (Dunnes Payments)*. Dublin: Stationery Office.

McCullagh, David (2012) '"A Particular View of What Was Possible": Labour in Government', in Daly, Paul, Ronan O'Brien and Paul Rouse (eds), *Making the Difference: The Irish Labour Party, 1912–2012*. Cork: Collins Press, 107–24.

McDaid, Jim (1993). 'On the Campaign Trail', in Gallagher, Michael and Michael Laver (eds), *How Ireland Voted 1992*. Dublin: PSAI Press, 39–43.

McGrath, Conor (2009). 'The Lobbyist with "Balls of Iron and a Spine of Steel": Why Ireland Needs Lobbying Reform', *Journal of Public Affairs*, 9, 256–71.

McGrath, Conor (2010). 'Lobbying Regulation: An Irish Solution to a Universal Problem?', in Hogan, John, Paul F. Donnelly and Brendan O'Rourke (eds), *Irish Business and Society: Governing, Participating and Transforming in the Twenty-First Century*. Dublin: Gill and Macmillan, 215–34.

McGrath, Conor (2011). 'Lobbying in Ireland: A Reform Agenda', *Journal of Public Affairs*, 11:2, 127–34.

McGraw, Sean (2008). 'Managing Changes: Party Competition in the New Ireland', *Irish Political Studies*, 23:4, 627–48.

McGraw, Sean D. (2015). *How Parties Win: Shaping the Irish Political Arena*. Ann Arbor: University of Michigan Press.

McMenamin, Iain (2013). *If Money Talks, What Does It Say?: Corruption and Business Financing of Political Parties*. Oxford: Oxford University Press.

McWilliams, David (2006). *The Pope's Children: Ireland's New Elite*. Dublin: Gill and Macmillan.

Meehan, Ciara (2013). *A Just Society for Ireland? 1964–1987*. London: Palgrave.

Minihan, Mary (2011). *A Deal with the Devil: The Green Party in Government*. Dublin: Maverick House.

Mitchell, Paul (2001). 'Divided Government in Ireland', in Elgie, Robert (ed.), *Divided Government in Comparative Perspective*. Oxford: Oxford University Press, 182–208.

Mitchell, Paul (2003). 'Government Formation in 2002: You Can Have Any Government as Long as It's Fianna Fáil', in Gallagher, Michael, Michael Marsh and Paul Mitchell (eds), *How Ireland Voted 2002*. Basingstoke: Palgrave, 214–29.

Moriarty, Mr Justice Michael (2006, 2011). *The Moriarty Tribunal Report. Report of the Tribunal of Inquiry into Payments to Politicians and Related Matters, Parts 1 and 2*. Dublin: Stationery Office.

Murphy, Brian, Mary O'Rourke and Noel Whelan (eds) (2014). *Brian Lenihan: In Calm and Crisis*. Dublin: Merrion Press.

Murphy, David and Martina Devlin (2009). *Banksters: How a Powerful Elite Squandered Ireland's Wealth*. Dublin: Hachette Books.

Murphy, Gary (1998). 'The 1997 General Election in the Republic of Ireland', *Irish Political Studies*, 13, 127–34.

Murphy, Gary (2000). 'A Culture of Sleaze: Political Corruption and the Irish Body Politic 1997–2000', *Irish Political Studies*, 15, 193–200.

Murphy, Gary (2003a). 'The Background to the Election', in Gallagher, Michael, Michael Marsh and Paul Mitchell (eds), *How Ireland Voted 2002*. Basingstoke: Palgrave, 1–20.

Murphy, Gary (2003b). 'Pluralism and the Politics of Morality', in Adshead, Maura and Michelle Millar (eds), *Public Administration and Public Policy in Ireland: Theory and Methods*. London: Routledge, 20–36.

Murphy, Gary (2006a). 'Payments for No Political Response? Political Corruption and Tribunals of Inquiry in Ireland, 1991–2003', in Garrard, John and James L. Newell (eds), *Scandals in Past and Contemporary Politics*. Manchester: Manchester University Press, 91–105.

Murphy, Gary (2006b). 'Assessing the Relationship Between Neoliberalism and Political Corruption: The Fianna Fáil – Progressive Democrat Coalition, 1997–2006', *Irish Political Studies*, 21:2, 297–317.

Murphy, Gary (2008). 'The Background to the Election', in Gallagher, Michael and Michael Marsh (eds), *How Ireland Voted 2007: The Full Story of Ireland's General Election*. Basingstoke: Palgrave, 1–18.

Murphy, Gary (2009). *In Search of the Promised Land: The Politics of Post War Ireland*. Cork: Mercier Press.

Murphy, Gary (2010a). 'Interest Groups in the Policy-Making Process', in Coakley, John and Michael Gallagher (eds), *Politics in the Republic of Ireland*, 5th edn. Abingdon: Routledge and PSAI Press, 327–58.

Murphy, Gary (2010b). 'Access and Expectation: Interest Groups in Ireland', in Hogan, John, Paul F. Donnelly and Brendan O'Rourke (eds), *Irish Business and Society: Governing, Participating and Transforming in the Twenty–First Century*. Dublin: Gill and Macmillan, 489–504.

Murphy, Gary (2010c). 'Influencing Political Decision-Making: Interest Groups and Elections in Independent Ireland', *Irish Political Studies*, 25:4, 563–80.

Murphy, Gary (2011). 'The Background to the Election', in Gallagher, Michael and Michael Marsh (eds), *How Ireland Voted 2011: The Full Story of Ireland's Earthquake Election*. Basingstoke: Palgrave, 1–28.

Murphy Gary (2012). 'Seeking the Fianna Fáil Vote: Why Do Interest Groups Run for Office in Ireland?', in Weeks, Liam and Alistair Clark (eds), *Radical or Redundant: Minor Parties in Irish Politics*. Dublin: The History Press, 142–58.

Murphy, Gary and John Hogan (2008). 'Fianna Fáil, the Trade Union Movement and the Politics of Macroeconomic Crises, 1970–1982', *Irish Political Studies*, 23:4, 577–98.

Murphy, Gary, John Hogan, and Raj Chari (2011). 'Lobbying Regulation in Ireland: Some Thoughts from the International Evidence', *Journal of Public Affairs*, 11:2, 111–19.

Murphy, Gary and Conor McGrath (2011). 'The Curious Case of Lobbying in Ireland', *Journal of Public Affairs*, 11:2, 71–3.

Murphy, Gary and Niamh Puirséil (2010). '"Is it a new allowance?": Irish Entry to the EEC and Popular Opinion', in Girvin, Brian and Gary Murphy (eds), *Continuity, Change and Crisis in Contemporary Ireland*. Abingdon: Routledge, 76–96.

Murphy, Gary and Theresa Reidy (2012). 'Presidential Elections in Ireland: From Partisan Predictability to the End of Loyalty'. *Irish Political Studies*, 27:4, 615–34.

Murphy, Gary and Theresa Reidy (2014). 'Presidential Elections: The Collapse of Partisanship?', in Coakley, John and Kevin Rafter (eds), *The Irish Presidency: Power, Ceremony and Politics*. Dublin: Irish Academic Press, 148–69.

Murphy, Mary C. (2006). 'Reform of Dáil Éireann: The Dynamics of Parliamentary Change', *Parliamentary Affairs*, 59:3, 437–53.

Murphy, Mary P. (2014). 'Ireland: Celtic Tiger in Austerity – Explaining Irish Path Dependency', *Journal of Contemporary European Studies*, 22:2, 132–42.

Murphy, Ronan J. and David M. Farrell (2002). 'Party Politics in Ireland: Regularizing a Volatile System', in Webb, Paul, David M. Farrell and Ian Holliday (eds), *Political Parties in Advanced Industrial Democracies*. Oxford: Oxford University Press, 217–47.

Nyberg, Peter (2011). *Misjudging Risk: Causes of the Systemic Banking Crisis in Ireland*, available at www.bankinginquiry.gov.ie.

O'Brennan, John (2009). 'Ireland Says No Again: The 12 June 2008 Referendum on the Lisbon Treaty', *Parliamentary Affairs*, 62:2, 258–77.

O'Brien, Mark (2008). *The Irish Times: A History*. Dublin: Four Courts Press.

O'Brien, Mark and Donnacha Ó Beacháin (eds) (2014). *Political Communication in the Republic of Ireland*. Liverpool: Liverpool University Press.

Ó Broin, Eoin (2009). *Sinn Féin and the Politics of Left Republicanism*. London: Pluto Press.

O'Byrnes, Stephen (1986). *Hiding Behind a Face: Fine Gael under FitzGerald*. Dublin: Gill and Macmillan.

O'Carroll, J. P. (1987). 'Strokes, Cute Hoors and Sneaking Regarders: the Influence of Local Culture on Irish Political Style', *Irish Political Studies*, 2, 77–92.

O'Connell, Hugh (2015). '"Not much of a f***ing ambush": An Oral History of the Heave against Enda Kenny', available at www.thejournal.ie/fine-gael-enda-kenny -heave-2155318-Jun2015/.

O'Connell, Philip (2000). 'The Dynamics of the Irish Labour Market in Comparative Perspective', in Nolan, Brian, Philip J. O'Connell and Christopher T. Whelan (eds), *Bust to Boom? The Irish Experience of Growth and Inequality*. Dublin: Institute of Public Administration, 58–89.

O'Connor, Emmet (2002). 'Ireland in Historical Perspective: The Legacies of Colonialism – Edging Towards Policy Concertation', in Berger, Stefan and Hugh Compston (eds), *Policy Concertation and Social Partnership in Western Europe*. New York: Berghahn Books, 155–66.

O'Donnell, Rory (2008). 'The Partnership State: Building the Ship at Sea', in Adshead, Maura, Peadar Kirby, and Michelle Millar (eds), *Contesting the State: Lessons from the Irish Case*. Manchester: Manchester University Press, 73–99.

O'Donnell, Rory and Colm O'Reardon (2000). 'Social Partnership in Ireland's Economic Transformation', in Fajertag, Giuseppe and Philippe Pochet (eds), *Social Pacts in Europe: New Dynamics*. Brussels: European Trade Union Institute, 237–57.

O'Donnell, Rory and Damian Thomas (1998). 'Partnership and Policy Making', in Healy, Seán and Brigid Reynolds (eds), *Social Policy in Ireland: Principles, Practice and Problems*. Dublin: Oak Tree Press, 117–46.

O'Donnell, Rory and Damian Thomas (2002). 'Ireland in the 1990s: Policy Concertation Triumphant', in Berger, Stefan and Hugh Compston (eds), *Policy Concertation and Social Partnership in Western Europe*. New York: Berghahn Books, 167–91.

O'Donoghue, Martin (1990). 'Irish Economic Policy, 1977–79', *Studies*, 79, 307–13.

O'Grada, Cormac (1997). *A Rocky Road: The Irish Economy since the 1920s*. Manchester: Manchester University Press.

O'Halloran, Anthony (2005). 'Transformation in Contemporary Ireland's Society, Economy and Polity: An Era of Post-Parliamentary Governance?', *Administration*, 53:1, 54–79.

O'Halpin, Eunan (2000). '"Ah they've given us a good bit of stuff …": Tribunals and Irish Political Life at the Turn of the Century', *Irish Political Studies*, 15, 183–92.

O'Halpin, Eunan and Eileen Connolly (1998). 'Parliaments and Pressure Groups: The Irish Experience of Change', in Norton, Philip (ed.), *Parliaments and Pressure Groups in Western Europe*. London: Frank Cass, 124–44.

O'Leary, Brendan (1993). 'Affairs, Partner-Swapping, and Spring Tides: The Irish General Election of 1992', *West European Politics*, 16:3, 401–12.

O'Leary, John (2015). *On The Doorsteps: Memoirs of a Long-Serving TD*. Killarney: Irish Political Memoirs.

O'Mahony, Jane (2001). 'Not so Nice: The Treaty of Nice, the International Criminal Court, the Abolition of the Death Penalty – the 2001 Referendum Experience', *Irish Political Studies*, 16, 201–13.

O'Malley, Des (2014). *Conduct Unbecoming: A Memoir*. Dublin: Gill and Macmillan.

O'Malley, Eoin (2006). 'Ministerial Selection in Ireland: Limited Choice in a Political Village', *Irish Political Studies*, 21:3, 319–36.

O'Malley, Eoin (2008a). 'Government Formation in 2007', in Gallagher, Michael and Michael Marsh (eds), *How Ireland Voted 2007: The Full Story of Ireland's General Election*. Basingstoke: Palgrave, 205–17.

O'Malley, Eoin (2008b). 'Why Is There No Radical Right Party in Ireland', *West European Politics*, 31:5, 960–77.

O'Malley, Eoin (2011a). *Contemporary Ireland*. Basingstoke: Palgrave Macmillan.

O'Malley, Eoin (2011b). 'Government Formation in 2011', in Gallagher, Michael and Michael Marsh (eds), *How Ireland Voted 2011: The Full Story of Ireland's Earthquake Election*. Basingstoke: Palgrave, 264–82.

O'Malley, Eoin and Matthew Kerby (2004). 'Chronicle of a Death Foretold? Understanding the Decline of Fine Gael', *Irish Political Studies*, 19:1, 39–58.

O'Malley, Eoin and Muris MacCarthaigh (eds) (2011). *Governing Ireland: From Cabinet Government to Delegated Governance*. Dublin: Institute for Public Administration.

O'Malley, Eoin and Shane Martin (2010). 'The Government and the Taoiseach', in Coakley, John and Michael Gallagher, *Politics in the Republic of Ireland*, 5th edn. Abingdon: Routledge and PSAI Press, 295–326.

O'Malley, Eoin and Gary Murphy (2012). 'Rewards for High Public Office in Ireland: Ratcheting Pay in the Public Sector', in Peters, B. Guy and Marleen Brans (eds), *Rewards for High Public Office in Europe and North America*, Abingdon: Routledge, 50–63

O'Muineacháin, Séin (2012). 'The Party that Ran Out of Lives: The Progressive Democrats', in Weeks, Liam and Alistair Clark (eds), *Radical or Redundant: Minor Parties in Irish Politics*. Dublin: The History Press, 126–41.

O'Neill, Bairbre (2000). 'Political and Legal Issues Arising out of Recent Tribunals of Inquiry', *Irish Political Studies*, 15, 201–12.

O'Reilly, Emily (1991). *Candidate: The Truth Behind the Presidential Campaign*. Dublin: Attic Press.

O'Reilly, Emily (1992). *Masterminds of the Right*. Dublin: Attic Press.

Ó Riain, Seán (2014). *The Rise and Fall of Ireland's Celtic Tiger: Liberalism, Boom and Bust*. Cambridge: Cambridge University Press.

O'Rourke, Brendan and John Hogan (2014). 'Guaranteeing Failure: Neoliberal Discourse in the Irish Economic Crisis', *Journal of Political Ideologies*, 19:1, 41–59.

O'Rourke, Mary (2012). *Just Mary: A Memoir*. Dublin: Gill and Macmillan.

O'Shea, Mary (2000). 'The 1999 Local Government Elections in the Republic of Ireland', *Irish Political Studies*, 15, 143–51.

O'Sullivan, Eoin (1991). 'The 1990 Presidential Election in the Republic of Ireland', *Irish Political Studies*, 6, 85–98.

O'Toole, Fintan (1995). *Meanwhile Back at the Ranch: The Politics of Irish Beef.* London: Vintage.

O'Toole, Fintan (2010). *Ship of Fools: How Stupidity and Corruption Sank the Celtic Tiger.* London: Faber and Faber.

O'Toole, Fintan (2011). *Enough Is Enough: How to Build a New Republic.* London: Faber and Faber.

O'Toole, Jason (2008). *Brian Cowen: The Path to Power.* Dublin: Transworld.

Patterson, Henry (2002). *Ireland since 1939.* Oxford: Oxford University Press.

Puirséil, Niamh (2012). '"If it's Socialism You Want, Join Some Other Party": Labour and the Left', in Daly, Paul, Ronan O'Brien and Paul Rouse (eds), *Making the Difference: The Irish Labour Party, 1912–2012.* Cork: Collins Press, 67–81.

Quinlan, Stephen (2009). 'The Lisbon Treaty Referendum 2008', *Irish Political Studies*, 24:1, 107–21.

Quinlan, Stephen (2010). 'The 2009 European Parliament Election in Ireland', *Irish Political Studies*, 25:2, 289–301.

Quinlivan, Aodh (2015). 'The 2014 Local Elections in the Republic of Ireland', *Irish Political Studies*, 30:1, 132–42.

Quinlivan, Aodh and Emmanuelle Schon-Quinlivan (2004). 'The 2004 European Parliament Election in the Republic of Ireland', *Irish Political Studies*, 19:2, 85–95.

Quinlivan, Aodh and Liam Weeks (2010). 'The 2009 Local Elections in the Republic of Ireland', *Irish Political Studies*, 25:2, 315–24.

Quinn, Ruairi (2005). *Straight Left: A Journey in Politics.* Dublin: Hodder Headline.

Rafter, Kevin (2003). 'Leadership Changes in Fine Gael and the Labour Party, 2002', *Irish Political Studies*, 18:1, 108–19.

Rafter, Kevin (2009). *Fine Gael: Party at the Crossroads.* Dublin: New Island.

Rafter, Kevin (2011a). *Democratic Left: The Life and Death of an Irish Political Party.* Dublin: Irish Academic Press.

Rafter, Kevin (2011b). *The Road to Power: How Fine Gael Made History.* Dublin: New Island.

Rafter, Kevin (2014). 'Voices in the Crisis: The Role of Media Elites in Interpreting Ireland's Banking Collapse', *European Journal of Communication*, 29:5, 598–607.

Regling, Klaus and Max Watson (2010). *A Preliminary Report on Ireland's Banking Crisis*, available at www.bankinginquiry.gov.ie.

Reidy, Theresa (2011). 'Candidate Selection', in Gallagher, Michael and Michael Marsh (eds), *How Ireland Voted 2011: The Full Story of Ireland's Earthquake Election.* Basingstoke: Palgrave, 47–67.

Reynolds, Albert (2009). *My Autobiography.* London: Transworld.

Roche, Bill (2009). 'Social Partnership: From Lemass to Cowen', *The Economic and Social Review*, 40:2, 183–205.

Roche, William K. and Terry Cradden (2003). 'Neo-Corporatism and Social Partnership', in Adshead, Maura and Michelle Millar (eds), *Public Administration and Public Policy in Ireland: Theory and Methods.* London: Routledge, 69–87.

Ross, Shane (2009). *The Bankers: How the Banks Ruined the Irish Economy*. Dublin: Penguin.

Ryan, Eamon (2014). 'Unprecedented Circumstances', in Murphy, Brian, Mary O'Rourke and Noel Whelan (eds), *Brian Lenihan: In Calm and Crisis*. Dublin: Merrion Press, 226–39.

Ryle Dwyer, T. (1992). *Haughey's Thirty Years of Controversy*. Cork: Mercier Press.

Ryle Dwyer, T. (1999). *Short Fellow: A Biography of Charles J. Haughey*. Dublin: Marino Books.

Sinnott, Richard (1995). *Irish Voters Decide: Voting Behaviour in Elections and Referendums since 1918*. Manchester: Manchester University Press.

Sinnott, Richard (2010). 'The Electoral System', in Coakley, John and Michael Gallagher, *Politics in the Republic of Ireland*, 5th edn. Abingdon: Routledge and PSAI Press, 111–36.

Sinnott, Richard and Johan A. Elkink (2010). 'Attitudes and Behaviour in the Second Referendum on the Treaty of Lisbon', Report prepared for the Department of Foreign Affairs, available at www.ucd.ie/t4cms/Attitudes%20and%20Behaviour%20in%20the%20Second%20Referendum%20on%20the%20Treaty%20of%20Lisbon.pdf.

Sinnott, Richard, Johan A. Elkink, Kevin O'Rourke and James McBride (2009). 'Attitudes and Behaviour in the Referendum on the Treaty of Lisbon', Report prepared for the Department of Foreign Affairs, available at http://web.dfa.ie/uploads/documents/ucd%20geary%20institute%20report.pdf.

Smyth, Sam (1997). *Thanks a Million Big Fella*. Dublin: Blackwater Press.

Stafford, Peter (2011). 'The Rise and Fall of Social Partnership: Its Impact on Interest Group Lobbying in Ireland', *Journal of Public Affairs*, 11:2, 74–9.

Suiter, Jane and David M. Farrell (2011). 'The Parties' Manifestoes', in Gallagher, Michael and Michael Marsh (eds), *How Ireland Voted 2011: The Full Story of Ireland's Earthquake Election*. Basingstoke: Palgrave, 29–46.

Tanzi, Vito (1998). 'Corruption around the World', *IMF Staff Papers*, Washington, 45:4, 559–94.

Taylor, George (2002). 'Hailing with an Invisible Hand: A "Cosy" Political Dispute amid the Rise of Neoliberal Politics in Ireland', *Government and Opposition*, 37:4, 501–23.

Taylor, George (2005). *Negotiated Governance and Public Policy in Ireland*. Manchester: Manchester University Press.

Taylor, George (2011). 'Risk and Financial Armageddon in Ireland: The Politics of the Galway Tent', *The Political Quarterly*, 82:4, 596–608.

Tonge, Jonathan (2005). *The New Northern Irish Politics?* Basingstoke: Palgrave.

Walsh, John (2008). *Patrick Hillery: The Official Biography*. Dublin: New Island.

Walshe, John (2014). *An Education: How an Outsider Became an Insider and Learned What Really Goes on in Irish Government*. Dublin: Penguin.

Weeks, Liam (2009). 'We Don't Like (to) Party. A Typology of Independents in Irish Political Life, 1922–2007', *Irish Political Studies*, 24:1, 1–27.

Weeks, Liam (2010). 'Parties and the Party System', in Coakley, John and Michael Gallagher (eds), *Politics in the Republic of Ireland*, 5th edn. Abingdon: Routledge and PSAI Press, 137–67.

Weeks, Liam and Alistair Clark (eds) (2012). *Radical or Redundant: Minor Parties in Irish Politics*. Dublin: The History Press.

Weeks, Liam and Aodh Quinlivan (2009). *All Politics Is Local: A Guide to Local Elections in Ireland*. Cork: The Collins Press.

Whelan, Ken and Eugene Masterson (1998). *Bertie Ahern: Taoiseach and Peacemaker*. Dublin: Blackwater Press.

Whelan, Noel (2007). *Showtime or Substance: A Voter's Guide to the 2007 General Election*. Dublin: New Island.

Whelan, Noel (2011). *Fianna Fáil: A Biography of the Party*. Dublin: Gill and Macmillan.

Whelan, Noel (2014). 'Introduction', in Murphy, Brian, Mary O'Rourke and Noel Whelan (eds). *Brian Lenihan: In Calm and Crisis*. Dublin: Merrion Press, 1–12.

Yates, Ivan (2014). *Full On: A Memoir*. Dublin: Hachette Books.

Index

Thatcher, Margaret, and
    Thatcherism 18, 21, 122
Traynor, Des, 76
tribunals of inquiry 3, 7, 53–4, 81, 90,
    100–2
   see also Hamilton; Mahon;
    McCracken; Moriarty
Troika bailout (2010) 1, 2, 3, 8,
    148–54, 157, 158, 161, 162

unemployment *see* employment and
    unemployment
United Left Alliance 156

Watson, Max 141
Whelan, Noel 33
Whelehan, Harry 63, 66–71
Workers' Party 17, 37, 38, 59
   see also Democratic Left Party
Wright, G. V., 83

X (abortion) case 4, 67–8